ASP.NET Core 1.1 MVC
For Beginners

How to build a Video Course Website

Overview 1

    Setup 2

    Book Version 2

    Other Titles by the Author 3

        Books by the Author 3

        MVC 5 – How to Build a Membership Website (video course) 4

        Store Secret Data in .NET Core Web App with Azure Key Vault (video course) 4

    Source Code 5

    Disclaimer – Who Is This Book for? 5

    Rights 6

    About the Author 6

Part 1: ASP.NET Core 1.1 MVC Your First Application 9

1. Your First ASP.NET Core Application 11

    Creating the Solution and Project 11

        The Project Layout and the File System 14

        Important Files 15

        Compiling the Solution 16

        The Startup.cs File 17

    Adding a Configuration Service 18

    Creating a Service 21

        Example 21

            Adding the Interface 22

            Adding the HardcodedMessageService Class 23

            Configure and Use the HardcodedMessageService Class 23

            Add and Use the ConfigurationMessageService Class 25

    Summary 27

2. Middleware 29

How Does Middleware Work? 29

IApplicationBuilder 30

Handling Exceptions 32

Serving Up Static Files 35

Serving Up Default Files 37

Setting Up ASP.NET MVC 37

Adding the MVC NuGet Package 38

Summary 40

3. MVC Controllers 41

Routing 42

Convention-Based Routing 43

Implement Routing 43

Adding Another Controller 44

Attribute Routing 45

IActionResult 48

Implementing ContentResult 49

Using a Model Class 49

Introduction to Views 51

A View with a Data Collection 53

Adding a Data Service 55

Summary 59

4. Models 61

View Model Example 62

Changing the Folder Structure 62

Adding the View Model 62

Using the View Model 63

Adding a Details View 64

Adding a Create View 68

Refactoring the Application 69

Adding the HTTP GET Create Action and the Create View 71

Adding the VideoEditViewModel Class 73

Adding the HTTP POST Create Action 74

Data Annotations 79

Preparing the Create View for Validation 80

Adding Validation to the Create View 80

Validating the Model on the Server 81

Adding Data Annotations in the Video Entity and VideoEditViewModel Class 82

Summary 85

5. Entity Framework 87

Installing Entity Framework and User Secrets 87

Adding the VideoDbContext Class 89

Configuration in the Startup Class 90

Adding the Initial Migration and Creating the Database 92

Adding the SqlVideoData Service Component 94

Implementing the SqlVideoData Service Component Class 94

Summary 97

6. Razor Views 99

Layout Views 99

Adding the _Layout View 100

Altering the Content Views 100

The _ViewStart file 104

The _ViewImports file 105

Tag Helpers 106

Altering the Index View 107

Adding an Edit View and Its Actions 108

Refactoring the IVideoData Service 111

Partial Views 113

View Components 116

Adding a View Component for the IMessageService Service 116

Summary 119

7. Forms Authentication 121

Adding the Authorize and AlowAnonymous Attributes 122

Configuring the Identity Framework 123

Creating the AspNet Identity Database Tables 125

User Registration 126

Login and Logout 131

Adding the _Login Partial View 131

Adding the Logout Action 133

Adding the LoginViewModel Class 134

Adding the HTTP GET Login Action 134

Adding the HTTP POST Login Action 135

Adding the Login View 137

Summary 140

8. Front-End Frameworks 141

Installing Bower and the Frameworks 141

Styling with Bootstrap 144

Adding a Navigation Bar 145

Styling the Index View 147

Adding Client-Side Validation 149

Summary 151

Part 2: ASP.NET Core 1.1 MVC How to Build a Video Course Website 153

9. The Use Case... 155

Introduction... 155

The Use Case 155

    The User Interface 155

    Login and Register User... 156

    The Administrator Views 156

Conclusion 156

    Login and Register 157

    The Dashboard View... 157

    The Course View 158

    The Video View 160

    A Typical Administrator Index View 161

    A Typical Administrator Create View.. 161

    A Typical Administrator Edit View 162

    A Typical Administrator Delete View.. 163

    A Typical Administrator Details View 164

10. Setting Up the Solution 165

Introduction... 165

    Technologies Used in This Chapter... 165

Overview... 165

Creating the Solution.. 165

Installing AutoMapper.. 167

Summary... 168

11. Login 169

Introduction... 169

    Technologies Used in This Chapter... 169

Creating the Database 169

Redirecting to the Login View 171

Styling the Login View 173

    Adding the login.css Stylesheet 174

    Changing the Layout of the View 175

    Styling the Login View 179

Summary.. 181

12. Register User 183

Introduction... 183

    Technologies Used in This Chapter.. 183

Overview... 183

    Changing the Layout of the View 184

    Styling the Register View 186

    Testing the Registration Form 188

Summary.. 190

13. Modifying the Navigation Bar... 191

Introduction... 191

    Technologies Used in This Chapter.. 191

Overview... 191

Styling the Navigation Bar 192

Remove the Register and Login links... 193

Add the Drop-Down Menu 194

    Style the Drop-Down Menu... 196

Summary.. 197

14. Data Transfer Objects... 199

Introduction... 199

    Technologies Used in This Chapter.. 199

Overview.. 199

The DTOs 199

Adding the DTOs.. 204

The View Models 206

Adding the View Models 207

Summary... 208

15. Entity Classes 209

Introduction.. 209

Technologies Used in This Chapter.. 209

Overview... 209

The Entities 209

The Video Entity 209

The Download Entity 210

The Instructor Entity.. 211

The Course Entity 211

The Module Entity 212

The UserCourse Entity 212

Adding the Entity Classes 213

Summary... 216

16. Mock Data Repository 217

Introduction.. 217

Technologies Used in This Chapter.. 217

Overview... 217

Add the IReadRepository Interface and MockReadRepository Class.......................... 217

Add Data to the MockReadRepository Class.. 218

The Course List 218

The UserCourses List 219

The Modules List...219

The Downloads List...219

The Instructors List 220

The Videos List...220

The GetCourses Method 221

Testing the GetCourses Method...222

The GetCourse Method 222

Testing the GetCourse Method 224

The GetVideo Method...225

Testing the GetVideo Method 225

The GetVideos Method 226

Testing the GetVideos Method 227

Summary...230

17. The Membership Controller and AutoMapper..231

Introduction..231

Technologies Used in This Chapter...231

Overview...231

Adding the Membership Controller 232

Adding the Controller 232

Configuring AutoMapper...235

Implementing the Action Methods 237

The Dashboard Action Method 237

The Course Action Method...241

The Video Action Method 245

Summary...250

18. The Dashboard View..251

Introduction..251

Technologies Used in This Chapter... 251

Overview... 251

Implementing the Dashboard View... 252

Adding the Dashboard View 252

Iterating Over the Courses in the Dashboard View.. 254

Creating the _CoursePanelPartial Partial View 256

Styling the Dashboard View and the _CoursePanelPartial Partial View 259

Summary... 263

19. The Course View 265

Introduction... 265

Technologies Used in This Chapter... 265

Overview... 265

Adding the Course View 266

Adding the Back to Dashboard Button 268

Adding the Course.css Style Sheet 269

Adding the Course Information to the View 270

Styling the Course Information Section... 272

Adding Columns for the Modules and the Instructor Bio 273

Adding the Modules 274

Adding the Videos 275

Styling the _ModuleVideosPartial View 279

Adding the Downloads 281

Styling the _ModuleDownloadsPartial View 284

Adding the Instructor Bio 284

Styling the _InstructorBioPartial Partial View 286

Summary... 287

20. The Video View.. 289

Introduction.. 289

Technologies Used in This Chapter.. 289

Overview... 289

Adding the Video View 291

Adding the Back to Course Button 293

Adding Row and Columns for the Video View Content........................... 294

Adding the _VideoPlayerPartial Partial View 295

Styling the _VideoPlayerPartial Partial View..................................... 298

Add JWPlayer.. 299

Create a Video Player 300

Add the Video Player to the Video View 300

Adding Properties to the LessonInfoDTO Class.................................... 301

Adding the _VideoComingUpPartial Partial View 302

Styling the _VideoComingUpPartial Partial View 307

Adding the _InstructorBioPartial Partial View.................................... 307

Summary... 309

21. SQL Data Repository 311

Introduction... 311

Technologies used in this chapter 311

Overview... 311

Adding the Tables... 312

Adding the Entity Classes to the ApplicationDbContext 312

Adding Seed Data 313

Creating the Tables.. 320

Adding the SqlReadRepository 321

Implementing the GetCourses method.. 321

Implementing the GetCourse Method 323

Implementing the GetVideo Method 325

Implementing the GetVideos Method 325

Summary... 326

22. The Admin Menu 327

Introduction... 327

Technologies Used in This Chapter.. 327

Overview.. 327

Adding the _AdminMenuPartial Partial View.. 328

Summary.. 331

23. Controllers and Views.. 333

Introduction... 333

Technologies used in this chapter 333

Overview.. 333

Adding Controllers and Views 337

Fixing the Drop-Downs in the Views 340

The Index Action.. 343

The Index View 345

The Details Action... 346

The Details View 347

The HTTP GET Delete Action 348

The HTTP POST DeleteConfirmed Action 348

The Delete View.. 348

The HTTP GET Create Action 349

The HTTP POST Create Action 349

The Create View 350

The HTTP GET Edit Action.. 352

The HTTP POST Edit Action.. 353

The Edit View... 354

Summary.. 354

24. The UserCourse Controller 355

Technologies used in this chapter 355

Overview... 355

The UserCourse Controller 355

Creating the UserCoursesController Class.................................... 356

Adding the Index Action and View 357

Adding the Details Action and View 361

Adding the HTTP GET Create Action and View............................ 364

Adding the HTTP POST Create Action... 367

Adding the HTTP GET Edit Action and View 369

Adding the HTTP POST Edit Action 373

Adding the HTTP GET Delete Action and View............................ 376

Adding the HTTP POST DeleteConfirmed Action......................... 379

Authorize and Route Attributes in the Admin Controllers............. 380

Changing the Route and Adding Authorization........................... 381

Summary.. 381

25. Custom Tag Helper 383

Introduction.. 383

Technologies Used in This Chapter... 383

Overview... 384

Implementing the Button-Container Tag Helper 384

Creating the Tag Helper... 385

Multiple Actions and Descriptions 388

URL Parameter Values.. 390

Glyphicons 393

Turning Links into Buttons 395

Styling the Views 395

Replacing Links with Buttons 398

An Alternate Button-Container Tag Helper 400

Summary 403

Other Titles by the Author 405

Books 405

Books by the Author 405

Video Courses 406

MVC 5 – How to Build a Membership Website (video course) 406

Store Secret Data in a .NET Core Web App with Azure Key Vault (video course) ... 406

Overview

I would like to welcome you to *ASP.NET Core 1.1 MVC for Beginners*. This book will guide you through creating your very first MVC applications. To get the most from this book, you should have a basic understanding of HTML and be familiar with the C# language.

ASP.NET Core is a new framework from Microsoft. It has been designed from the ground up to be fast and flexible and to work across multiple platforms. ASP.NET Core is the framework to use for your future ASP.NET applications.

The first application you build will evolve into a basic MVC application, starting with an empty template. You will add the necessary pieces one at a time to get a good understanding of how things fit together. The focus is on installing and configuring middleware, services, and other frameworks. Styling with CSS is not a priority in this application; you'll learn more about that in the second application you build.

You will install middleware to create a processing pipeline, and then look at the MVC framework. If you already are familiar with MVC or Web API from previous versions of ASP.NET, you will notice some similarities.

There still are model classes, which are used as data carriers between the controller and its views. There are, however, many new features that you will learn, such as Tag Helpers and view components. You will also work with Entity Framework to store and retrieve data, implement authentication with ASP.NET Identity framework, install CSS libraries such as Bootstrap, and install JavaScript libraries such as JQuery. Note that dependency injection now is a first-class design pattern.

The second application you will create, starts from a pre-existing MVC template, where the main pipeline already has been added. Things like database support, authentication, and routing have already been implemented, ready to use.

By the end of this book you will be able to create simple ASP.NET Core MVC applications on your own, which can create, edit, delete, and view data in a database.

Both applications you will build revolve around video data and playing videos. In the first application, you will be able to add and edit video titles, and in the second you will build a more sophisticated customer portal, where users can view the course videos that they have access to.

Setup

In this book, you will be using C# and any Visual Studio 2017 version that you have access to. You can even use the free Visual Studio Community 2017 version, which you can download from www.visualstudio.com/downloads.

You can develop ASP.NET Core applications on Mac OS X and Linux, but then you are restricted to the ASP.NET Core libraries that don't depend on .NET Framework, which requires Windows. The applications in this book are created with the ASP.NET 1.1 Core project template.

You will install additional libraries using NuGet packages when necessary, throughout the book.

The complete code for both applications is available on GitHub with a commit for each task. If you open the code in a Visual Studio version greater than 15.0.0, you might have to edit the .csproj file for the project to build successfully. Right click on the file and delete the <ItemGroup> element listing the file names of the files located in the *css*, *images* and *js* folders. Save the file ands close it, now the solution should build successfully.

The first application: https://github.com/csharpschool/AspNetCoreVideoCore
The second application: https://github.com/csharpschool/VideoOnDemandCore

Book Version

The current version of this book: 1.2

Errata: https://github.com/csharpschool/VideoOnDemandCore/issues

Other Titles by the Author

The author has written other books and produced video courses that you might find helpful.

Books by the Author

Below is a list if the most recent books by the author. The books are available on Amazon.

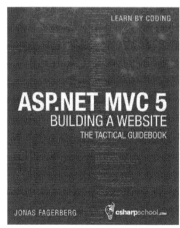 

ASP.NET Core 1.1 – Building a Website: http://www.amazon.com/dp/1546832068

ASP.NET Core 1.1 – Building a Web API: www.amazon.com/dp/1975798929

ASP.NET MVC 5 – Building a Website: www.amazon.com/dp/B01IF63FIY

C# for Beginners: https://www.amazon.com/dp/B017OAFR8I

MVC 5 – How to Build a Membership Website (video course)

This is a comprehensive video course on how to build a membership site using ASP.NET MVC 5. The course has more than **24 hours** of video.

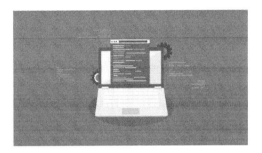

In this video course you will learn how to build a membership website from scratch. You will create the database using Entity Framework code-first, scaffold an Administrator UI, and build a front-end UI using HTML5, CSS3, Bootstrap, JavaScript, C#, and MVC 5. Prerequisites for this course are: a good knowledge of the C# language and basic knowledge of MVC 5, HTML5, CSS3, Bootstrap, and JavaScript.

You can watch this video course on Udemy at this URL:
www.udemy.com/building-a-mvc-5-membership-website

Store Secret Data in .NET Core Web App with Azure Key Vault (video course)

In this Udemy course you will learn how to store sensitive data in a secure manner. First you will learn how to store data securely in a file called *secrets.json* with the User Manager. The file is stored locally on your machine, outside the project's folder structure. It is therefore not checked into your code repository. Then you will learn how to use Azure Web App Settings to store key-value pairs for a specific web application. The third and final way to secure your sensitive data is using Azure Key Vault, secured with Azure Active Directory in the cloud.

The course is taught using a ASP.NET Core 1.1 Web API solution in Visual Studio 2015.

You really need to know this if you are a serious developer.

You can watch this video course on Udemy at this URL:
www.udemy.com/store-secret-data-in-net-core-web-app-with-azure-key-vault

Source Code

The source code accompanying this book is shared under the MIT License and can be downloaded on GitHub, with a commit for each task.

The first application: https://github.com/csharpschool/AspNetCoreVideoCore
The second application: https://github.com/csharpschool/VideoOnDemandCore

Errata: https://github.com/csharpschool/VideoOnDemandCore/issues

Disclaimer – Who Is This Book for?

It's important to mention that this book is not meant to be a *get-to-know-it-all* book; it's more on the practical and tactical side, where you will learn as you progress through the exercises and build real applications in the process. Because I personally dislike having to read hundreds upon hundreds of pages of irrelevant fluff (filler material) not necessary for the tasks at hand, and also view it as a disservice to the readers, I will assume that we are of the same mind on this, and will therefore only include important information pertinent for the tasks at hand, thus making the book both shorter and more condensed and also saving you time and effort in the process. Don't get me wrong, I will describe the important things in great detail, leaving out only the things that are not directly relevant to your first experience with a ASP.NET Core 1.1 MVC Web Application. The goal is for you to have created a working MVC application upon finishing this book. You can always look into details at a later time when you have a few projects under your belt. *If you prefer encyclopedic books describing everything in minute detail with short examples, and value a book by how many pages it has, rather than its content, then this book is NOT for you*.

The examples in this book are presented using the free Visual Studio 2017 Community version and ASP.NET Core 1.1. You can download Visual Studio 2017 here: www.visualstudio.com/downloads

Rights

About the Author

Jonas started a company back in 1994 focusing on teaching Microsoft Office and the Microsoft operating systems. While still studying at the university of Skovde in 1995, he wrote his first book about Widows 95, as well as a number of course materials.

In the year 2000, after working as a Microsoft Office developer consultant for a couple of years, he wrote his second book about Visual Basic 6.0.

Between 2000 and 2004, he worked as a Microsoft instructor with two of the largest educational companies in Sweden teaching Visual Basic 6.0. When Visual Basic.NET and C# were released, he started teaching those languages, as well as the .NET Framework. He was also involved in teaching classes at all levels, from beginner to advanced developers.

From the year 2005, Jonas shifted his career towards consulting once again, working hands-on with the languages and framework he taught.

Jonas wrote his third book, *C# Programming*, aimed at beginner to intermediate developers in 2013, and in 2015 his fourth book *C# for Beginners – The Tactical Guide* was published. Shortly thereafter his fifth book, ASP.NET MVC 5 – Building a Website: The Tactical Guidebook, was published.

Jonas has also produced a 24h+ video course titled *Building a ASP.NET MVC 5 Membership Website* (www.udemy.com/building-a-mvc-5-membership-website), showing in great detail how to build a membership website.

And a course on how to secure sensitive data in web applications titled <u>Store Secret Data in a .NET Core Web App with Azure Key Vault</u> is also available on Udemy.

All the books and video courses, including **C# for Beginners – The Tactical Guide**, **MVC 5 – How to Build a Membership Website (book and video)**, **Store Secret Data in a .NET Core Web App with Azure Key Vault**, and this book, have been specifically written with the student in mind.

Part 1:
ASP.NET Core 1.1 MVC
Your First Application

1. Your First ASP.NET Core Application

Now that you have Visual Studio 2017 installed on your computer, it's time to create your first project.

Creating the Solution and Project

1. Open Visual Studio 2017.
2. Select **File-New-Project** (Ctrl+Shift+N) in the main menu.
3. Make sure that the **Templates-Visual C#-Web** node is selected in the **New Project** dialog.
   There are three templates available:
   a. ASP.NET Core Web Application (.NET Core)
      Can be used to create cross-platform ASP.NET Core web applications without the .NET Framework (not restricted to Windows).
   b. ASP.NET Web Application (.NET Framework)
      Can be used to create traditional ASP.NET web applications (without .NET Core).
4. Select the **ASP.NET Core Web Application** template.
5. Give the application a name and select which folder to place it in. You can name it *AspNetCoreVideo*.
6. Make sure that the **Create directory for solution** checkbox is checked.
7. Learning how to use GitHub is not part of this course, so if you are unfamiliar with GitHub, you should make sure that the **Create new Git repository** checkbox is unchecked.
8. Click the **OK** button.

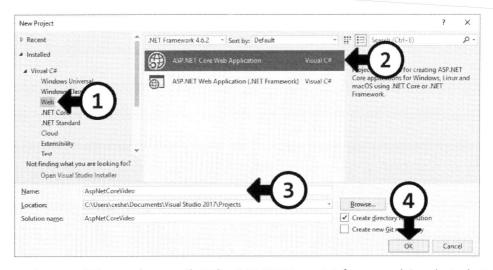

9. In the next dialog, make sure that the **ASP.NET Core 1.1** framework is selected at the top left of the dialog.
10. Select the **Empty** template.
11. Click the **OK** button.

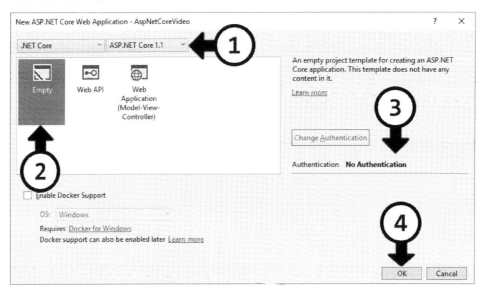

12. When the solution has been created in the folder you selected, it will contain all the files in the *AspNetCoreVideo* project.
13. Press Ctrl+F5 on the keyboard, or select **Debug-Start Without Debugging** in the main menu, to run the application in the browser.

14. Note that the application only can do one thing right now, and that is to display the text *Hello World!* Later in this, and the next, module you will learn why that is, and how you can change that behavior.

For now, just note that the application is running on *localhost:51457* (the port number might be different on your machine).

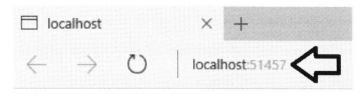

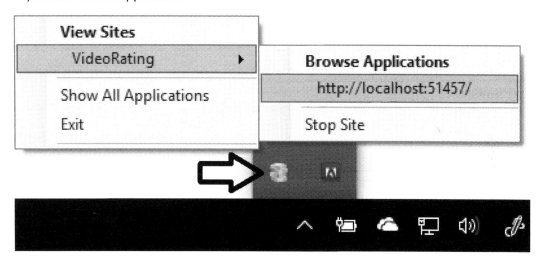

If you right click on the IIS icon in the system tray, you can see that ISS is hosting the *AspNetCoreVideo* application.

The Project Layout and the File System

There is a direct correlation between the files in the solution folder and what is displayed in the Solution Explorer in Visual Studio. To demonstrate this, you will add a file to the file structure in the File Explorer and see it show up in the Solution Explorer in real-time.

1. Right click on the **Solution** node in the Solution Explorer and select **Open Folder in File Explorer**.
2. When the File Explorer has opened, you can see that the solution file *AspNetCoreVideo.sln* is in that folder, along with the project folder with the same name.
3. Double click on the project folder in the File Explorer to open it.
4. Right click in the File Explorer window and select **New-Text Document** and press **Enter** on the keyboard.
5. A new file with the name *New Text File* should have been created in the folder.
6. Now look in the Solution Explorer in Visual Studio; the same file should be available there.
7. Double click the icon for the *New Text File* document in the Solution Explorer in Visual Studio, to open it.
8. Write the text *Some text from Visual Studio* in the document and save it.
9. Now switch back to the File Explorer and open the file. It should contain the text you added.
10. Change the text to *Some text from Notepad* using the text editor (not in Visual Studio) and save the file.
11. Switch back to Visual Studio and click the **Yes** button in the dialog. The altered text should now be displayed in Visual Studio.

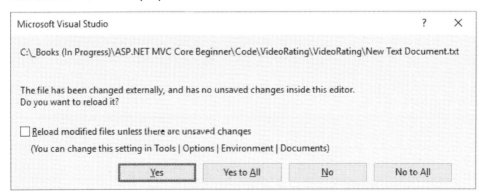

12. Close the text document in Visual Studio and in the text editor.

13. Right click on the file in the Solution Explorer in Visual Studio and select **Delete** to remove the file permanently.
14. Go to the File Explorer and verify that the file was deleted from the folder structure.

As you can see, the files in the project are in sync with the files in the file system, in real-time.

Important Files

There are a couple of files that you need to be aware of in ASP.NET Core 1.1, and these have changed from previous versions.

The **Properties** folder in the Solution Explorer contains a file called *launchSettings.json*, which contains all the settings needed to launch the application. It contains IIS settings, as well as project settings, such as environment variables and the application URL.

One major change from ASP.NET Core 1.0 is that the project.json file no longer exists; instead the installed NuGet packages are listed in the *.csproj* file. It can be opened and edited directly from Visual Studio (which is another change) or its content can be changed using the NuGet Package Manager.

To open the *.csproj* file, you simply right click on it and select **Edit AspNetCoreVideo.csproj** (substitute *AspNetCoreVideo* with the name of the project you are in).

You can add NuGet packages by adding **PackageReference** nodes to the file *.csproj,* or by opening the NuGet Package Manager. Right click on the **project node** or the **References** node, and select **Manage NuGet Packages** to open the NuGet Manager.

Open the *.csproj* file and the NuGet manager side by side and compare them. As you can see, the same packages are listed in the dialog and in the file.

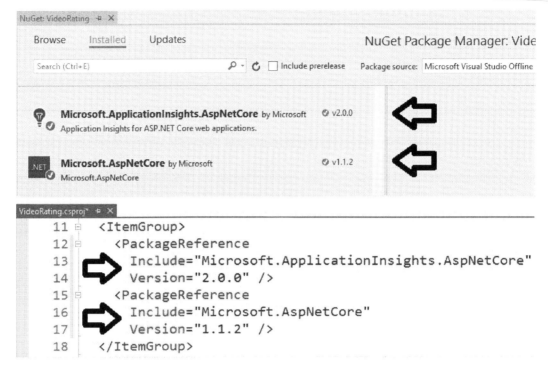

```
NuGet: VideoRating   + ×

  Browse    Installed    Updates                    NuGet Package Manager: Vide

  Search (Ctrl+E)                    ⌕ ▾  ⟳  ☐ Include prerelease   Package source: Microsoft Visual Studio Offline


  ☼   Microsoft.ApplicationInsights.AspNetCore by Microsoft   ⊘ v2.0.0      ⇦
   ⊘  Application Insights for ASP.NET Core web applications.

  NET  Microsoft.AspNetCore by Microsoft                      ⊘ v1.1.2      ⇦
   ⊘  Microsoft.AspNetCore
```

```
VideoRating.csproj*  + ×

11      <ItemGroup>
12        <PackageReference
13   ⇨      Include="Microsoft.ApplicationInsights.AspNetCore"
14   ⇨      Version="2.0.0" />
15        <PackageReference
16   ⇨      Include="Microsoft.AspNetCore"
17   ⇨      Version="1.1.2" />
18      </ItemGroup>
```

You will be adding more NuGet packages (frameworks) as you build the projects.

Compiling the Solution

It is important to know that ASP.NET will monitor the file system and recompile the application when files are changed and saved. Because ASP.NET monitors the file system and recompiles the code, you can use any text editor you like, such as Visual Studio Code, when building your applications. You are no longer bound to Visual Studio; all you need to do is to get the application running in the web server (IIS). Let's illustrate it with an example.

1. Start the application without debugging (Ctrl+F5) to get it running in IIS, if it isn't already open in a browser.
2. Open the *Startup.cs* file with Notepad (or any text editor) outside of Visual Studio. This file is responsible for configuring your application when it starts.
3. Locate the line of code with the string *Hello World*. This line of code is responsible for responding to every HTTP request in your application.
   ```
   await context.Response.WriteAsync("Hello World!");
   ```
4. Change the text to *Hello, from My World!* and save the file.
   ```
   await context.Response.WriteAsync("Hello, from My World!");
   ```

5. Refresh the application in the browser. Do not build the solution in Visual Studio before refreshing the page.
6. The text should change from *Hello World!* To *Hello, from My World!*
   The reason this works is because ASP.NET monitors the file system and recompiles the application when changes are made to a file.

As mentioned earlier you can create cross-platform applications using ASP.NET Core 1.1, but this requires the *.NET Core* template. As of this writing, this template has limitations compared with the *.NET Framework* template. This, because .NET Framework contains features that are relying on the Windows operating system. In a few years' time, this gap will probably not be as significant, as the .NET Core platform evolves. So, if you don't need the added features in .NET Framework, then use the *.NET Core* template, as it is much leaner and cross-platform ready.

The Startup.cs File

Gone are the days when the *web.config* file ruled the configuration universe. Now the *Startup.cs* file contains a **Startup** class, which ASP.NET will look for by convention. The application and its configuration sources are configured in that class.

The **Configure** and **ConfigureServices** methods in the **Startup** class handle most of the application configuration. The HTTP processing pipeline is created in the **Configure** method, located at the end of the class. The pipeline defines how the application responds to requests; by default, the only thing it can do is to print *Hello World!* to the browser.

If you want to change this behavior, you will have to add additional code to the pipeline in this method. If you for instance want to serve up static files, like HTML or JSON, you will need to add that behavior to the pipeline.

If you want to add a pretty error page, or handle route request in an ASP.NET MVC application, you have to modify the pipeline.

In the **Configure** method, you setup the HTTP request pipeline (the middleware) that is called when the application starts. In the second part of this book, you will add an object-to-object mapper called AutoMapper to this method. AutoMapper transforms objects from one type to another.

The **ConfigureServices** method is where you set up the services, such as MVC. You can also register your own services and make them ready for Dependency Injection (DI), for instance the services that you implement using the **IMessageService** interface at the beginning of the book.

You will learn more about how to configure your application in the next chapter.

For now, all you need to know about dependency injection is that, instead of creating instances of a class explicitly, they can be handed to a component when asked for. This makes your application loosely coupled and flexible.

Adding a Configuration Service

Let's say that the hard-coded string *Hello, from My World* is a string that shouldn't be hardcoded, and you want to read it from a configuration source. The source is irrelevant; it could be a JSON file, a database, a web service, or some other source. To solve this, you could implement a configuration service that fetches the value when asked.

Let's implement this scenario in your application

1. Right click on the project folder and select **Add-New Item**.
2. Search for *JSON* in the dialog's search field.
3. Select the **ASP.NET Configuration File** template.
4. Make sure the name of the file is *appsettings.json*. The file could be named anything, but *appsettings* is convention for this type of configuration file.
5. Click the **Add** button.
6. As you can see, a default connection string is already in the file. Remove the connection string property and add the following key-value pair: *"Message":"Hello, from configuration"*. This is the file content after you have changed it.
   ```
   {
       "Message": "Hello, from configuration"
   }
   ```

7. To read configuration information from the *appsettings.json* file you have to add a constructor to the **Startup** class. You can do that by typing *ctor* and hitting the **Tab** key twice.

```
public class Startup
{
    public Startup()
    {
    }
    ...
}
```

8. You need to create an instance of the **ConfigurationBulder** class called **builder** in the constructor, and chain on the **SetBasePath** method with the application's current directory as an argument. Without specifying the base path, the application will not know where to search for files.

```
var builder = new ConfigurationBuilder()
    .SetBasePath(Directory.GetCurrentDirectory());
```

9. To read the JSON *appsettings.json* file you need to chain on the **AddJsonFile** method, with *appsettings.json* as an argument, to the **builder** object. If you need to include more files, you can chain on the method multiple times.

```
var builder = new ConfigurationBuilder()
    .SetBasePath(Directory.GetCurrentDirectory())
    .AddJsonFile("appsettings.json");
```

10. Add a property called **Configuration**, of type **IConfiguration**, to the **Startup** class. To get access to the interface you have to add a **using** statement to the **Microsoft.Extensions.Configuration** namespace.

```
public IConfiguration Configuration { get; set; }
```

11. Now, you need to build the configuration structure from the **ConfigurationBuilder** object, and store it in the **Configuration** property. You do this by calling the **Build** method on the **builder** variable in the constructor.

```
Configuration = builder.Build();
```

12. To replace the hardcoded text *Hello, from My World!* With the value stored in the **Message** property in the *appsettings.json* file, you have to index into the **Configuration** property. Store the value in a variable in the **Configure** method.

```
var message = Configuration["Message"];
```

13. Now, replace the hardcoded text with the variable.

```
await context.Response.WriteAsync(message);
```

14. Save all the files and go to the browser. Refresh the application to see the new message.

Hello, from configuration

The **Startup** class' code, so far:

```
public class Startup
{
    public IConfiguration Configuration { get; set; }

    public Startup()
    {
        var builder = new ConfigurationBuilder()
            .SetBasePath(Directory.GetCurrentDirectory())
            .AddJsonFile("appsettings.json");

        Configuration = builder.Build();
    }

    public void Configure(IApplicationBuilder app,
    IHostingEnvironment env, ILoggerFactory loggerFactory)
    {
        loggerFactory.AddConsole();

        if (env.IsDevelopment())
        {
            app.UseDeveloperExceptionPage();
        }

        app.Run(async (context) =>
        {
            var message = Configuration["Message"];
            await context.Response.WriteAsync(message);
        });
    }
}
```

Creating a Service

Instead of using one specific source to fetch data, you can use services to fetch data from different sources, depending on the circumstance. This mean that you, through the use of configuration, can use different data sources according to the need at hand.

You might want to fetch data from a JSON file when building the service, and later switch to another implementation of that service, to fetch real data.

To achieve this, you create an interface that the service classes implement, and then use that interface when serving up the instances. Because the service classes implement the same interface, instances from them are interchangeable.

To get access to the services from the **Configure** method in the **Startup** class, or any other constructor, model, or view, you must use dependency injection. That is, pass in the interface as a parameter to the method.

You must register the service interface, and the desired service class, with the **services** collection in the **ConfgureServices** method, in the **Startup** class. This determines which class will be used to create the instance, when dependency injection is used to pass in an instance of a class implementing the interface.

In the upcoming example, you will inject a service class into the **Configure** method, but it works just as well with regular classes that you want to inject into a constructor, model, or view, using dependency injection. The same type of registration that you did in the **ConfigureServices** method could be applied to this scenario, but you wouldn't have to implement it as a service.

You might ask how the **IApplicationBuilder** parameter gets populated in the **Configure** method, when no configuration has been added for it in the **ConfigureServices** method. The answer is that certain service objects will be served up for interfaces automatically by ASP.NET; one of those interfaces is the **IApplicationBuilder**. Another is the **IHosting-Environment** service, which handles different environments, such as development, staging, and production.

Example

Let's implement an example where you create two service classes that retrieve data in two different ways. The first will simply return a hardcoded string (you can pretend that the data is fetched from a database or a web service if you like), and the second class will return the value from the **Message** property that you added to the *appsettings.json* file.

You will begin by adding an interface called **IMessageService**, which will define a method called **GetMessage**, which returns a string.

Then you will implement that interface in a service class called **HardcodedMessageService**, which will return a hardcoded string. After implementing the class, you will add configuration for it and the interface in the **ConfigureServices** method and test the functionality.

Then you will implement another class called **ConfigurationMessageService**, which reads from the *application.json* file and returns the value from the **Message** property. To use the new service class, you must change the configuration. Then you will refresh the application in the browser to make sure that the configuration value is returned.

Adding the Interface
1. Right click on the project node in the Solution Explorer and select **Add-New Folder**.
2. Name the folder *Services*.
3. Right click on the *Services* folder and select **Add-New Item**.
4. Select the **Interface** template, name the interface **IMessageService**, and click the **Add** button.
5. Add the **public** access modifier to the interface (make it public).
6. Add a method called **GetMessage**, which return a **string** to the interface. It should not take any parameters.
7. Save the file.

The complete code for the interface:

```
public interface IMessageService
{
    string GetMessage();
}
```

Adding the HardcodedMessageService Class
1. Right click on the *Services* folder and select **Add-Class**.
2. Name the class **HardcodedMessageService** and click the **Add** button.
3. Implement the **IMessageService** interface in the class by clicking on the lightbulb icon that appears when you hover over the interface name when you have added it to the class. Select **Implement interface** in the menu that appears.
4. Remove the code line with the **throw** statement and return the string *Hardcoded message from a service.*
5. Save all files by pressing Ctrl+Shift+S on the keyboard.

The complete code for the **HardcodedMessageService** class:

```
public class HardCodedMessageService : IMessageService
{
    public string GetMessage()
    {
        return "Hardcoded message from a service.";
    }
}
```

Configure and Use the HardcodedMessageService Class
1. Open the *Startup.cs* file.
2. Locate the **ConfigureServices** method.
3. To create instances that can be swapped for the **IMessageService** interface when dependency injection is used, you must add a definition for it to the **services** collection. In this example, you want ASP.NET to swap out the interface with an instance of the **HardcodedMessageService** class. Add the definition by calling the **AddSingleton** method on the **services** object, specifying the interface as the first type and the class as the second type.
   ```
   services.AddSingleton<IMessageService, HardcodedMessageService>();
   ```
4. Now you can use dependency injection to access the **IMessageService** from the **Configure** method, and then call the **GetMessage** method on the passed-in **HardcodedMessageService** object named **msg**.
   ```
   public void Configure(IApplicationBuilder app, IHostingEnvironment env,
   ILoggerFactory loggerFactory, IMessageService msg)
   {
       ...
   }
   ```

5. Remove the line that declares the **message** variable from the **Run** block.
6. Replace the **message** variable name in the **WriteAsync** method with a call to the **GetMessage** method on the **msg** object.
   ```
   await context.Response.WriteAsync(msg.GetMessage());
   ```
7. Save all files, switch to the browser, and refresh the application. The message *Hardcoded message from a service* should appear.

Hardcoded message from a service.

The complete code for the **ConfigureServices** method:

```
public void ConfigureServices(IServiceCollection services)
{
    services.AddSingleton<IMessageService, HardcodedMessageService>();
}
```

The complete code for the **Configure** method:

```
public void Configure(IApplicationBuilder app, IHostingEnvironment env,
ILoggerFactory loggerFactory, IMessageService msg)
{
    loggerFactory.AddConsole();

    if (env.IsDevelopment())
    {
        app.UseDeveloperExceptionPage();
    }

    app.Run(async (context) =>
    {
        await context.Response.WriteAsync(msg.GetMessage());
    });
}
```

When adding a service to the service collection, you can choose between several **Add** methods. Here's a rundown of the most commonly used.

Singleton creates a single instance that is used throughout the application. It creates the instance when the first dependency-injected object is created.

Scoped services are lifetime services, created once per request within the scope. It is equivalent to **Singleton** in the current scope. In other words, the same instance is reused within the same HTTP request.

Transient services are created each time they are requested and won't be reused. This lifetime works best for lightweight, stateless services.

Add and Use the ConfigurationMessageService Class

1. Right click on the *Services* folder and select **Add-Class**.
2. Name the class **ConfigurationMessageService** and click the **Add** button.
3. Implement the **IMessageService** interface in the class.
4. Add a constructor to the class (you can use the *ctor* code snippet).
5. Inject the **IConfiguration** interface into the constructor and name it **configuration**.
6. Save the **configuration** object in a private class level variable called **_configuration**. You can let Visual Studio create the variable for you by writing the variable name in the method, clicking the lightbulb icon, and selecting **Generate field...**
```
private IConfiguration _configuration;

public ConfigurationMessageService(IConfiguration configuration)
{
    _configuration = configuration;
}
```
7. Remove the **throw** statement from the **GetMessage** method and return the string from the **Message** property stored in the *appsettings.json* file. You achieve this by indexing into the **Configuration** object.
```
return _configuration["Message"];
```
8. Open the *Startup.cs* file and locate the **ConfigureServices** method.
9. Change the **HardcodedMessageService** type to the **ConfigurationMessageService** type in the **AddSingleton** method call.

```
services.AddSingleton<IMessageService,
ConfigurationMessageService>();
```

10. Add another call to the **AddSingleton** method <u>above</u> the previous **AddSingleton** method call. This time use the existing **Configuration** object and pass it to the method's provider using a Lambda expression. This is another way to use the **Add** methods when you already have an object. You must add this line of code to prepare the **configuration** object for dependency injection.

```
services.AddSingleton(provider => Configuration);
```

11. Save all files by pressing Ctrl+Shift+S on the keyboard.
12. Switch over to the browser and refresh the application. You should now see the message *Hello, from configuration*, from the *appsettings.json* file.

Hello from configuration

The complete code for the **ConfigurationMessageService** class:

```
public class ConfigurationMessageService : IMessageService
{
    private IConfiguration _configuration;

    public ConfigurationMessageService(IConfiguration configuration)
    {
        _configuration = configuration;
    }

    public string GetMessage()
    {
        return _configuration["Message"];
    }
}
```

The complete code for the **ConfigureServices** method:

```
public void ConfigureServices(IServiceCollection services)
{
    //services.AddSingleton<IMessageService, HardCodedMessageService>();
    services.AddSingleton(provider => Configuration);
    services.AddSingleton<IMessageService,
        ConfigurationMessageService>();
}
```

Summary

In this chapter, you created your first ASP.NET application and added only the necessary pieces to get it up and running. Throughout the first part of this book you will add new functionality using services and middleware.

You also added a configuration file, and created and registered a service to make it available through dependency injection in other parts of the application.

In the next chapter, you will learn about middleware.

2. Middleware

In this chapter, you will add middleware that handles HTTP requests, and how the application behaves if there is an error. One key aspect of the middleware is to perform user authentication and authorization.

By the end of this chapter you will have built a middleware pipeline for a MVC application.

How Does Middleware Work?

Let's have a look at how middleware works and what it is used for.

When a HTTP request comes to the server, it is the middleware components that handle that request.

Each piece of middleware in ASP.NET is an object with a very limited, specific, and focused role. This means that you will have to add many middleware components for an application to work properly.

The following example illustrates what can happen when a HTTP POST request to a URL, ending with *reviews*, reaches the server.

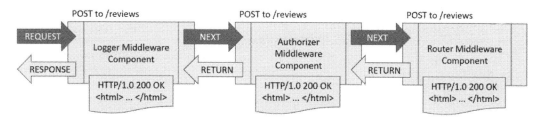

Logging is a separate middleware component that you might want to use to log information about every incoming HTTP request. It can see every piece of data, such as the headers, the query string, cookies, and access tokens. Not only can it read data from the request, it can also change information about it, and/or stop processing the request.

The most likely scenario with a logger is that it will log information and pass the processing onto the next middleware component in the pipeline.

This mean that middleware is a series of components executed in order.

The next middleware component might be an authorizer that can look at access tokens or cookies to determine if the request will proceed. If the request doesn't have the correct credentials, the authorizer middleware component can respond with a HTTP error code or redirect the user to a login page.

If the request is authorized, it will be passed to the next middleware component, which might be a routing component. The router will look at the URL to determine where to go next, by looking in the application for something that can respond. A method on a class could be called, returning a JSON, XML, or HTML page for instance. If it can't find anything that can respond, the component could throw a *404 Not Found* error.

Let's say that it found an HTML page to respond, then the pipeline starts to call all the middleware components in reverse order, passing along the HTML. When the response ultimately reaches the first component, which is the logger in our example, it might log the time the request took and then allow the response to go back over the network to the client's browser.

This is what middleware is, a way to configure how the application should behave. A series of components that handle specific, narrow tasks, such as handle errors, serve up static files and send HTTP requests to the MVC framework. This will make it possible for you to build the example video application.

This book will not go into the nitty-gritty of middleware, only the basics that you need to build an MVC application.

IApplicationBuilder

The **IApplicationBuilder** interface injected into the **Startup** class' **Configure** method is used when setting up the middleware pipeline.

```
public void Configure(IApplicationBuilder app, IHostingEnvironment env,
ILoggerFactory loggerFactory, IMessageService msg)
{
    loggerFactory.AddConsole();

    if (env.IsDevelopment())
    {
        app.UseDeveloperExceptionPage();
    }
```

```
app.Run(async (context) =>
{
    await context.Response.WriteAsync(msg.GetMessage());
});
}
```

To add middleware, you call extension methods on the **app** parameter, which contains the dependency injected object for the **IApplicationBuilder** interface. Two middleware components are already defined in the **Configure** method.

The **UseDeveloperExceptionPage** middleware component will display a pretty error page to the developer, but not the user; you can see that it is encapsulated inside an if-block that checks if the environment variable is set to the development environment.

The **UseDeveloperExceptionPage** middleware component then calls the **Run** middleware component that is used to process every response. **Run** is not frequently used because it is a terminal piece of middleware, which means that it is the end of the pipeline. No middleware component added after the **Run** component will execute, because **Run** doesn't call into any other middleware components.

```
app.Run(async (context) =>
{
    await context.Response.WriteAsync(msg.GetMessage());
});
```

By using the **context** object passed-into the **Run** method, you can find out anything about the request through its **Request** object, the header information for instance. It will also have access to a **Response** object, which currently is used to print out a string.

In the previous chapter, you called the **GetMessage** method on the message service in the **Run** method .

Most middleware components will be added by calling a method beginning with **Use** on the **app** object, such as **app.UseDeveloperExceptionPage**.

As you can see, there are several middleware components available out of the box using the **app** object. You can add more middleware components by installing NuGet packages containing middleware.

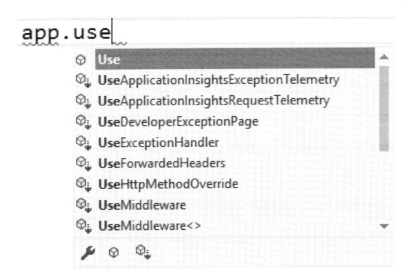

Handling Exceptions

Let's have a look at how exception messages are handled by the pipeline. As previously mentioned the **app.UseDeveloperExceptionPage** middleware is in place to help the developer with any exceptions that might occur. To test this behavior, you can add a **throw** statement at the top of the **Run**-block and refresh the application in the browser.

1. Open the *Startup.cs* file and locate the **Run** middleware in the **Configure** method.

2. Add a generic **throw** statement that returns the string *Fake Exception!* to the **Run**-block.

```
app.Run(async (context) =>
{
    throw new Exception("Fake Exception!");
    await context.Response.WriteAsync(msg.GetMessage());
});
```

3. If you haven't already started the application, press Ctrl+F5 to start it without debugging. Otherwise switch to the browser and refresh the application.

4. A pretty error message will be displayed. Note that this message only will be displayed when in development mode. On this page, you can read detailed information about the error, query strings, cookie information, and header content.

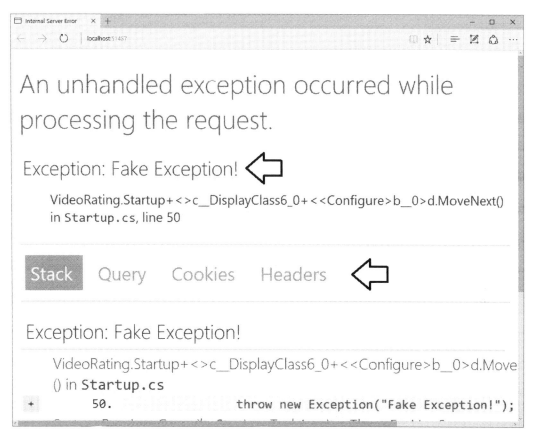

Now let's see what happens if you change the environment variable to *Production* and refresh the page.

1. Select **Project-*AspNetCoreVideo* Properties** in the main menu.
2. Click on the **Debug** tab on the left side of the dialog.
3. Change the **ASPNETCORE_ENVIRONMENT** property to *Production*.
4. Save all files (Ctrl+Shift+S).
5. Refresh the application in the browser.
6. Now you will get a *HTTP 500 - Can't display this page* error, which is what a regular user would see. If you don't see this message, then you have to manually build the project with Ctrl+F5.

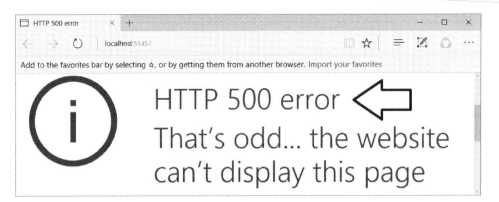

7. Switch back to Visual Studio and change back the **ASPNETCORE_ENVIRONMENT** property to *Development*.
8. Save all files.
9. Refresh the application in the browser; you should now be back to the pretty error page.

Now let's see what happens if we comment out the **app.UseDeveloperExceptionPage** middleware.

1. Open the *Setup.cs* file and locate the **Configure** method.
2. Comment out the call to the **app.UseDeveloperExceptionPage** middleware.
   `//app.UseDeveloperExceptionPage();`

3. Save the file.
4. Refresh the application in the browser.
5. The plain HTTP 500 error should be displayed because you no longer are loading the middleware that produces the pretty error message.
6. Uncomment the code again and save the file.
7. Refresh the browser one last time to make sure that the pretty error message is displayed.
8. Remove the **throw** statement from the **Run**-block and save the file.

You can use the **IHostingEnvironment** object, passed in through dependency injection, to find out information about the environment. You have already used this to determine if you are in the development environment, and if so, display a pretty error page. You can also use it to find out the absolute path to the **wwwroot** directory in the project with the **WebRootPath** property.

Serving Up Static Files

A feature that nearly all web applications need is the ability to serve up static files, such as JSON, CSS, and HTML files. To allow ASP.NET to serve up files, you must add a new middleware component that is called with the **UseStaticFiles** method, located in the **Microsoft .AspNetCore.StaticFiles** NuGet package.

Without that middleware component, the application will display the message from the **Run** middleware.

Let's add an HTML file to the **wwwroot** folder and see what happens, and why. Static files must be added to the **wwwroot** folder for ASP.NET to find them.

1. Right click on the **wwwroot** folder and select **Add-New Item**.
2. Search for the **HTML Page** template and select it.
3. Name the file *index.html* and click the **Add** button.
4. Add the text *An HTML Page* to the **<title>** tag, and *Hello, from index.html* in the **<body>** tag.
5. Save all files and navigate to the */index.html* page in the browser.
6. The message *Hello, from configuration* is displayed, which probably isn't what you expected.

The reason why the message *Hello, from configuration* is displayed is that there currently is no middleware that can serve up the static file. Instead the message in the **Run** middleware, which is accessible, will be displayed.

Let's fix this by adding a new middleware located in the **Microsoft.AspNetCore.StaticFiles** NuGet package.

When the **UseStaticFiles** method is called on the app object, ASP.NET will look in the **wwwroot** folder for the desired file. If a suitable file is found the next piece of middleware will not be called.

1. Right click on the project node in the Solution Explorer and select **Manage NuGet Packages**.
2. Click the **Browse** link at the top of the manager window.
3. Search for **Microsoft.AspNetCore.StaticFiles** in the search field.
4. Select the **Microsoft.AspNetCore.StaticFiles** package and click the **Install** button.

5. Click **OK** and **Accept** in the pop-up dialogs.
6. Close the NuGet manager.
7. Open the *Startup.cs* file and locate the **Configure** method.
8. Add a call to the **UseStaticFiles** method on the **app** object <u>above</u> the **Run** middleware.
   ```
   app.UseStaticFiles();
   ```
9. Save all the files and refresh the application in the browser.
10. The *index.html* file should be served up and displayed.

Hello from index.html

The complete code for the **Configure** method:

```
public void Configure(IApplicationBuilder app, IHostingEnvironment env,
ILoggerFactory loggerFactory, IMessageService msg)
{
    loggerFactory.AddConsole();

    if (env.IsDevelopment())
    {
        app.UseDeveloperExceptionPage();
    }

    app.UseStaticFiles();
```

```
    app.Run(async (context) =>
    {
        await context.Response.WriteAsync(msg.GetMessage());
    });
}
```

Serving Up Default Files

One of the features of ASP.NET is the ability to serve up default files for the root of the web application. Currently there is no middleware component added to the pipeline with that functionality. To add it you can call the **UseDefaultFiles** method before the **UseStatic-Files** method call; it must be added before that method call for the pipeline to recognize it and modify the HTTP request.

```
app.UseDefaultFiles();
app.UseStaticFiles();
```

Instead of adding the two previously mentioned middleware components, you can call the **UseFileServer** method, which contains a call to the two previously mentioned methods, as well as other functionality.

```
app.UseFileServer();
```

When you navigate to the root of the web application the *index.html* file will be served up to the user, because it is a default file.

If you try to reach a resource that is unavailable, the application falls through to the **Run** middleware and displays that message.

Setting Up ASP.NET MVC

The last thing you will do in this chapter is to set up the ASP.NET MVC middleware and add a simple controller to test that it works.

Three things need to be added to the application to enable MVC. First you need to add the **Microsoft.AspNetCore.Mvc** (version 1.1.4) NuGet package, then you need to add the MVC services, and lastly you need to add the MVC middleware.

Then you need to add a controller class with an **Index** action method that can be requested from the browser. In ASP.NET MVC, static HTML files, such as *index.html*, are not used. Instead views are usually used to serve up the HTML, JavaScript, and CSS content to the user. You will learn more about MVC in the next chapter. For now, let's look at a simple example.

Adding the MVC NuGet Package

To add the **Microsoft.AspNetCore.Mvc** (version 1.1.4) NuGet package, you can either use the NuGet Manager or type in the package name into the *.csproj* file manually.

1. Right click on the project node in the Solution Explorer and select **Edit AspNetCoreVideo.csproj**.
2. Locate the **ItemGroup** element in the file.
3. Add a new **PackageReference** element and assign the NuGet package name to its **Include** attribute.
4. Choose the version number with the **Version** attribute; the *1.1.4* version is used in this example.
    ```
    <ItemGroup>
        <PackageReference Include="Microsoft.AspNetCore.Mvc"
            Version="1.1.4" />
        . . .
    </ItemGroup>
    ```
5. Save the file to install the NuGet package.
6. You must add a controller that can respond to the HTTP requests coming in to the application pipeline. The convention is to add controller classes to a folder named *Controllers*. Right click on the project node and select **Add-New Folder** and name it *Controllers*.
7. Right click on the *Controllers* folder and select **Add-Class**.
8. Name the class **HomeController** (the convention for a default controller) and click the **Add** button. The class doesn't have to inherit from any other class.
    ```
    public class HomeController
    {
    }
    ```
9. Add a **public** method named **Index** that returns a **string**, to the **HomeController** class. Return the string *Hello, from the controller!* in the method.
    ```
    public string Index()
    {
        return "Hello, from the controller!";
    }
    ```

10. Save all files and refresh the application in the browser. Note that the *index.html* file still is being served up to the user, displaying the text *Hello, from index.html*. This, because you haven't yet added the MVC service and middleware.

11. Delete the *index.html* file you added to the **wwwroot** folder; you won't be needing it anymore since you want the controller to respond instead. You can do this either from the Solution Explorer or a File Explorer window in Windows.

12. Open the *Startup.cs* file and locate the **Configure** method.

13. Add the MVC middleware after the **UseFileServer** middleware method call, by calling the **UseMvcWithDefaultRoute** method. Adding it before the **UseFileServer** middleware would give the application a different behavior.
    `app.UseMvcWithDefaultRoute();`

14. Save the file and refresh the application in the browser. You will be greeted by an exception message telling you that the necessary MVC service hasn't been added.

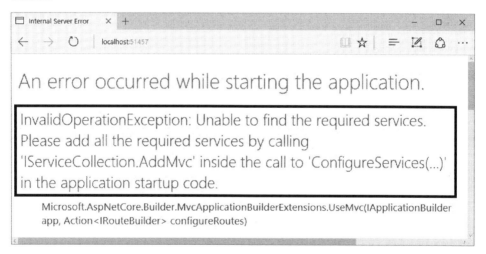

15. Open the **Startup** class and locate the **ConfigureServices** method.

16. Add the MVC services to the **services** collection at the top of the method. This will give ASP.NET everything it needs to run a MVC application.
    ```
    public void ConfigureServices(IServiceCollection services)
    {
        services.AddMvc();

        ...
    }
    ```

17. Save the file and refresh the application in the browser. Now the message *Hello, from the controller!* will be displayed to the user. This means that MVC is installed and working correctly. In the next chapter, you will implement a more sophisticated controller using HTML.

Summary

In this chapter, you learned how to configure middleware in the **Configure** method of the **Startup** class.

The application now has several middleware components, including a developer error page and MVC. The MVC middleware can forward a request to an action method in a controller class to serve up content.

In the next chapter, you will learn more about controllers, and that you can use many different controllers in the same application, and how to route the HTTP requests to the appropriate one.

You will also create controller actions that return HTML, instead of just a string, as in the previous example.

3. MVC Controllers

In this chapter, you will learn about MVC, which is a popular design pattern for the user interface layer in applications, where *M* stands for Model, *V* stands for View, and *C* stands for Controller. In larger applications, MVC is typically combined with other design patterns, like data access and messaging patterns, to create a full application stack. This book will focus on the MVC fundamentals.

The controller is responsible for handling any HTTP requests that come to the application. It could be a user browsing to the */videos* URL of the application. The controller's response-bility is then to gather and combine all the necessary data and package it in model objects, which act as data carriers to the views.

The model is sent to the view, which uses the data when it's rendered into HTML. The HTML is then sent back to the client browser as a HTML response.

The MVC pattern creates a separation of concerns between the model, view, and con-troller. The sole responsibility of the controller is to handle the request and to build a model. The model's responsibility is to transport data and logic between the controller and the view, and the view is responsible for transforming that data into HTML.

For this to work, there must be a way to send HTTP requests to the correct controller. That is the purpose of ASP.NET MVC routing.

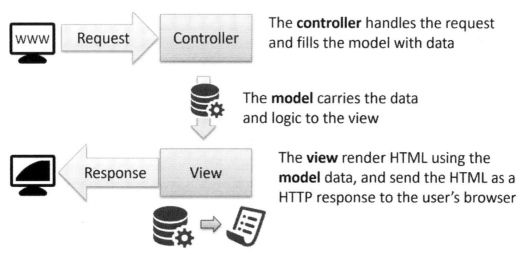

The **controller** handles the request and fills the model with data

The **model** carries the data and logic to the view

The **view** render HTML using the model data, and send the HTML as a HTTP response to the user's browser

1. The user sends a HTTP request to the server by typing in a URL.
2. The controller on the server handles the request by fetching data and creating a model object.
3. The model object is sent to the view.
4. The view uses the data to render HTML.
5. The view is sent back to the user's browser in a HTTP response.

Routing

The ASP.NET middleware you implemented in the previous chapter must be able to route incoming HTTP requests to a controller, since you are building an ASP.NET Core MVC application. The decision to send the request to a controller action is determined by the URL, and the configuration information you provide.

It is possible to define multiple routes. ASP.NET will evaluate them in the order they have been added. You can also combine convention-based routing with attribute routing if you need. Attribute routing is especially useful in edge cases where convention-based routing is hard to use.

One way to provide the routing configuration is to use convention-based routing in the **Startup** class. With this type of configuration, you tell ASP.NET how to find the controller's name, action's name, and possibly parameter values in the URL. The controller is a C# class, and an action is a public method in a controller class. A parameter can be any value that can be represented as a string, such as an integer or a GUID.

The configuration can be done with a Lambda expression, as an inline method:

```
app.UseMvc(routes =>
{
    routes.MapRoute(
        name: "default",
        template: "{controller=Home}/{action=Index}/{id?}");
});
```

ASP.NET looks at the route template to determine how to pull apart the URL. If the URL contains */Home* it will locate the **HomeController** class by convention, because the name begins with *Home*. If the URL contains */Home/Index* ASP.NET will look for a public action method called **Index** inside the **HomeController** class. If the URL contains */Home/Index/ 123* ASP.NET will look for a public action method called **Index** with an **Id** parameter inside the **HomeController** class. The *Id* is optional when defined with a question mark after its name. The controller and action names can also be omitted, because they have default values in the **Route** template.

Another way to implement routing is to use attribute routing, where you assign attributes to the controller class and its action methods. The metadata in those attributes tell ASP.NET when to call a specific controller and action.

Attribute routing requires a **using** statement to the **Microsoft.AspNetCore.Mvc** name-space.

```
[Route("[controller]/[action]")]
public class HomeController
{
}
```

Convention-Based Routing

In the previous chapter, you created a C# controller class named **HomeController**. A controller doesn't have to inherit from any other class when returning basic data such as strings. You also implemented routing using the **UseMvcWithDefaultRoute** method, which comes with built-in support for default routing for the **HomeController**. When building an application with multiple controllers, you want to use convention-based routing, or attribute routing to let ASP.NET know how to handle the incoming HTTP requests.

Let's implement the default route explicitly, first with a method and then with a Lambda expression. To set this up you replace the **UseMvcWithDefaultRoute** method with the **UseMvc** method in the **Startup** class. In the **UseMvc** method, you then either call a method or add a Lambda expression for an inline method.

Implement Routing
1. Open the **Startup** class and locate the **Configure** method.
2. Replace the **UseMvcWithDefaultRoute** method with the **UseMvc** method and add a Lambda expression with the default route template.
```
app.UseMvc(routes =>
{
    routes.MapRoute(
        name: "default",
        template: "{controller=Home}/{action=Index}/{id?}");
```

```
});
```

3. Save the file and refresh the application in the browser. As you can see, the **Index** action was reached with the explicit URL */home/index*.

4. Now change to a URL without the action's name, and only the controller's name (*/Home*). You should still get the message from the action method, because you specified the **Index** action method as the default action in the routing template.

5. Now call the root URL. A root URL is a URL with only the localhost and the port specified (*http://localhost:xxxxx*). This should also call the **Index** action because both *Home* and *Index* are declared as default values for the controller and the action in the routing template.

Adding Another Controller

Now that you have implemented default routing, it's time to add another controller and see how you can reach that controller.

1. Right click on the **Controllers** folder and select **Add-Class**.

2. Name the controller **EmployeeController** and click the **Add** button.
   ```
   public class EmployeeController
   {
   }
   ```

3. Add an action method called **Name** that returns a string to the controller. Return your name from the method.
   ```
   public string Name()
   {
       return "Jonas";
   }
   ```

4. Add another action method called **Country** that also returns a string. Return your country of residence from the method.

5. Save the file and switch to the browser. Try with the root URL first. This should take you to */Home/Index* as defined in the default route.

6. Change the URL to */Employee/Name*; this should display your name in the browser. In my case *Jonas*.

7. Change the URL to */Employee/Country*; this should display your country of residence in the browser. In my case *Sweden*.

8. Change the URL to */Employee*. ASP.NET passes the request on to the **Run** middleware, which returns the string *Hello from configuration*, using the **ConfigurationMessageService** that you implemented earlier. The reason is that

the **EmployeeController** class has no action method called **Index**, which is the name defined as the default action in the default route.

9. Add a new method called **Index** that returns the string *Hello from Employee* to the **EmployeeController** class.
10. Save the file and refresh the application in the browser, or use the */Employee* URL. Now the text *Hello from Employee* should be displayed.

The complete code for the **EmployeeController** class:

```
public class EmployeeController
{
    public string Name()
    {
        return "Jonas";
    }

    public string Country()
    {
        return "Sweden";
    }

    public string Index()
    {
        return "Hello from Employee";
    }
}
```

Attribute Routing
Let's implement an example of attribute routing, using the **EmployeeController** and its actions.

1. Open the **EmployeeController** class.
2. If you want the controller to respond to */Employee* with attribute routing, you add the **Route** attribute above the controller class, specifying *employee* as its parameter value. You will have to bring in the **Microsoft.AspNetCore.Mvc** namespace for the **Route** attribute to be available.
    ```
    [Route("employee")]
    public class EmployeeController
    ```

3. Save the file and navigate to the */Employee* URL. An exception is displayed in the browser. The reason for this exception is that ASP.NET can't determine which of the three actions is the default action.

4. To solve this, you can specify the **Route** attribute for each of the action methods, and use an empty string for the default action. Let's make the **Index** action the default action, and name the routes for the other action methods the same as the methods.

```
[Route("")]
public string Index()
{
    return "Hello from Employee";
}

[Route("name")]
public string Name()
{
    return "Jonas";
}

[Route("country")]
public string Country()
{
    return "Sweden";
}
```

5. Save the file and refresh the application in the browser. Make sure that the URL ends with */Employee*. You should see the message *Hello from Employee* in the browser.
6. Navigate to the other actions by tagging on the route name of the specific actions to the */Employee* URL, for instance */Employee/Name*. You should be able to navigate to them and see their information.
7. Let's clean up the controller and make its route more reusable. Instead of using a hardcoded value for the controller's route, you can use the **[controller]** token

that represents the name of the controller class (*Employee* in this case). This makes it easier if you need to rename the controller for some reason.

```
[Route("[controller]")]
public class EmployeeController
```

8. You can do the same for the action methods, but use the **[action]** token instead. ASP.NET will then replace the token with the action's name.

```
[Route("[action]")]
public string Name()
{
    return "Jonas";
}
```

9. Save the file and refresh the application in the browser. Make sure that the URL ends with */Employee/Name*. You should see your name in the browser.

10. You can also use literals in the route. Let's say that you want the route for the **EmployeeController** to be *Company/Employee*; you could then prepend the controller's route with *Company/*.

```
[Route("company/[controller]")]
public class EmployeeController
```

11. Save the file and refresh the application in the browser. Make sure that the URL ends with */Employee/Name*. You will not see your name in the browser; instead ASP.NET displays the text from the **Run** middleware. The reason for this is that there isn't a route to */Employee/Name* anymore; it has changed to */Company/Employee/Name*. Change the URL in the browser to */Company/Employee/Name*. You should now see your name again.

12. If you don't want a default route in your controller, you can clean it up even more by removing all the action attributes and changing the controller route to include the **[action]** token. This means that you no longer can go to */Company/Employee* and reach the **Index** action; you will have to give an explicit URL in the browser to reach each action.

```
[Route("company/[controller]/[action]")]
public class EmployeeController
```

13. Remove all the **Route** attributes from the action methods and change the controller's **Route** attribute to include the **[action]** token. Save the file and refresh the browser with the URL */Company/Employee/Name*. You should now see your name.

14. Now navigate to the */Company/Employee* URL. You should see the message from the **Run** middleware because ASP.NET couldn't find any default action in the **EmployeeController**. Remember, you must give a specific URL with an action specified.

The complete code in the **EmployeeController** class:

```
[Route("company/[controller]/[action]")]
public class EmployeeController
{
    public string Name()
    {
        return "Jonas";
    }

    public string Country()
    {
        return "Sweden";
    }

    public string Index()
    {
        return "Hello from Employee";
    }
}
```

IActionResult

The controller actions that you have seen so far have all returned strings. When working with actions, you rarely return strings. Most of the time you use the **IActionResult** return type, which can return many types of data, such as objects and views. To gain access to **IActionResult** or derivations thereof, the controller class must inherit the **Controller** class.

There are more specific implementations of that interface, for instance the **ContentResult** class, which can be used to return simple content such as strings. Using a more specific return type can be beneficial when unit testing, because you get a specific data type to test against.

Another return type is **ObjectType**, which often is used in Web API applications because it turns the result into an object that can be sent over HTTP. JSON is the default return type, making the result easy to use from JavaScript on the client. The data carrier can be configured to deliver the data in other formats, such as XML.

A specific data type helps the controller decide what to do with the data returned from an action. The controller itself does not do anything with the data, and does not write anything into the response. It is the framework that acts on that decision, and transforms the data into something that can be sent over HTTP. That separation of letting the controller decide what should be returned, and the framework doing the actual transformation, gives you flexibility and makes the controller easier to test.

Implementing ContentResult

Let's change the **Name** action to return a **ContentResult**.

1. Open the **EmployeeController** class.
2. Have the **EmployeeController** class inherit the **Controller** class.
   ```
   public class EmployeeController : Controller
   ```

3. Change the **Name** action's return type to **ContentResult**.
   ```
   public ContentResult Name()
   ```

4. Change the **return** statement to return a content object by calling the **Content** method, and pass in the string to it.
   ```
   public ContentResult Name()
   {
       return Content("Jonas");
   }
   ```

5. Save all files, open the browser, and navigate to the *Company/Employees/Name* URL.
6. Your name should be returned to the browser, same as before.

Using a Model Class

Using a model class, you can send objects with data and logic to the browser. By convention, model classes should be stored in a folder called **Models**, but in larger applications it's not uncommon to store models in a separate project, which is referenced from the application. A model is a POCO (*Plain Old CLR Object* or *Plain Old C# Object*) class that can have attributes specifying how the browser should behave when using it, such as checking the length of a string or displaying data with a certain control.

Let's add a **Video** model class that holds data about a video, such as a unique id and a title. Typically you don't hardcode a model into a controller action; the objects are usually fetched from a data source such as a database (which you will do in another chapter).

1. Right click on the project node in the Solution Explorer and select **Add-New Folder**.
2. Name the folder *Models*.
3. Right click on the *Models* folder and select **Add-Class**.
4. Name the class **Video** and click the **Add** button.
5. Add an **int** property called **Id**. This will be the unique id when it is used as an entity in the database later.
6. Add a **string** property called **Title**. Let's keep it simple for now; you will add more properties later.

```
public class Video
{
    public int Id { get; set; }
    public string Title { get; set; }
}
```

7. Open the **HomeController** class and inherit the **Controller** class.

```
public class HomeController : Controller
```

8. Instead of returning a string from the **Index** action, you will change the return type to **ObjectResult**.

```
public ObjectResult Index()
```

9. Create an instance of the **Video** model class and store it in a variable called **model**. Assign values to its properties when you instantiate it.

```
var model = new Video { Id = 1, Title = "Shreck" };
```

10. Return an instance of the **ObjectResult** class passing in the **model** object as its parameter.

```
return new ObjectResult(model);
```

11. Save the file and browse to the */Home* URL. As you can see, the object has been sent to the client as a JSON object.

```
{"id":1,"title":"Shreck"}
```

The complete code for the **HomeController** class:

```
public class HomeController : Controller
{
    public ObjectResult Index()
    {
        var model = new Video { Id = 1, Title = "Shreck" };
        return new ObjectResult(model);
    }
}
```

Introduction to Views

The most popular way to render a view from a ASP.NET Core MVC application is to use the Razor view engine. To render the view, a **ViewResult** is returned from the controller action using the **View** method. It carries with it the name of the view in the filesystem, and a model object if needed.

The framework receives that information and produces the HTML that is sent to the browser.

Let's implement a view for the **Index** action and pass in a **Video** object as its model.

1. Open the **HomeController** class.
2. Change the return type of the **Index** action to **ViewResult**.
    ```
    public ViewResult Index()
    ```
3. Call the **View** method and pass in the **model** object that you created earlier.
    ```
    return View(model);
    ```
4. Save the file and refresh the application in the browser.
5. By convention ASP.NET will look for a view with the same name as the action that produced the result. It will look in two places, both subfolders to a folder called *Views*: the first is a folder with the same name as the controller class, the second a folder named *Shared*. In this case, there is no view for the **Index** action, so an exception will be thrown.

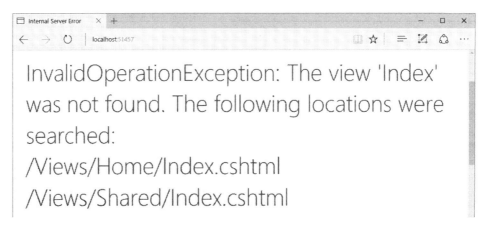

6. To fix this you must add a view called **Index**. Right click on the project node in the Solution Explorer and select **Add-New Folder**.
7. Name the folder *Views*.
8. Right click on the *Views* folder and select **Add-New Folder**; name it *Home*.
9. Right click on the *Home* folder and select **Add-New Item**.
10. Select the **MVC View Page** template and click the **Add** button (it should be named *Index* by default).
11. Delete everything in the *Index.cshtml* view that was added.
12. Type *html* and press the **Tab** key on the keyboard to insert a skeleton for the view.
13. Add the text *Video* to the <title> element.
    `<title>Video</title>`

14. Although you can use the passed-in model and have it inferred from the actual object, it is in most cases better to explicitly specify it to gain access to IntelliSense and pre-compilation errors. You specify the model using the **@model** directive at the top of the view. Note that it should be declared with a lower-case *m*.
    `@model AspNetCoreVideo.Models.Video`

15. To display the value from the **Title** property in the <body> element, you use the **@Model** object (note the capital-letter *M*, and that it is prefixed with the @-sign to specify that it is Razor syntax). The IntelliSense will show all properties available in the model object passed to the view.
    `<body>@Model.Title</body>`

16. Save the **Index** view and refresh the application in the browser. You should now see the video title in the browser and the text *Video* in the browser tab.

Shreck

A View with a Data Collection

Now that you know how to display one video, it's time to display a collection of videos. To achieve this, you'll first have to create the video collection and then pass it to the view displaying the data. In the view, you'll use a Razor **foreach** loop to display the data as HTML.

1. Open the **HomeController** class.
2. Replace the single **Video** object with a list of **Video** objects.
   ```
   var model = new List<Video>
   {
       new Video { Id = 1, Title = "Shreck" },
       new Video { Id = 2, Title = "Despicable Me" },
       new Video { Id = 3, Title = "Megamind" }
   };
   ```
3. Switch to the browser and navigate to */Home/Index*, or start the application without debugging (Ctrl+F5), if it's not already started.
4. An error message will appear, telling you that you are sending in a collection (list) of **Video** objects to the **Index** view, when it is designed for a single **Video** object.

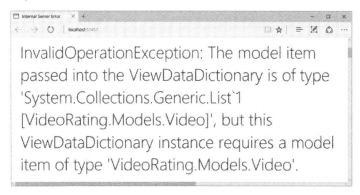

5. To solve this, you will have to change the **@model** directive in the **Index** view. You can use the **IEnumerable** interface, which is a nice abstraction to many different collections.
    ```
    @model IEnumerable<AspNetCoreVideo.Models.Video>
    ```

6. When you change the **@model** directive, the **@Model** object no longer is a single instance of the **Video** class; you therefore must implement a loop to display the data in the model. Remove the **@Model.Title** property and add a table by typing *table* in the <body> element and press the **Tab** key.
    ```
    <table>
        <tr>
            <td></td>
        </tr>
    </table>
    ```

7. Add a **foreach** loop around the <tr> element with Razor to loop over the **Model** object. Using Razor makes it possible to mix C# and HTML. Note that you don't add the @-sign when already inside Razor code, but you use it when in HTML. Use the loop variable to add the **Id** and **Title** properties to the table row. The **video** variable in the loop doesn't have an @-sign because the **foreach** loop has one. When the **video** variable is used in HTML, however, the @-sign must be used.
    ```
    @foreach (var video in Model)
    {
        <tr>
            <td>@video.Id</td>
            <td>@video.Title</td>
        </tr>
    }
    ```

8. Save all files, switch to the browser, and refresh the application. The three films should now be displayed.

The full code for the **Index** action:

```
public ViewResult Index()
{
    var model = new List<Video>
    {
        new Video { Id = 1, Title = "Shreck" },
        new Video { Id = 2, Title = "Despicable Me" },
        new Video { Id = 3, Title = "Megamind" }
    };
    return View(model);
}
```

The full markup for the **Index** view:

```
@model IEnumerable<AspNetCoreVideo.Models.Video>

<html xmlns="http://www.w3.org/1999/xhtml">
<head>
    <title>Video</title>
</head>
<body>
    <table>
        @foreach (var video in Model)
        {
        <tr>
            <td>@video.Id</td>
            <td>@video.Title</td>
        </tr>
        }
    </table>
</body>
</html>
```

Adding a Data Service

Hardcoding data in a controller is not good practice. Instead you want to take advantage of dependency injection to make data available in a constructor, using a service component, like the **Message** service you added earlier.

One big benefit of implementing a service is that its interface can be used to implement different components. In this book you will implement one for Mock data and one for a SQL Server database.

In this section, you will implement a **MockVideoData** component that implements an interface called **IVideoData**.

The data will be implemented as a **List<Video>**. Note that a **List** collection isn't thread safe, and should be used with caution in web applications; but this code is for experimental purposes, and the component will only ever be accessed by one user at a time.

To begin with, the interface will only define one method, called **GetAll**, which will return a **IEnumerable<Video>** collection.

1. Right click on the *Services* folder and select **Add-New Item**.
2. Select the **Interface** template, name it **IVideoData**, and click the **Add** button.
3. Add the **public** access modifier to the interface to make it publicly available.
```
public interface IVideoData
{
}
```

4. Add a method called **GetAll** that returns a **IEnumerable<Video>** collection.
```
IEnumerable<Video> GetAll();
```

5. Right click on the *Services* folder and select **Add-Class**.
6. Name the class **MockVideoData** and click the **Add** button.
7. Implement the **IVideoData** interface in the class.
```
public class MockVideoData : IVideoData
{
    public IEnumerable<Video> GetAll()
    {
        throw new NotImplementedException();
    }
}
```

8. Add a private field called **_videos** of type **IEnumerable<Video>** to the class. This field will hold the video data, loaded from a constructor.
```
private IEnumerable<Video> _videos;
```

9. Add a constructor below the **_videos** field in the class. You can use the *ctor* snippet and hit the **Tab** key.
```
public MockVideoData()
{
}
```

10. Open the **HomeController** class and copy the video list, then paste it into the **MockVideoData** constructor. Remove the **var** keyword and rename the **model** variable **_videos** to assign the list to the field you just added.
```
_videos = new List<Video>
{
    new Video { Id = 1, Title = "Shreck" },
    new Video { Id = 2, Title = "Despicable Me" },
    new Video { Id = 3, Title = "Megamind" }
};
```

11. Remove the **throw** statement in the **GetAll** method and return the **_videos** list.
```
public IEnumerable<Video> GetAll()
{
    return _videos;
}
```

12. Now that the service is complete, you must add it to the **services** collection in the **Startup** class' **ConfigureServices** method. Previously you registered the **IMessageService** interface with the services collection using the **AddSingleton** method; this would ensure that only one instance of the defined class would exist. Let's use another method this time. Register the **IVideoData** interface using the **AddScoped** method; this will ensure that one object is created for each HTTP request. The HTTP request can then flow through many services that share the same instance of the **MockVideoData** class.
```
services.AddScoped<IVideoData, MockVideoData>();
```

13. Open the **HomeController** class and add a private field of type **IVideoData** called **_videos** on class level. This field will hold the data fetched from the service.
```
private IVideoData _videos;
```

14. Add a constructor to the **HomeController** class and inject the **IVideoData** interface into it. Name the parameter **videos**. Assign the **videos** parameter to the **_videos** field, inside the constructor. This will make the video service available throughout the controller.
```
public HomeController(IVideoData videos)
{
    _videos = videos;
}
```

15. Replace the hardcoded **List<Video>** collection assigned to the **model** variable in the **Index** action, with a call to the **GetAll** method on the service.
```
var model = _videos.GetAll();
```

16. Save all the files.
17. Switch to the browser and refresh the application. You should now see the list of videos.

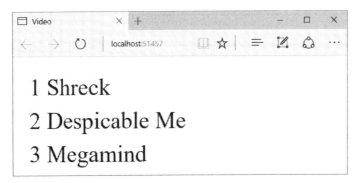

The complete code for the **IVideoData** interface:

```
public interface IVideoData {
    IEnumerable<Video> GetAll();
}
```

The complete code for the **MockVideoData** class:

```
public class MockVideoData : IVideoData
{
    private List<Video> _videos;

    public MockVideoData()
    {
        _videos = new List<Video>
        {
            new Video { Id = 1, Genre = Models.Genres.Romance,
                Title = "Shreck" },
            new Video { Id = 2, Genre = Models.Genres.Comedy,
                Title = "Despicable Me" },
            new Video { Id = 3, Genre = Models.Genres.Action,
                Title = "Megamind" }
        };
    }

    public IEnumerable<Video> GetAll() {
        return _videos;
    }
}
```

Summary

In this chapter, you learned about the MVC (Model-View-Controller) design pattern; how the controller receives an HTTP request, gathers data from various sources, and creates a model, which is then processed into HTML by the view, along with its own markup.

You will continue to use MVC throughout the book and create more sophisticated views and models that can be used to view and edit data.

4. Models

In this chapter, you will learn more about different types of model classes in the MVC framework and how to use them.

Up until now, you have used the **Video** class as a model for the **Index** view. In simple solutions that might be fine, but in more complex solutions, you need to use entity models and view models. Sometimes you even make a more granular distinction between the models, using Data Transfer Objects (DTOs) with the view models.

An entity model is typically used to define a table in a database. A view model is used to transport data from the controller to the view, but sometimes the view model needs to contain objects, and that's where the DTOs come into play. Some might argue that DTOs are view models, and in some scenarios they are.

You will create a new folder called *Entities* and move the **Video** class to that folder. The reason for moving the file is that the **Video** class later will be used to define a table in a SQL Server database. A class used to define a database table is referred to as an entity. You will also add a new folder named *ViewModels*, which will hold the view models created throughout the first part of the book.

Important to note is that the view model typically contains other data than the entity model, although some properties are the same. One example is when a video is being added in a **Create** view. The view model needs some properties from the entity model, but could also need other information that is not stored in the **Video** entity and must be fetched from another database table, or an **enum**.

A view model is never used to directly update the database. To update the database the data from the view model is added to an entity model, which then in turn updates the database table.

Let's look at an example where an **enum** is used to display the genre a video belongs to. For simplicity, a video can only belong to one genre.

View Model Example

First you need to add an *Entities* folder and a *ViewModels* folder to the folder structure.

Changing the Folder Structure

1. Create a new folder called *Entities* in the project.
2. Move the *Video.cs* file from the *Models* folder to the *Entities* folder, using drag-and-drop.
3. Open the **Video** class and change the **Models** namespace to **Entities**.
   ```
   namespace AspNetCoreVideo.Entities
   ```

4. Open the **MockVideoData** class and change the **Models** namespace to **Entities**.
5. Open the **IVideoData** interface and change the **Models** namespace to **Entities**.
6. Open the **Index** view and change the **Models** namespace to **Entities**.
7. Open the **HomeController** class and remove any unused **using** statements.

Adding the View Model

1. Add a new folder called *ViewModels* to the project.
2. Add a class called **Genres** to the *Models* folder.
3. Replace the **class** keyword with the **enum** keyword and add some genres.
   ```
   public enum Genres
   {
       None,
       Horror,
       Comedy,
       Romance,
       Action
   }
   ```

4. Open the **Video** class and add an **int** property called **Genreld** to the class. This will hold the **enum** value for the video's genre.
   ```
   public class Video
   {
       public int Id { get; set; }
       public string Title { get; set; }
       public int GenreId { get; set; }
   }
   ```

5. Open the **MockVideoData** class and add a genre id for each video.
   ```
   new Video { Id = 3, GenreId = 2, Title = "Megamind" }
   ```

6. Add a class called **VideoViewModel** to the *ViewModel* folder.

7. The view model will contain the **Id** and **Title** properties, but you don't want to display the genre id; it would be nicer to display the actual genre. To achieve this, you add a **string** property called **Genre** to the **VideoViewModel** class, but not to the **Video** class.

```
public class VideoViewModel
{
    public int Id { get; set; }
    public string Title { get; set; }
    public string Genre { get; set; }
}
```

Using the View Model

Now that the view model has been created, you need to send it to the view as its model. This requires some changes to the **HomeController** class and the **Index** view. You need to fetch the video from the **_videos** collection using its id, and then convert the genre id to the name for the corresponding value in the **Genres enum**.

When the view model has been assigned values from the entity object and the **enum** name, it is sent to the view with the **View** method.

1. Open the **HomeController** class.
2. Use the LINQ **Select** method in the **Index** action to convert each video into a **VideoViewModel** object, and store it in the **model** field. Use the **Enum.GetName** method to fetch the genre corresponding to the video's genre id.

```
public ViewResult Index()
{
    var model = _videos.GetAll().Select(video =>
    new VideoViewModel
    {
        Id = video.Id,
        Title = video.Title,
        Genre = Enum.GetName(typeof(Genres), video.GenreId)
    });
    return View(model);
}
```

3. Open the **Index** view and change the **@model** directive to an **IEnumerable<VideoViewModel>**.

```
@model IEnumerable<AspNetCoreVideo.ViewModels.VideoViewModel>
```

4. Add a new <td> for the genre.

```
<td>@video.Genre</td>
```

5. Switch to the browser and refresh the application. As you can see, the genres are now displayed beside each of the video titles.

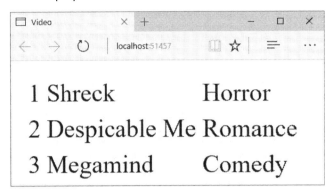

Adding a Details View

Now that you know how to use the **VideoViewModel** to send data to the **Index** view, it is time to add a new view to the **Views** folder.

The **Details** view will display a single video in the browser, based on the id sent to the **Details** action you will add next.

1. Add a new public action method called **Details** to the **HomeController**. It should have an **int** parameter named **id**, which will match a video id from the URL or the request data. The return type should be **IActionResult**, which makes it possible to return different types of data.
   ```
   public IActionResult Details(int id)
   {
   }
   ```

2. To fetch the video matching the passed-in id, you must add a new method called **Get** to the **IVideoData** interface. The method should have an **int** parameter called **id** and return a video object.
   ```
   Video Get(int id);
   ```

3. Now you need to implement that method in the **MockVideoData** class, and have it return the video matching the **id** parameter value. Use LINQ to fetch the video with the **FirstOrDefault** method.
   ```
   public Video Get(int id)
   {
       return _videos.FirstOrDefault(v => v.Id.Equals(id));
   }
   ```

4. Add a variable called **model** to the **Details** action in the **HomeController** class. Call the **Get** method to fetch the videos matching the passed-in id and assign them to the **model** variable.
```
var model = _videos.Get(id);
```

5. To test the **Get** method, return the **model** variable using an **ObjectResult** instance.
```
return new ObjectResult(model);
```

6. Save all files and switch to the browser. Navigate to the */Home/Details/2* URL. The video matching the id 2 should be displayed.

7. Change the **return** statement to return the **View** method and pass in an instance of the **VideoViewModel** class filled with data from the **model** variable.
```
return View(new VideoViewModel
    {
        Id = model.Id,
        Title = model.Title,
        Genre = Enum.GetName(typeof(Genres), model.GenreId)
    }
);
```

8. Add a new **MVC View Page** file called *Details.cshtml* to the *Views/Home* folder in the Solution Explorer.

9. Delete all content in the **Details** view.

10. Type *html* and hit **Tab** to add the HTML skeleton to the view.

11. Add the **@model** directive for a single **VideoViewModel** to the view. This enables the view to display information about one video.
```
@model AspNetCoreVideo.ViewModels.VideoViewModel
```

12. Add the text *Video* to the <title> element.

13. Add a <div> element inside the <body> element for each property.
```
<div>Id: @Model.Id</div>
<div>Title: @Model.Title</div>
<div>Genre: @Model.Genre</div>
```

14. Save all the files and switch to the browser and refresh. You should see the data for the video matching the id in the URL.

15. Change the id in the URL and make sure that the correct film is displayed.
16. Change to an id that doesn't exist. An error should be displayed in the browser. The reason for the error is that the **Get** method will return **null** if the video doesn't exist, and the view can't handle **null** values for the model.

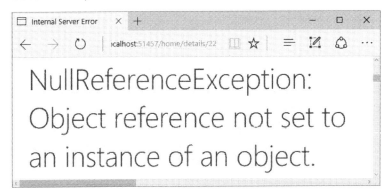

17. One way to solve this is to redirect to another action; in this case the **Index** action is appropriate. Add an if-statement above the previous **return** statement, which checks if the **model** is **null**; if it is, redirect to the **Index** action. Implementing this check will ensure that the action won't show the error message, and instead display the video list.
```
if (model == null)
    return RedirectToAction("Index");
```

18. Switch to the browser and refresh. The **Index** view should be displayed.
19. Let's add a link to the **Index** view in the **Details** view, for easy navigation back to the root. You can use a traditional HTML <a> tag, or you can use the Razor

ActionLink HTML helper method. There is a new, third way to add a link, using Tag Helpers. You will explore Tag Helpers shortly.

```
@Html.ActionLink("Home", "Index")
```

20. Switch to the browser and navigate to */Home/Details/2* URL. The view should have a link with the text *Home*. Click the link to get back to the **Index** view.

21. Now open the **Index** view and add links for the video ids. To achieve this, you must pass in an anonymous object as an extra parameter, and add an id property to that object.

```
<td>@Html.ActionLink(video.Id.ToString(), "Details",
    new { id = video.Id })</td>
```

22. Switch to the browser and go to the root (/). Click one of the links to view the details for that video.

The complete markup for the **Details** view:

```
@model AspNetCoreVideo.ViewModels.VideoViewModel

<html xmlns="http://www.w3.org/1999/xhtml">
<head>
    <title>Video</title>
</head>
<body>
    <div>Id: @Model.Id</div>
    <div>Title: @Model.Title</div>
    <div>Genre: @Model.Genre</div>
    @Html.ActionLink("Home", "Index")
</body>
</html>
```

The complete markup for the **Index** view:

```
@model IEnumerable<AspNetCoreVideo.ViewModels.VideoViewModel>

<html xmlns="http://www.w3.org/1999/xhtml">
<head>
    <title>Video</title>
</head>
```

```
<body>
    <table>
        @foreach (var video in Model)
        {
            <tr>
            <td>@Html.ActionLink(video.Id.ToString(), "Details",
                    new { id = video.Id })</td>
            <td>@video.Title</td>
            <td>@video.Genre</td>
            </tr>
        }
    </table>
</body>
</html>
```

Adding a Create View

When creating a new record in the data source with a **Create** view, you have to implement two action methods. The first is a method using HTTP GET to render the **Create** view in the browser, filling select lists and other controls that need data. The second method is an HTTP POST method that receives data from the client through a HTTP POST request.

The post from the client can be done in several ways, for instance with JavaScript or a form post. In this example, you will use a form post to call back to the server when the user clicks a **Submit** button.

The HTTP POST action method can fetch data from several places in the posted data: the header, the query string, and the body of the request. The data is then matched against properties in a model object, which is a parameter of the action method. The action can also handle simple types such as **int** and **string**, without them being encapsulated in a model object.

There is a naming convention that you need to be aware of, to properly match posted form data with properties in model objects and other parameters. The rule states that the element names in the form data must match the property names to be matched.

The default behavior of a view using an **enum** is to display it as a text field. This is not the best way to display a selected item in a list of values. In this section, you will remove the **Video** class' **GenreId** property, and add a new property of the **enum** type **Genres** called **Genre**. This makes it easier to work with **enum** data, especially when working with a SQL Server database entity model.

You will also add the **enum** as a property to a new view model called **VideoEditView-Model**, which can be used both when creating a new video and when editing one.

Refactoring the Application

1. Open the **Video** class.
2. Delete the **GenreId** property.
3. Add a new property of type **Genres** and name it **Genre**. This property will hold the current genre for the video.
   ```
   public Genres Genre { get; set; }
   ```
4. Open the **MockVideoData** class.
5. Replace the **GenreId** property with the **Genre** property and assign its value form the **enum** directly.
   ```
   new Video { Id = 1, Genre = Models.Genres.Comedy, Title = "Shreck"
   },
   ```
6. Open the **HomeController** class.
7. Locate the **Index** action and change the assignment of the **Genre** string in the **VideoViewModel** object to use the value stored in the **Genre** property of the **Video** object. You can use the **ToString** method to fetch the name of the **enum** value.
   ```
   Genre = video.Genre.ToString()
   ```
8. Repeat step 7 for the **Details** action method.
9. Switch to the browser and refresh the application. It should look and work the same as before.

The complete code for the **Video** class, after the changes:

```
public class Video
{
    public int Id { get; set; }
    public string Title { get; set; }
    public Genres Genre { get; set; }
}
```

The complete code for the **MockVideoData** class, after the changes:

```
public class MockVideoData : IVideoData
{
    private IEnumerable<Video> _videos;
```

```
    public MockVideoData()
    {
        _videos = new List<Video>
        {
            new Video { Id = 1, Genre = Models.Genres.Romance,
                Title = "Shreck" },
            new Video { Id = 2, Genre = Models.Genres.Comedy,
                Title = "Despicable Me" },
            new Video { Id = 3, Genre = Models.Genres.Action,
                Title = "Megamind" }
        };
    }

    public Video Get(int id)
    {
        return _videos.FirstOrDefault(v => v.Id.Equals(id));
    }

    public IEnumerable<Video> GetAll()
    {
        return _videos;
    }
}
```

The complete **HomeController** class after the changes:

```
public class HomeController : Controller
{
    private IVideoData _videos;
    public HomeController(IVideoData videos)
    {
        _videos = videos;
    }

    public ViewResult Index()
    {
        var model = _videos.GetAll().Select(video => new VideoViewModel
        {
            Id - video.Td,
            Title = video.Title,
            Genre = video.Genre.ToString()
        });
        return View(model);
    }
```

```
public IActionResult Details(int id)
{
    var model = _videos.Get(id);

    if (model == null) return RedirectToAction("Index");

    return View(new VideoViewModel
        {
            Id = model.Id,
            Title = model.Title,
            Genre = model.Genre.ToString()
        });
}
}
```

Adding the HTTP GET Create Action and the Create View

The HTTP GET **Create** action method renders the **Create** view to the browser, displaying the necessary controls to create a new video and to post the form to the server.

1. Open the **HomeController** class.
2. Add a new action method called **Create**, with the return type **IActionResult**. Return the **View** method.
   ```
   public IActionResult Create()
   {
       return View();
   }
   ```
3. Add a **MVC View Page** to the *Views/Home* folder in the Solution Explorer and name it *Create.cshtml*.
4. Delete all the content in the view.
5. Add a **@using** statement to the *Models* folder, to get access to the **enum** definition for the select list.
   ```
   @using AspNetCoreVideo.Models
   ```
6. Add a **@model** directive with the **Video** class as the view model.
   ```
   @model AspNetCoreVideo.Entities.Video
   ```
7. To be able to use Tag Helpers, which is the new way to add ASP.NET specific markup to views, you have to add a **@addTagHelper** directive to the view, or a shared file. You will learn more about Tag Helpers later.
   ```
   @addTagHelper *, Microsoft.AspNetCore.Mvc.TagHelpers
   ```

8. Add an <h2> heading with the text *Create Video*.

9. Add a <form> element and use the **asp-action** Tag Helper to specify the action to post to when the **Submit** button is clicked. Make the form post to the server by assigning **post** to the **method** attribute.

```
<form asp-action="Create" method="post">
```

10. Add a table with two rows to the form, one for the **Title** and one for the **Genre enum**.

11. Use the **asp-for** Tag Helper to specify which property the controls should bind to. Add a <label> and a <input> element for the **Title** property.

```
<tr>
    <td><label asp-for="Title"></label></td>
    <td><input asp-for="Title"/></td>
</tr>
```

12. Use the same Tag Helper when you add the <label> and <select> elements for the **Genre enum**. To list the **enum** items, you must add the **asp-items** Tag Helper to the <select> element and call the **GetEnumSelectList** method on the **Html** class.

```
<tr>
    <td><label asp-for="Genre"></label></td>
    <td><select asp-for="Genre"
        asp-items="Html.GetEnumSelectList<Genres>()"></select>
    </td>
</tr>
```

13. Add a **submit** button with the text *Create* to the form.

```
<input type="submit" value="Create" />
```

14. Add an anchor tag with the text *Back to List* below the form. Use the **asp-action** Tag Helper to specify that the link should navigate to the **Index** action.

```
<a asp-action="Index">Back to List</a>
```

15. Save all files and switch to the browser. Navigate to the */Home/Create* URL. You should see a form with a text field, a drop-down with all genres listed, a **Submit** button, and a link leading back to the **Index** view. The **Submit** button won't work yet, because you haven't added the required action method.

16. Click the link to navigate to the **Index** view.

The complete code for the HTTP GET **Create** action:

```
public IActionResult Create()
{
    return View();
}
```

The complete markup for the **Create** view:

```
@using AspNetCoreVideo.Models
@model AspNetCoreVideo.Entities.Video
@addTagHelper *, Microsoft.AspNetCore.Mvc.TagHelpers

<h2>Create Video</h2>

<form asp-action="Create" method="post">
    <table>
        <tr>
            <td><label asp-for="Title"></label></td>
            <td><input asp-for="Title" /></td>
        </tr>
        <tr>
            <td><label asp-for="Genre"></label></td>
            <td><select asp-for="Genre" asp-items=
                "Html.GetEnumSelectList<Genres>()"></select></td>
        </tr>
    </table>

    <input type="submit" value="Create" />
</form>

<div>
    <a asp-action="Index">Back to List</a>
</div>
```

Adding the VideoEditViewModel Class

This view model will be used when the controller receives a post from a video's **Edit** or **Create** view.

1. Create a new class called **VideoEditViewModel** in the *ViewModels* folder.
2. Add an **int** property named **Id** and a **string** property named **Title**.

3. Add a property called **Genre** of type **Genres**. This property will contain the genre selected in the form when the **submit** button is clicked, and a post is made back to the controller on the server.
```
public Genres Genre { get; set; }
```

The complete code for the **VideoEditViewModel** class:

```
public class VideoEditViewModel
{
    public int Id { get; set; }
    public string Title { get; set; }
    public Genres Genre { get; set; }
}
```

Adding the HTTP POST Create Action

A <form> element is used when a user should enter data in a view. There are a few steps that are performed when a user posts data. The first you already know: the user sends an HTTP request to the HTTP GET action in the controller, which fetches the necessary data after which the view is rendered.

To handle the form's post back to the server, an HTTP POST version of the action method is called with the form values. The names of the form controls are matched against the model properties or parameters available in the action's parameter list.

The POST action then uses that data to create, update, or delete data in the data source.

When passing data from the view to the action, MVC will, by default, match all properties in the form with properties in the model. This can be risky, especially if you use an entity class as the model. In many scenarios, you don't want to receive all data the form sends to the action. So how do you tell MVC to use only the values of interest? You create a separate view model, like you did in the previous section.

Let's implement the HTTP POST **Create** action in the **HomeController** class.

1. Open the **HomeController** class.
2. Add a new action method called **Create** that takes the **VideoEditViewModel** as a parameter named **model**.
```
public IActionResult Create(VideoEditViewModel model) {
    return View();
}
```

3. Save all files and switch to the browser. Navigate to the */Home/Create* URL. You should see an error message telling you that multiple actions were found with the same name.

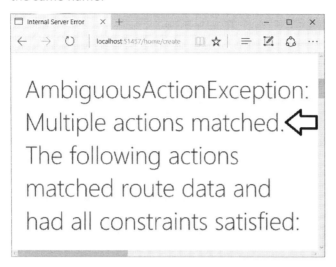

4. To fix this, you need to decorate the GET action with the **[HttpGet]** attribute, and the POST action with the **[HttpPost]** attribute. This will tell ASP.NET which method to call when the view is rendered and which method to call by the client when posting data.

```
[HttpGet]
public IActionResult Create()
{
    return View();
}

[HttpPost]
public IActionResult Create(VideoEditViewModel model)
{
    return View();
}
```

5. Place a breakpoint on the **return** statement in the POST action.
6. Save all files and start the application with debugging (F5). Navigate to the */Home/Create* URL. The **Create** view should be displayed again.
7. Fill out the form and click the **Create** button. The execution should halt at the breakpoint, proving that the **Create** button posts to the server. Inspect the

content in the **model** object; it should contain the values you entered in the form.

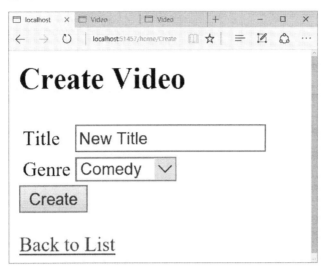

```
[HttpPost]
public IActionResult Create(
    VideoEditViewModel model)
{
    return View();
}
```

8. Stop the application in Visual Studio.
9. Because the purpose of the **Create** method is to add a new video to the data source, you will have to create an instance of the **Video** class and assign values to it from the **model** object properties. Note that you don't have to assign the **Id** property. The video doesn't exist in the data source yet, and therefore doesn't have an id.

```
var video = new Video
{
    Title = model.Title,
    Genre = model.Genre
};
```

10. Because you have implemented the **IVideoData** Interface as a service that is injected to the constructor, you have to add an **Add** method to it, and **implement** it in the **MockVideoData** class. This will make it possible to call the **Add** method on the **_videos** variable to add a new video. Let's implement it one step at a time. Begin by opening the **IVideoData** Interface.

11. Add a new **void** method called **Add** that takes a **Video** parameter called **newVideo**.
    ```
    void Add(Video newVideo);
    ```

12. Add the method to the **MockVideoData** class. You can use the lightbulb button if you hover over the interface name.

13. Remove the **throw** statement from the method.

14. Because the data source is a collection that is unable to generate new ids, you have to create a new id for the video object. You can fake an id by using LINQs **Max** method to fetch the highest id and add 1 to it.
    ```
    newVideo.Id = _videos.Max(v => v.Id) + 1;
    ```

15. To add the new video to the videos collection, you must change its data type to **List**. You can't add values to an **IEnumerable** collection. To preserve the values between HTTP requests, you will later change the scope of the **IVideoData** service in the **Startup** class.
    ```
    private List<Video> _videos;
    ```

16. Make a call to the **Add** method on the **_videos** collection, to add the new video in the **Add** method you created in the **MockVideoData** class.
    ```
    public void Add(Video newVideo)
    {
        newVideo.Id = _videos.Max(v => v.Id) + 1;
        _videos.Add(newVideo);
    }
    ```

17. Open the **HomeController** class and call the **Add** method you just created, from the HTTP POST **Create** action, and pass in the **video** object to it.
    ```
    _videos.Add(video);
    ```

18. To prevent the user from submitting the create form multiple times by refreshing the page, you must replace the **View** method with a call to the **RedirectToAction** method and redirect them to another view, like the **Details** view. Because the **Details** view has an **id** parameter you must pass in the name of the view, and the video id wrapped in an anonymous object.

```
        return RedirectToAction("Details", new { id = video.Id });
```

19. Open the **Startup** class and locate the **ConfigureServices** method. Change the scope of the **IVideoData** service to singleton by calling the **AddSingleton** method instead of the **AddScoped** that is currently used. You do this to preserve the data between HTTP requests.
    ```
    services.AddSingleton<IVideoData, MockVideoData>();
    ```

20. Save all the files and navigate to the */Home/Create* URL. Fill out the form and click the **Create** button. Instead of remaining on the **Create** view, you are redirected to the **Details** view, which displays the added video. Note that the URL changed to */Home/Details/4* with the redirect.

The complete code for the **IVideoData** interface:

```
public interface IVideoData
{
    IEnumerable<Video> GetAll();
    Video Get(int id);
    void Add(Video newVideo);
}
```

The complete code for the **Add** method in the **MockVideoData** class:

```
public void Add(Video newVideo)
{
    newVideo.Id = _videos.Max(v => v.Id) + 1;
    _videos.Add(newVideo);
}
```

The complete code for the **Create** actions:

```
[HttpGet]
public IActionResult Create()
{
    return View();
}

[HttpPost]
public IActionResult Create(VideoEditViewModel model)
{
    var video = new Video
    {
        Title = model.Title,
        Genre = model.Genre
    };

    _videos.Add(video);
    return RedirectToAction("Details", new { id = video.Id });
}
```

Data Annotations

Data annotations are attributes you add to properties in a model, to enforce rules about them. You can specify that a field is required or must have a maximum number of characters. The text displayed in a label is normally the property name, but that can be overridden with the [Display] attribute.

Many data annotations can be found in the **System.ComponentModel.DataAnnotations** namespace. You can specify one annotation per code line, or multiple annotations as a comma-separated list inside a set of square brackets.

```
[Required]
[MaxLength(80)]
```

Or

```
[Required, MaxLength(80)]
```

Below is a list of commonly used data annotations.

Name	Purpose
MinLength / MaxLength	Enforces length of strings
Range	Enforces min and max for numbers
RegularExpression	Makes a string match a pattern
Display	Sets the label text for a property
DataType	Determines how the output control will be rendered in the browser, for instance password or email
Required	The model value is mandatory
Compare	Compares the values of two input controls, often used for password validation

Preparing the Create View for Validation

To validate the annotations in the browser, the view must be altered to display possible errors. You usually do this by adding a <span> or a <div> element decorated with the **asp-validation-for** Tag Helper, specifying which property it displays errors for. You can also add a validation summary that displays all errors as an unordered list inside a <div> element decorated with the **asp-validation-summary** Tag Helper.

Adding Validation to the Create View

Let's add both types of validation to the **Create** view to see what it looks like.

1. Open the **Create** view.
2. Add a validation summary <div> at the top of the form.
    ```
    <form asp-action="Create">
        <div asp-validation-summary="All"></div>
    ```
3. Add validation to the **Title** property. Add a <span> decorated with the **asp-validation-for** Tag Helper inside a <td> element below the **Title** <input>.
    ```
    <td><span asp-validation-for="Title"></span></td>
    ```
4. Repeat step 3 for the **Genre** property.

The complete **Create** view after the changes:

```
@using AspNetCoreVideo.Models
@model AspNetCoreVideo.Entities.Video
@addTagHelper *, Microsoft.AspNetCore.Mvc.TagHelpers

<h2>Create Video</h2>
<form asp-action="Create">
    <div asp-validation-summary="All"></div>
    <table>
        <tr>
            <td><label asp-for="Title"></label></td>
            <td><input asp-for="Title" /></td>
            <td><span asp-validation-for="Title"></span></td>
        </tr>
        <tr>
            <td><label asp-for="Genre"></label></td>
            <td><select asp-for="Genre" asp-items=
                "Html.GetEnumSelectList<Genres>()"></select></td>
            <td><span asp-validation-for="Genre"></span></td>
        </tr>
    </table>
    <input type="submit" value="Create" />
</form>

<div>
    <a asp-action="Index">Back to List</a>
</div>
```

Validating the Model on the Server

Since no JavaScript validation libraries has been added to the application, you must validate the model on the server. To enforce model validation in the HTTP POST **Create** action, you must check if the model is valid before taking any action. If the model is valid, the video will be added to the data source, otherwise it will re-render the view so that the user can change the values and resubmit.

The **ModelState** object's **IsValid** property can be used in the HTTP POST action to check if the model is valid. Surround the code that creates and adds the video to the data source with an if-statement that checks the **IsValid** property value. Return the view below the if-block if the model state is invalid.

1. Open the **HomeController** class.
2. Add an if-block that checks the model state; it should surround all the code inside the HTTP POST **Create** action.
   ```
   if (ModelState.IsValid)
   {
       ...
   }
   ```
3. Return the view below the if-block.
   ```
   return View();
   ```

The complete code for the HTTP POST **Create** action:

```
[HttpPost]
public IActionResult Create(VideoEditViewModel model)
{
    if (ModelState.IsValid)
    {
        var video = new Video
        {
            Title = model.Title,
            Genre = model.Genre
        };

        _videos.Add(video);

        return RedirectToAction("Details", new { id = video.Id });
    }

    return View();
}
```

Adding Data Annotations in the Video Entity and VideoEditViewModel Class

Data annotations added to an entity class can affect both the controls in a view and the database table it represents.

In the project you are building, the **Video** entity is used as the view model for the **Create** view. To enforce some rules on that model, you add attributes to its properties that restrict or enhance them.

Let's implement some annotations in the **Video** entity model that alter how the controls in the view is rendered, and later restrict the database columns.

1. Open the **Video** entity model.
2. Add the **Required** annotation to the **Title** property. This will restrict the value in the database table to non-null values, and force the user to enter a value in the control, for the **model** object to be valid.
   ```
   [Required]
   public string Title { get; set; }
   ```
3. Open the **VideoEditViewModel** and repeat step 2.
4. Save all files and switch to the browser. Navigate to the */Home/Create* URL.
5. Click the **Create** button without entering a title. The validation message should appear beside the input field.

6. Add the **MinLength** annotation, with a min length of 3, to the **Title** property in both the **Video** and **VideoEditViewModel** classes.
   ```
   [Required, MinLength(3)]
   ```
7. Save all files and switch to the browser. Navigate to the */Home/Create* URL.
8. Enter 2 characters in the **Title** input field and click the **Create** button. The validation message should tell you that too few characters have been entered in the input field.
9. Enter at least 3 characters in the **Title** input field and click the **Create** button. The video should be successfully added to the data source.

10. Add the **MaxLength** annotation, with a max length of 80, to the **Title** property in both the **Video** and **VideoEditViewModel** classes. This will ensure that the **Title** property can have at most 80 characters when saved to the data source, and that the input control only will accept that many characters.

11. You can use the **Display** annotation to change the label text for a property. Let's change the text for the **Genre** property to *Film Genre*. Add the **Display** attribute to the **Genre** property in the **Video** class. Set its **Name** parameter to the text *Film Genre*. You only have to add the attribute to the **Video** model, since it only is applied to labels in a view.
    ```
    [Display(Name ="Film Genre")]
    ```

12. Save all files and switch to the browser. Navigate to the */Home/Create* URL. The label for the **Genre** select list should display the text *Film Genre*.

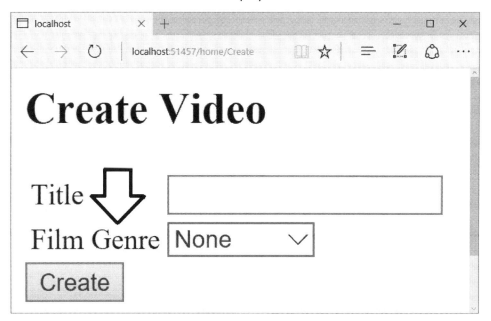

13. Let's try the **DataType** annotation next. Add it to the **Title** property in the **Video** class and select the **Password** type. This should display the entered text as password characters, typically dots or asterisks. Specifying a data type In the model can change its control's appearance on some devices, and can even change the layout of the keyboard displayed on the device screen, when the control has focus.
    ```
    [DataType(DataType.Password)]
    ```

14. Save all files and switch to the browser. Navigate to the */Home/Create* URL. Enter text in the **Title** input field. It should be displayed as password characters.

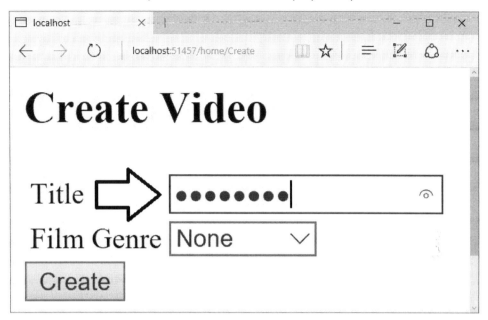

15. Remove the **Password** annotation and save the file.

Summary

In this chapter, you learned about different models that can be used with MVC, and how data annotations can be used to influence the labels and input controls, created with HTML and Tag Helpers in the view.

You also implemented validation checks on the server and displayed validation messages on the client.

5. Entity Framework

In this chapter, you will set up Entity Framework (EF) and get familiar with how it works. To work with EF, you must install the proper services, either manually in the *.csproj* file or by using the NuGet manager.

When the services have been installed and configured in the **Startup** class, you need to add a data context class that inherits from the **DbContext** class. This class will be the context that you use to interact with the database. To add a table to the database, the table's entity class must be added as a **DbSet** property in the context class.

When the services are installed and configured in the **Startup** class, you create the first migration by using the Package Manager Console and the **Add-Migration** command. When the initial migration has been added, the database can be generated with the **Update-Database** command.

If you make any changes to the database, like adding or changing columns or tables, then you must execute the **Add-Migration** and **Update-Database** commands again for the application to work properly.

Installing Entity Framework and User Secrets

Now you will install the Entity Framework NuGet packages needed to create and interact with a database. The database you add later will use the built-in local development SQL Server version, which installs with Visual Studio 2017. You will also use User Secrets, stored in a *secrets.json* file, to store the database connection string securely.

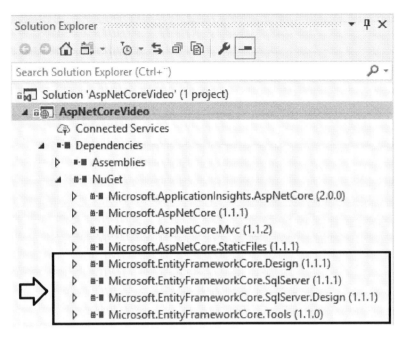

1. Open the NuGet Manager. Right click on the project node and select **Manage NuGet Packages**.

2. Install the following four packages: **Microsoft.EntityFrameworkCore.Design**, **Microsoft.EntityFrameworkCore.SqlServer**, **Microsoft.EntityFrameworkCore.SqlServer.Design**, **Microsoft.EntityFrameworkCore.Tools**.

3. Open the .csproj file and verify that the packages have been installed.
```
<PackageReference
    Include="Microsoft.EntityFrameworkCore.Design"
    Version="1.1.2" PrivateAssets="All" />
<PackageReference
    Include="Microsoft.EntityFrameworkCore.SqlServer"
    Version="1.1.2" />
<PackageReference
    Include="Microsoft.EntityFrameworkCore.SqlServer.Design"
    Version="1.1.2" PrivateAssets="All" />
<PackageReference Include="Microsoft.EntityFrameworkCore.Tools"
    Version="1.1.1" PrivateAssets="All" />
```

4. Add the *User Secrets* NuGet packages to be able to store and retrieve data in the *secrets.json* file.

```
<PackageReference
    Include="Microsoft.Extensions.Configuration.UserSecrets"
    Version="1.1.2" />
<DotNetCliToolReference
    Include="Microsoft.Extensions.SecretManager.Tools"
    Version="1.0.0" />
```

Adding the VideoDbContext Class

Now that the NuGet packages have been installed, you can add a class called **VideoDb-Context** that inherits form the **DbContext** class. This class will be your connection to the database. It defines the entity classes as **DbSet** properties, which are mirrored as tables in the database.

For the **AddDbContext** method to be able to add the context to the services collection, the **VideoDbContext** must have a constructor with a **DbContextOptions<VideoDbContext>** parameter, which passes the parameter object to its base constructor. The **OnModelCreating** method must be overridden to enable Entity Framework to build the entity model for the database.

1. Add a new folder called *Data* to the project.
2. Add a class called **VideoDbContext** to the *Data* folder in the Solution Explorer.
3. Inherit the **DbContext** class in the **VideoDbContext** class. **DbContext** is in the **Microsoft.EntityFrameworkCore** namespace.
   ```
   public class VideoDbContext : DbContext { }
   ```
4. Add a **DbSet** property for the **Video** class in the **VideoDbContext** class.
   ```
   public DbSet<Video> Videos { get; set; }
   ```
5. Add the constructor with the a **DbContextOptions<VideoDbContext>** parameter.
   ```
   public VideoDbContext(DbContextOptions<VideoDbContext> options)
   : base(options)
   {
   }
   ```
6. Override the **OnModelCreating** method.
   ```
   protected override void OnModelCreating(ModelBuilder builder)
   {
       base.OnModelCreating(builder);
   }
   ```
7. Save all the files.

The complete code for the **VideoDbContext** class:

```
public class VideoDbContext : DbContext
{
    public DbSet<Video> Videos { get; set; }

    public VideoDbContext(DbContextOptions<VideoDbContext> options)
        : base(options)
    {
    }

    protected override void OnModelCreating(ModelBuilder builder)
    {
        base.OnModelCreating(builder);
    }
}
```

Configuration in the Startup Class

Before the initial migration can be applied, you have to configure Entity Framework to use the **VideoDbContext**, and read the connection string from the sercrets.json file. Using the secrets.json file has two purposes: It stores the connection string in a safe place that is not checked into source control. It also renders the appsettings.json obsolete for storing secret or sensitive data, which is a good thing, since it is checked into source control.

If the *appsettings.json* file isn't optional, the migration might fail.

1. Right click on the project node in the Solution Explorer and select **Manage User Secrets**.
2. Add the following connection string property. Note that the database name is **VideoDb**. The connection string should be on one row in the file.
   ```
   "ConnectionStrings": {
       "DefaultConnection": "Server=(localdb)\\mssqllocaldb;
           Database=VideoDb;Trusted_Connection=True;
           MultipleActiveResultSets=true"
   }
   ```
3. Open the **Startup** class and locate the constructor.
4. Add the **optional: true** parameter value temporarily to the **AddJsonFile** method for the *appsettings.json* file.
   ```
   .AddJsonFile("appsettings.json", optional: true);
   ```

5. To be able to check the environment the **IHostingEnvironment** interface must be injected into the constructor.
   ```
   IHostingEnvironment env
   ```

6. Add an if-statement, checking if the development environment is active, and use the **AddUserSecrets** method to add it to the **builder** object. Add it above the **Build** method call.
   ```
   if (env.IsDevelopment())
       builder.AddUserSecrets<Startup>();
   ```

7. Locate the **ConfigureServices** method and fetch the connection string from the *secrets.json* file using the **Configuration** object. Store the connection string in a variable called **conn**.
   ```
   var conn = Configuration.GetConnectionString("DefaultConnection");
   ```

8. Use the **AddDbContext** method on the **services** collection to add the database context and the EF services at the beginning of the **ConfigureServices** method. Call the **UseSqlServer** method on the **options** action in its constructor to specify that you want to use a SQL Server database provider. The **UseSqlServer** method is in the **Microsoft.EntityFrameworkCore** namespace. Note that **DefaultConnection** is the name of the property you added to the *secrets.josn* file.
   ```
   services.AddDbContext<VideoDbContext>(options =>
       options.UseSqlServer(conn));
   ```

The complete code for the *secrets.json* file:

```
{
    "ConnectionStrings": {
        "DefaultConnection": "Server=(localdb)\\mssqllocaldb;
            Database=VideoDb;Trusted_Connection=True;
            MultipleActiveResultSets=true"
    }
}
```

Note that the **DefaultConnection** property value should be one line of code.

The complete code for the **Startup** class' constructor:

```
public Startup(IHostingEnvironment env)
{
    var builder = new ConfigurationBuilder()
        .SetBasePath(Directory.GetCurrentDirectory())
        .AddJsonFile("appsettings.json", optional: true);

    if (env.IsDevelopment())
        builder.AddUserSecrets<Startup>();

    Configuration = builder.Build();
}
```

The complete code for the **Startup** class' **ConfigureServices** method:

```
public void ConfigureServices(IServiceCollection services)
{
    var conn = Configuration.GetConnectionString("DefaultConnection");
    services.AddDbContext<VideoDbContext>(options =>
        options.UseSqlServer(conn));

    services.AddMvc();

    //services.AddSingleton<IMessageService, HardCodedMessageService>();
    services.AddSingleton(provider => Configuration);
    services.AddSingleton<IMessageService,
        ConfigurationMessageService>();
    services.AddSingleton<IVideoData, MockVideoData>();
}
```

Adding the Initial Migration and Creating the Database

To add the initial migration and create the database, you execute the **Add-Migration** and **Update-Database** commands in the Package Manager Console (**View-Other Windows-Package Manager Console**).

When the **Add-Migration** command has been successfully executed, a new folder called *Migrations* will appear in the project. The current and all future migrations will be stored in this folder.

If you encounter the error message *No parameterless constructor was found on 'VideoDbContext': Either add a parameterless constructor to 'VideoDbContext' or add an implementation of 'IDbContextFactory<VideoDbContext>' in the same assembly as*

'VideoDbContext', then check that your connection string in *secrets.json* is correct and that it is being loaded in the **Startup** class, before doing any other troubleshooting.

1. Open the package Manager Console.
2. Type in the command *add-migration Initial* and press **Enter**. Note the *Migrations* folder, and the migration files in it.
3. Execute the command *update-database* in the Package Manager Console to create the database.
4. Open the **SQL Server Object Explorer** from the **View** menu.
5. Expand the **MSSQLLocalDb** node, and then the **Databases** node. If the **VideoDb** database isn't visible, right click on the **Databases** node and select **Refresh**.
6. Expand the **VideoDb** node, and then the **Tables** node. You should now see the **Videos** table in the **VideoDb** database that you just created.
7. Expand the **Videos** table and then the **Columns** node. You should now see the columns in the table. Note that they match the properties in the **Video** entity class, and that they have the restrictions from the attributes you added to its properties.

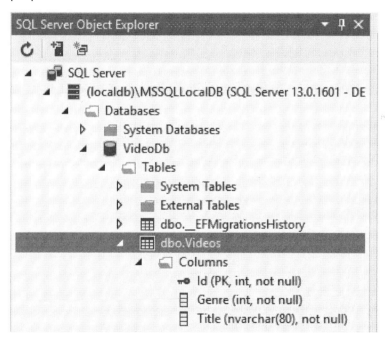

8. Right click on the **Videos** table and select **View Data**. This will open the table in edit mode. Add a genre id from the **Genres** enum (it is zero based) and a title.

Press **Enter** to commit the value to the database. Add a few more videos if you like.

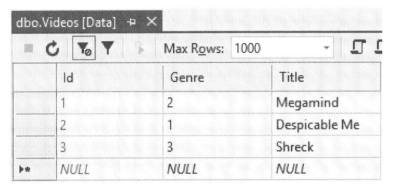

Adding the SqlVideoData Service Component

To use the database in the application, you can implement the **IVideoData** interface in a new service component class. Then, you change the service registration in the **Configure-Services** method in the **Startup** class to create instances of the new component.

Implementing the SqlVideoData Service Component Class

Let's begin by implementing the **SqlVideoData** class that will communicate with the database through the **VideoDbContext**.

1. Add a class called **SqlVideoData** to the *Services* folder.
2. Open the **Startup** class and change the service registration for the **IVideoData** interface to create instances of the **SqlVideoData** class.
   ```
   services.AddSingleton<IVideoData, SqlVideoData>();
   ```
3. Add a private field called **_db** to the **SqlVideoData** class. This variable will hold the context needed to communicate with the database.
   ```
   private VideoDbContext _db;
   ```
4. Add a constructor that is injected with an instance of the **VideoDbContext** class; name the parameter **db**. Assign the injected object in the **db** parameter to the **_db** variable.
   ```
   public SqlVideoData(VideoDbContext db)
   {
       _db = db;
   }
   ```

5. Implement the **IVideoData** interface. You can use the lightbulb button when hovering over the interface name.
```
public class SqlVideoData : IVideoData
```

6. Replace the **throw** statement in the **Add** method with a call to the **Add** method on the _**db** context and pass in the **video** object to the method. Then call the **SaveChanges** method on the _**db** context to persist the changes in the database.
```
public void Add(Video video)
{
    _db.Add(video);
    _db.SaveChanges();
}
```

7. Replace the **throw** statement in the **Get** method with a call to the **Find** method on the _**db** context to fetch the video matching the id passed-in to the method. Return the fetched video.
```
public Video Get(int id)
{
    return _db.Find<Video>(id);
}
```

8. Replace the **throw** statement in the **GetAll** method with a **return** statement that returns all the videos in the **Videos** table.
```
public IEnumerable<Video> GetAll()
{
    return _db.Videos;
}
```

9. Save all the files and navigate to the root URL *(/Home)*. The list of videos from the database should be displayed.

10. Add a new video by navigating to the *Home/Create* URL and fill out the form. When you click the **Create** button in the form, the **Details** view should display the new video.

11. Click the **Home** link and make sure that the video is in the list.

12. Open the **Video** table in the SQL Server Object Explorer and verify that the video is in the table.

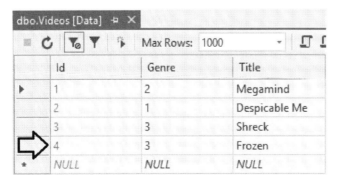

The complete code in the **SqlVideoData** class:

```
public class SqlVideoData : IVideoData
{
    private VideoDbContext _db;

    public SqlVideoData(VideoDbContext db)
    {
        _db = db;
    }

    public void Add(Video video)
    {
        _db.Add(video);
        _db.SaveChanges();
    }

    public Video Get(int id)
    {
        return _db.Find<Video>(id);
    }

    public IEnumerable<Video> GetAll()
    {
        return _db.Videos;
    }
}
```

Summary

In this chapter, you installed the Entity Framework services using the NuGet Package Manager and the User Secrets services using the *.csproj* file.

You also added a **DbContext** class that communicates with the database, and a new service component class that implements the **IVideoData** Interface, as a separation between the **DbContext** and the application.

Finally, you added a new video to the database using the **Create** view, and verified that it had been added to the database.

6. Razor Views

In this chapter, you will learn about different views that can be used for layout, to include namespaces, and to render partial content in a view.

Layout Views

The *_Layout.cshtml* Razor view gives the application more structure and makes it easier to display data that should be visible on every page, such as a navigation bar and a footer. You avoid duplication using this view. The underscore at the beginning of the name is not required, but it is a convention that is commonly used among developers. It signifies that the view shouldn't be rendered as a view result with the **View** method from a controller action.

The normal views, like the **Index** view, are rendered inside the **_Layout** view. This mean that they don't have any knowledge about the navigation and the footer; they only need to render what the action tells them to render.

If you look inside the views you have created, they have some code in common, such as the <html>, <head> and <body> elements. Because the markup is the same for all the views, it could be moved to the **_Layout** view.

Shared views, like **_Layout**, are placed in a folder called *Shared* inside the *Views* folder. These views are available anywhere in the application. The layout view doesn't have to be named **_Layout**; you can even have multiple layout views in the application if you like.

The **_Layout** view is a Razor view, which means that you can use C# inside the view, like you can in any other view. It should also have a method called **@RenderBody**, which is responsible for rendering the different content views the user navigates to, such as the **Index** and the **Details** views.

There is an object called **@ViewBag** in the **_Layout** view. It is a dynamic object that you can use to send data from the server to the view.

Another method that can be used in the **_Layout** view is the **@RenderSection**. This method can be used to render specific sections of HTML from the content view in the **_Layout** view. There is an asynchronous version of this method that you can use if you want that type of behavior.

Adding the _Layout View

1. Add a new folder called *Shared* to the *Views* folder.
2. Add an **MVC View Layout Page** called **_Layout** to the *Shared* folder using the **New Item** dialog.
3. Add a <footer> element at the bottom of the <body> element.
4. Add a call to the **@RenderSection** method to the <footer> element and pass in the name of the section that could be in any of the views. If you want the section to be optional, then pass in **false** for the second parameter. Name the section *footer* and pass in **false**.
   ```
   <footer>@RenderSection("footer", false)</footer>
   ```

The complete markup for the **_Layout** view:

```
<!DOCTYPE html>

<html>
<head>
    <meta name="viewport" content="width=device-width" />
    <title>@ViewBag.Title</title>
</head>
<body>
    <div>
        @RenderBody()
    </div>
    <footer>
        @RenderSection("footer", false)
    </footer>
</body>
</html>
```

Altering the Content Views

Now that the **_Layout** view has been added, you need to remove the markup shared among the content views.

Open the **Index** view and remove the <head> and <body> elements, and do the same for the other views in the *Home* folder. You can use the Ctrl+E, D keyboard command to format the HTML.

Since you removed the <title> element from the view, you can add it to the **ViewBag** object as a property called **Title**. Assign the name of the view to the property. Since the **ViewBag** is placed inside a C# block, it doesn't need the @-sign.

You can also use the **Layout** property in the C# block to tell the MVC framework which layout view to use with the view. The layout view must be specified with an explicit path, beginning with the tilde (~) sign.

The usual C# rules apply inside C# blocks, such as ending code lines with a semicolon.

1. Open the **Index** view and remove all the <html>, <head>, and <body> elements, but leave the table and the **@model** directive.

```
@model IEnumerable<AspNetCoreVideo.ViewModels.VideoViewModel>

<table>
    @foreach (var video in Model)
    {
        <tr>
            <td>@Html.ActionLink(video.Id.ToString(), "Details",
                new { id = video.Id })</td>
            <td>@video.Title</td>
            <td>@video.Genre</td>
        </tr>
    }
</table>
```

2. Add a C# block below the **@model** directive.

```
@{
}
```

3. Add a **Title** property to the **ViewBag** inside the C# block and assign a title to it (*Home*, in this case).

4. Add the **Layout** property inside the C# block and assign the explicit path to the *_Layout.cshtml* file.

```
@{
    ViewBag.Title = "Home";
    Layout = "~/Views/Shared/_Layout.cshtml";
}
```

5. Add a **@section** block named **footer** to the end of the **Index** view and place a <div> element with the text *This is the Index footer* inside it.

```
@section footer{
    <div>This is the Index footer</div>
}
```

6. Repeat steps 1-4 for all the views in the *Views/Home* folder.
7. Save all the files and switch to the browser. Navigate to the **Index** view (/). You should be able to see the footer text below the video list. This verifies that the layout view is used to render the **Index** view.

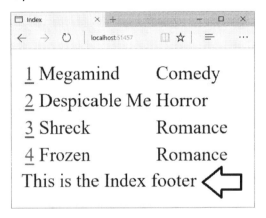

The complete code in the **Index** view, after removing the elements:

```
@model IEnumerable<AspNetCoreVideo.ViewModels.VideoViewModel>

@{
    ViewBag.Title = "Home";
    Layout = "~/Views/Shared/_Layout.cshtml";
}

<table>
    @foreach (var video in Model)
    {
        <tr>
            <td>@Html.ActionLink(video.Id.ToString(), "Details",
                new { id = video.Id })</td>
            <td>@video.Title</td>
            <td>@video.Genre</td>
        </tr>
    }
</table>
```

```
@section{
    <div>This is the Index footer</div>
}
```

The complete code in the **Details** view, after removing the elements:

```
@model AspNetCoreVideo.ViewModels.VideoViewModel

@{
    ViewBag.Title = "Details";
    Layout = "~/Views/Shared/_Layout.cshtml";
}

<div>Id: @Model.Id</div>
<div>Title: @Model.Title</div>
<div>Genre: @Model.Genre</div>

@Html.ActionLink("Home", "Index")
```

The complete code in the **Create** view, after removing the elements:

```
@using AspNetCoreVideo.Models
@model AspNetCoreVideo.Entities.Video
@addTagHelper *, Microsoft.AspNetCore.Mvc.TagHelpers

@{
    ViewBag.Title = "Create";
    Layout = "~/Views/Shared/_Layout.cshtml";
}

<h2>Create Video</h2>
<form asp-action="Create">
    <div asp-validation-summary="All"></div>
    <table>
        <tr>
            <td><label asp-for="Title"></label></td>
            <td><input asp-for="Title" /></td>
            <td><span asp-validation-for="Title"></span></td>
        </tr>
        <tr>
            <td><label asp-for="Genre"></label></td>
            <td><select asp-for="Genre" asp-items=
                "Html.GetEnumSelectList<Genres>()"></select></td>
```

```
            <td><span asp-validation-for="Genre"></span></td>
        </tr>
    </table>
    <input type="submit" value="Create" />
</form>

<div>
    <a asp-action="Index">Back to List</a>
</div>
```

The _ViewStart file

The Razor view engine has a convention that looks for a file called _ViewStart.cshtml. This file is executed before any other views, but it has no HTML output. One purpose it has is to remove duplicate code from code blocks in the views, like the **Layout** declaration. Instead of declaring the location of the **_Layout** view in each view, it can be placed inside the **_ViewStart** view. It is possible to override the settings in the **_ViewStart** view by adding the **Layout** declaration in individual views.

If you place this view directly in the Views folder, it will be available to all views. Placing it in another folder inside the Views folder makes it available to the views in that folder.

You can assign **null** to the **Layout** property in a specific view to stop any layout view from being used with the view.

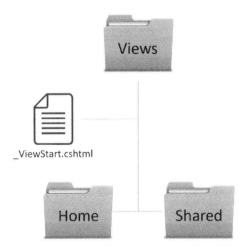

Let's create the **_ViewStart** view in the Views folder, and add the **Layout** declaration in it.

1. Add an **MVC View Start Page** to the *Views* folder (use the **New Item** dialog). It is important that you name it **_ViewStart**, to adhere to MVC conventions.
2. Copy the **_Layout** view path from the **Index** view.
3. Replace the current value for the **Layout** property in **_ViewStart** with the path you copied.

```
@{
    Layout = "~/Views/Shared/_Layout.cshtml";
}
```

4. Remove the **Layout** property from all the views in the *Views/Home* folder.
5. Save all the files and navigate to the root (/). You should still see the text *This is the Index footer* rendered by the **_Layout** view.

The _ViewImports file

The Razor view engine has a convention that looks for a file called *_ViewImports.cshtml*. This file is executed before any other views, but it has no HTML output. You can use this file to add **using** statements that will be used by all the views; this removes code duplication and cleans up the views.

So, if you know that many views will use the same namespaces, then add them to the *_ViewImports.cshtml* file. Add the file to the *Views* folder.

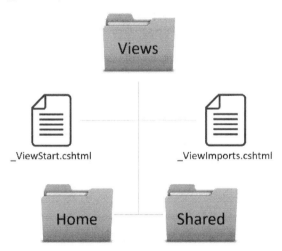

1. Add a **MVC View Imports Page** file named *_ViewImports.cshtml* to the *Views* folder.
2. Open the **Create** view and cut out the **@using** and **@addTagHelper** rows.

3. Open the **_ViewImports** view and paste in the code.
4. Add a **using** statement to the **AspNetCoreVideo.Entities** namespace.
5. Save the **_ViewImports** view.
6. Open the **Create** view and remove the namespace path in the **@model** directive. The view should be able to find the **Video** model from the **using** statement in the **_ViewImports** view.

   ```
   @model Video
   ```

7. Open the **Index** view and cut out the **AspNetCoreVideo.ViewModels** namespace path from the **@model** directive and add it as a **using** statement to the **_ViewImports** view and save it. Leave only the class name in the **@model** directive.

   ```
   @model IEnumerable<VideoViewModel>
   ```

8. Open the **Details** view and delete the **AspNetCoreVideo.ViewModels** namespace path. Leave only the class name in the **@model** directive.

   ```
   @model VideoViewModel
   ```

9. Save all the files and navigate to the different views in the browser, to verify that the application still works as before.

The complete code in the **_ViewImports** file:

```
@using AspNetCoreVideo.Models
@using AspNetCoreVideo.Entities
@using AspNetCoreVideo.ViewModels
@addTagHelper *, Microsoft.AspNetCore.Mvc.TagHelpers
```

Tag Helpers

Tag Helpers are new to ASP.NET Core, and can in many instances replace the old HTML helpers. The Tag Helpers blend in with the HTML as they appear to be HTML attributes or HTML elements.

You have already used Tag Helpers in the **Create** form. There you added the **asp-for** and **asp-validation-for** among others. They blend in much better than the alternatives: **Label-For**, **TextBoxFor**, **EditorFor**, and other HTML helpers that are used in previous versions of ASP.NET. You can still use Razor HTML Helpers in ASP.NET Core, and they have one benefit over Tag Helpers; they are tightly coupled to the model. This means that you get Intelli-Sense and can rename properties more easily. In a Tag Helper, the property is added as a string value.

To use the Tag Helpers, you need to add a **@addTagHelper** directive to the **_ViewImports** view, or in specific views where you want to use them. The first parameter, the asterisk, specifies that all Tag Helpers in that namespace should be available. You can change this to a specific Tag Helper if you don't want to import all helpers.

```
@addTagHelper *, Microsoft.AspNetCore.Mvc.TagHelpers
```

Let's add a link calling the **Create** action from the **Index** view using Tag Helpers, so that you don't have to type in the URL to the **Create** view in the browser. Let's also replace the **ActionLink** HTML helper for the **Id** property, with a Tag Helper that opens the **Details** view and has the description *Details*.

Altering the Index View

1. Open the **Index** view.
2. Add an anchor tag (<a>) between the </table> tag and the **@section** block. Add the text *Create* to the anchor tag.
   ```
   <a>Create</a>
   ```

3. Use the **asp-action** Tag Helper to specify which action in the **Home** controller you want the link to call. You can add the **asp-controller** Tag Helper if you want to navigate to a controller that the view doesn't belong to.
   ```
   <a asp-action="Create">Create</a>
   ```

4. Save the file and navigate to the **Index** view in the browser. You should see a link with the text *Create*. When you click the link, the **Create** view should appear.
5. Click the *Back to List* link to get back to the **Index** view.
6. Place a breakpoint inside the HTTP GET **Create** action in the **HomeController** class, and start the application <u>with</u> debugging (F5).
7. Click the **Create** link again. The execution should halt at the breakpoint. This demonstrates that the **Action** was called by the Tag Helper.
8. Remove the breakpoint and stop the application in Visual Studio.
9. Remove the **ActionLink** for the **Id** property.
10. Add an anchor tag that opens the **Details** view using the **asp-action** Tag Helper, and the **asp-route-id** Tag Helper to pass in the video id.
    ```
    <td>
        <a asp-action="Details" asp-route-id="@video.Id">Details</a>
    </td>
    ```

11. Start the application without debugging (Ctrl+F5). You should now see *Details* links. Click one to verify that the **Details** view for that video is displayed.

The complete markup for the **Index** view:

```
@model IEnumerable<VideoViewModel>

@{
    ViewBag.Title = "Home";
}

<table>
    @foreach (var video in Model)
    {
        <tr>
            <td>
                <a asp-action="Details" asp-route-id="@video.Id">
                Details</a>
            </td>
            <td>@video.Title</td>
            <td>@video.Genre</td>
        </tr>
    }
</table>

<a asp-action-"Create">Create</a>

@section footer{
    <div>This is the Index footer</div>
}
```

Adding an Edit View and Its Actions

There is one more view that is needed to complete the CRUD operations, and that is the **Edit** view. Let's add the **Edit** view by copying the **Create** view and modify the form. Then let's refactor the **IVideoData** interface, and the classes implementing it. Instead of saving data directly when a video is added or edited, this refactoring will make it possible to add or edit multiple videos before saving the changes to the database.

1. Copy the **Create** view and paste it into the *Home* folder. Rename the view *Edit*.
2. Visual Studio sometimes gets confused when a view is copied, pasted, and renamed. To avoid confusion, close the **Edit** view and open it again.
3. Change the title to *Edit* followed by the video title.

```
ViewBag.Title = $"Edit {Model.Title}";
```

4. Do the same for the view's heading; use the value from the **ViewBag**.
   ```
   <h2>@ViewBag.Title</h2>
   ```

5. Change the **asp-action** Tag Helper to call an action named **Edit**; you will add the action to the **HomeController** class later. Also specify that the form should use the **post** method; it is safer than using the default **get** method when posting a form.
   ```
   <form asp-action="Edit" method="post">
   ```

6. Change the **submit** button's text to *Edit*.
   ```
   <input type="submit" value="Edit" />
   ```

7. Open the **Index** view and add a link to the **Edit** view, like you did in the **Details** view. You can copy and change the **Details** anchor tag you added earlier. Move the links after the **Genre** table cell to make the form a little more pleasing to the eye.
   ```
   <td><a asp-action="Edit" asp-route-id="@video.Id">Edit</a></td>
   ```

8. To make the **Edit** link and view work, you have to add HTTP GET and HTTP POST **Edit** actions to the **HomeContgroller** class. Let's start with the HTTP GET action. Copy the HTTP GET **Details** action and paste it into the class. Rename it **Edit** and add the **HttpGet** attribute to it. This will make it possible to open the **Edit** view with the link you added in the **Index** view.
   ```
   [HttpGet]
   public IActionResult Edit(int id)
   {
       ...
   }
   ```

9. Rename the **model** variable **video**.
10. Replace the **return** statement with one that returns the **video** object to the view.
    ```
    return View(video);
    ```

11. Add an HTTP POST **Edit** action that has an **id** parameter of type **int** and a **VideoEditViewModel** parameter called **model**. Add the **HttpPost** attribute to the action.
    ```
    [HttpPost]
    public IActionResult Edit(int id, VideoEditViewModel model)
    {
        ...
    }
    ```

12. Fetch the video matching the passed-in **id** and store it in a variable called **video**.
    ```
    var video = _videos.Get(id);
    ```

13. Add an if-statement that checks if the model state is invalid, or the video object is null. If any of them are **true**, then return the view with the model.
    ```
    if (video == null || !ModelState.IsValid)
        return View(model);
    ```

14. Assign the **Title** and **Genre** values from the model to the **video** object you fetched. Entity Framework will keep track of changes to the video objects.
    ```
    video.Title = model.Title;
    video.Genre = model.Genre;
    ```

15. Call the **Commit** method on the **_Video** object. This method does not exist yet, but you will add it to the **IVideoData** service classes shortly. After you have refactored the **IVideoData** service, the method will work, and save any changes to the database. Since Entity Framework keeps track of any changes to the **DbContext**, you don't have to send in the video object to the **Commit** method.
    ```
    _videos.Commit();
    ```

16. Add a redirect to the **Details** view.
    ```
    return RedirectToAction("Details", new { id = video.Id });
    ```

The complete code for the HTTP GET **Edit** action:

```
[HttpGet]
public IActionResult Edit(int id)
{
    var video = _videos.Get(id);

    if (video == null) return RedirectToAction("Index");

    return View(video);
}
```

The complete code for the HTTP POST **Edit** action:

```
[HttpPost]
public IActionResult Edit(int id, VideoEditViewModel model)
{
    var video = _videos.Get(id);

    if (video == null || !ModelState.IsValid) return View(model);
```

```
video.Title = model.Title;
video.Genre = model.Genre;

_videos.Commit();

return RedirectToAction("Details", new { id = video.Id });
}
```

Refactoring the IVideoData Service

The idea is that you should be able to do multiple changes and add new videos before committing the changes to the database. To achieve this, you must move the **SaveChanges** method call to a separate method called **Commit**. Whenever changes should be persisted to the database, the **Commit** method must be called.

1. Open the **IVideoData** interface.
2. Add a definition for a method called **Commit** that returns an **int**. The **int** value will in some instances reflect the number of records that were affected by the commit.
   ```
   int Commit();
   ```

3. Open the **MockVideoData** class and add a **Commit** method that returns 0. You must add the method even though it isn't necessary for the mock data. The mock data is instantly saved when in memory. The interface demands that the **Commit** method is implemented.
   ```
   public int Commit()
   {
       return 0;
   }
   ```

4. Open the **SqlVideoData** class and add a **Commit** method that return the results from the call to the **SaveChanges** method.
   ```
   public int Commit()
   {
       return _db.SaveChanges();
   }
   ```

5. Remove the call to the **SaveChanges** method from the **Add** method.
   ```
   public void Add(Video video)
   {
       _db.Add(video);
   }
   ```

6. Open the **HomeController** and verify that the **Commit** method doesn't have a red squiggly line and therefore is working properly.

7. Call the **Commit** method in the **Create** action, below the call to the **Add** method. This is necessary since you refactored out the call to the **SaveChanges** method from the **Add** method in the **SqlVideoData** service.

8. Because you refactored the **SaveChanges** method call to a separate method, you have to add a call to the **Commit** method below the call to the **Add** method in the HTTP POST **Create** action.

9. Save all files and navigate to the root URL. The new **Edit** links should appear to the right of the videos in the listing, beside the **Details** links.

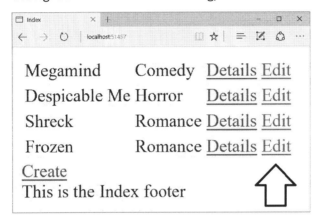

10. Click the **Edit** link for one of the videos to open the new **Edit** view.

11. Make some changes to the video and click the **Edit** button.

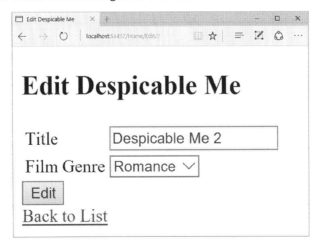

12. The **Details** view for the video is displayed. Click the **Home** link to get back to the video list in the **Index** view.

13. The **Index** view should reflect the changes you made to the video.

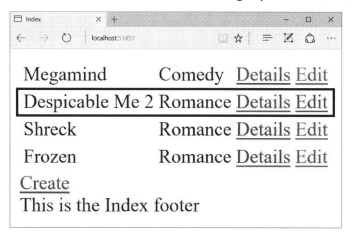

Partial Views

A partial view has two main purposes. The first is to render a portion of a view; the other is to enable reuse of markup to clean up the code in a view.

To render a partial view, you can use either the synchronous **@Html.Partial** method or the asynchronous **@Html.PartialAsync** method. Both methods take two parameters, where the first is the name of the partial view and the second is an optional model object.

Note that partial views always use data from the parent view model.

The following example would render a partial view called **_Video** that receives a video object from the parent view's model. The first code line is synchronous while the second is asynchronous; you choose which one you want to use.

```
@Html.Partial("_Video", video);
```

```
@await Html.PartialAsync("_Video", video);
```

Let's create a partial view called **_Video** to clean up the **Index** view. It will display the videos as panels, and get rid of that ugly table in the process.

1. Add a new **MVC View Page** called **_Video** to the **Home** folder.
2. Delete all code inside the view.
3. Add the **VideoViewModel** class as its model.
   ```
   @model VideoViewModel
   ```
4. Add a <section> element in the partial view.
5. Add a <h3> element inside the <section> element and add the video title to it using the **@Model** object.
   ```
   <h3>@Model.Title</h3>
   ```
6. Add a <div> element below the <h3> element and add the video genre to it using the **@Model** object.
   ```
   <div>@Model.Genre</div>
   ```
7. Add another <div> element below the previous <div> element.
8. Copy the **Details** and **Edit** links from the **Index** view and paste them into the newest <div> element. Change the **asp-route-id** Tag Helper to fetch its value from the **@Model** object.
   ```
   <div>
       <a asp-action="Details" asp-route-id="@Model.Id">Details</a>
       <a asp-action="Edit" asp-route-id="@Model.Id">Edit</a>
   </div>
   ```
9. Open the **Index** view and replace the <table> element and all its content with a **foreach** loop that renders the partial view. The **foreach** loop is the same as the one in the <table> element, so you can copy it before removing the <table> element.
   ```
   @foreach (var video in Model)
   {
       @Html.Partial("_Video", video);
   }
   ```

10. Place the remaining anchor tag inside a <div> element to make it easier to style.
```
<div>
    <a asp-action="Create">Create</a>
</div>
```

11. Remove the **@section footer** block. You will display other information at the bottom of the page using a View Component in the next section.

12. Save all the files and navigate to the root URL in the browser. The videos should now be stacked vertically as cards. They might not look pretty, but you can make them look great with CSS styling.

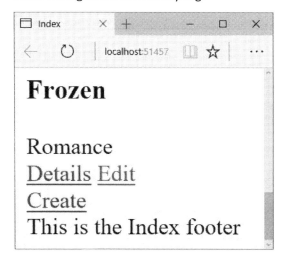

The complete code for the partial view:

```
@model VideoViewModel

<section>
    <h3>@Model.Title</h3>
    <div>@Model.Genre</div>
    <div>
        <a asp-action="Details" asp-route-id="@Model.Id">Details</a>
        <a asp-action="Edit" asp-route-id="@Model.Id">Edit</a>
    </div>
</section>
```

The complete code for the **Index** view:

```
@model IEnumerable<VideoViewModel>

@{
```

```
    ViewBag.Title = "Index";
}

@foreach (var video in Model)
{
    @Html.Partial("_Video", video)
}

<div>
    <a asp-action="Create">Create</a>
</div>
```

View Components

A View Component is almost a complete MVC abstraction. It is a partial view that has its own model, which it gets from a method called **Invoke** in a controller-like class. A View Component's model is independent from the current view's model. You should not use a regular partial view, with a model, from the **_Layout** view, since it has no model and it is difficult to get one into it. Use a View Component to render partial content in the **_Layout** view.

In previous versions of MVC, you use **@Html.ActionHelper** to execute a child action. In this version of MVC it has been replaced with the View Component.

You can look at a View Component as having a controller that you never route to.

View Component views are always placed in a folder called *Components* inside the *Views* folder. If you place the folder in the *Views/Shared* folder, the view can be used from any view. Each View Component has a subfolder in the *Components* folder with the same name as the View Component.

Adding a View Component for the IMessageService Service

Let's implement a View Component that uses the **IMessageService** service to display the configuration message in every view.

1. Create a new folder called *ViewComponents* under the project node. This folder will hold the necessary files for View Components to work.
2. Add a class called **Message** to the folder and inherit the **ViewComponent** class.
   ```
   public class Message : ViewComponent
   {
   }
   ```

3. Add a constructor and inject the **IMessageService** interface to it, name the parameter **message**, and store it in a private class level variable called **_message**.
```
private IMessageService _message;

public Message(IMessageService message)
{
    _message = message;
}
```

4. Add a public method called **Invoke** that returns an **IViewComponentResult**.
```
public IViewComponentResult Invoke()
{
}
```

5. Add a variable called **model** to the **Invoke** method, which stores the result from the **_message.GetMessage** method call.
```
var model = _message.GetMessage();
```

6. Return the **model** with the **View** method. Because the model is a string, the **View** method gets confused and thinks it is the name of the view to render. To fix this you pass in the name of the view as the first parameter and the **model** object as its second parameter.
```
return View("Default", model);
```

7. Create a new folder called *Components* inside the *Views/Shared* folder. And a folder called *Message* inside the *Components* folder.
8. Add a **MVC View Page** called *Default* in the *Message* folder.
9. Delete all code in the view.
10. Add a **@model** directive of type **string**.
```
@model string
```

11. Add a <section> element with a <small> element inside it. Add the **@Model** value to the <small> element.
```
<section>
    <small>@Model</small>
</section>
```

12. Open the **_Layout** view and call the **InvokeAsync** method on the **Component** property inside the <footer> element. Pass in the name of the View Component as a parameter. Remember to use **@await** when calling an asynchronous method.
```
<footer>
```

```
        @RenderSection("footer", false)
        @await Component.InvokeAsync("Message")
    </footer>
```

13. Save all the files.
14. Navigate to all the views, one at a time, to verify that the message from the configuration file (*Hello from configuration*) is displayed in each of their footers.

The complete code for the **Message** View Component:

```
public class Message : ViewComponent
{
    private IMessageService _message;

    public Message(IMessageService message)
    {
        _message = message;
    }

    public IViewComponentResult Invoke()
    {
        var model = _message.GetMessage();
        return View("Default", model);
    }
}
```

The complete markup for the **Default** view:

```
@model string

<section>
    <small>@Model</small>
</section>
```

The complete code for the **_Layout** view:

```
<!DOCTYPE html>

<html>
<head>
    <meta name="viewport" content="width=device-width" />
    <title>@ViewBag.Title</title>
</head>
<body>
```

```
    <div>
        @RenderBody()
    </div>
    <footer>
        @RenderSection("footer", false)
        @await Component.InvokeAsync("Message")
    </footer>
</body>
</html>
```

Summary

In this chapter, you worked with layout views and partial views. You also used new features, such as Tag Helpers, View Components, and the **_ViewStart** and **_ViewImport** views.

Using these features allow you to reuse code and decompose a large view into smaller, more maintainable, pieces. They give you the ability to write maintainable and reusable code.

7. Forms Authentication

In this chapter, you will learn about ASP.NET Identity and how you can use it to implement registration and login in your application. You will add the authentication from scratch to learn how all the pieces fit together.

ASP.NET Identity is a framework that you need to install either with the NuGet Manager, or by adding it manually in the *.csproj* file. It can handle several types of authentication, but in this chapter, you will focus on Forms Authentication.

The first thing you need to add is a **User** entity class that inherits from an identity base class, which gives you access to properties such as **Username**, **PasswordHash**, and **Email**. You can add as many properties to the **User** class as your application needs, but in this chapter, you will only use some of the inherited properties.

The **User** class needs to be plugged into a class called **UserStore**, provided by the **Identity** framework. It is used when creating and validating a user that then is sent to a database; Entity Framework is supported out of the box. You can implement your own **UserStore**, for a different database provider.

The **User** class needs to be plugged into an **IdentityDb** class that handles all communication with an Entity Framework supported database, through an Entity Framework **DbContext**. The way this is done is by making your existing **VideoDbContext** inherit from the **IdentityDbContext** class instead of the current **DbContext** class.

The **UserStore** and the **IdentityDbContext** work together to store user information and validate against the hashed passwords in the database.

Another class involved in the process is the **SignInManager**, which will sign in a user once the password has been validated. It can also be used to sign out already logged in users. A cookie is used to handle Forms Authentication sign-in and sign-out. The cookie is then sent with every subsequent request from the browser, so that the user can be identified.

The last piece is the Identity Middleware that needs to be configured to read the cookie and verify the user.

The **[Authorize]** attribute can be applied to a controller to restrict user access; a user must be signed in and verified to have access to the actions in that controller.

The **[AllowAnonymous]** attribute can be applied to actions to allow any visitor access to that action, even if they aren't registered or signed in.

You can use parameters with the **[Authorize]** attribute to restrict the access even beyond being logged in, which is its default behavior. You can for instance add the **Roles** parameter to specify one or more roles that the user must be in to gain access.

You can also place the **[Authorize]** attribute on specific actions, instead of on the controller class, to restrict access to specific actions.

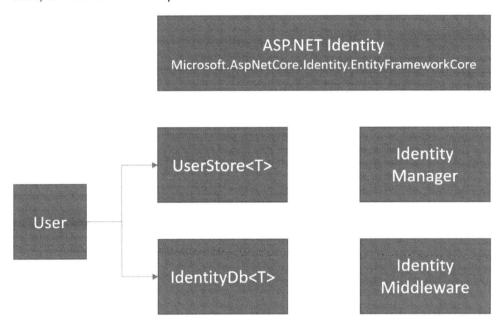

Adding the Authorize and AlowAnonymous Attributes

Let's start by adding the **[Authorize]** attribute to the **HomeController** class, to grant access only to logged in users. Let's also add the **[AllowAnonymous]** attribute to the **Index** action, so that any visitor can see the video list.

1. Open the **HomeController** class and add the **[Authorize]** attribute to it.
   ```
   [Authorize]
   public class HomeController : Controller
   {
       ...
   }
   ```

2. Add the **[AllowAnonymous]** attribute to the **Index** action.
```
[AllowAnonymous]
public ViewResult Index()
{
    ...
}
```

3. Save all files and navigate to the root URL in the browser. As you can see, the **[AllowAnonymous]** attribute lets you see the video list in the **Index** view.

4. Click the **Edit** link to edit a video. Instead of being greeted by the **Edit** view, an empty page is displayed. This confirms that the **[Authorize]** attribute is working. You are not logged in, and are therefore not allowed to use the **Edit** form.

Configuring the Identity Framework

The first thing you need to do is to install the **Microsoft.AspNetCore.Identity.EntityFrameworkCore** NuGet package; the version 1.1.1 is used in this book.

Once you have changed the inheritance on the **VideoDbContext** from the current **DbContext** to the **IdentityDbContext**, the Identity services can be configured in the **ConfigureServices** method, and in the Identity middleware installed in the **Configure** method, in the **Startup** class.

The services that need to be configured are the **UserStore** and **SignInManager**.

1. Add the **Microsoft.AspNetCore.Identity.EntityFrameworkCore** NuGet package to the application.
```
<PackageReference
    Include="Microsoft.AspNetCore.Identity.EntityFrameworkCore"
    Version="1.1.1" />
```

2. Add the **User** entity class to the **Entities** folder and inherit from the **IdentityUser** class to gain access to its user properties. It's in this **User** class that you can add your own user properties, specific to your application; it could be any property related to the user. Below is a list of all the properties the **IdentityUser** class will bring.
```
public class User : IdentityUser
{
}
```

3. Open the **VideoDbContext** and make it inherit the **IdentityDbContext** class instead of EFs default **DbContext**. You can specify the type of user it should store, which in this case is the **User** entity class you just added. the **IdentityDbContext** class is located in the **Microsoft.AspNetCore.Identity.EntityFrameworkCore** namespace.
```
public class VideoDbContext : IdentityDbContext<User>
{
    ...
}
```

4. Open the **Startup** class and locate the **ConfigureServices** method.

5. Add the **Identity** service to the **services** collection by calling the **AddIdentity** method. The method takes two generic type parameters: the first is the user you want it to use (the **User** entity class you just added) and the second is the identity role you want it to use (use the built-in **IdentityRole** class). You can inherit the **IdentityRole** class to another class if you want to implement your own identity role behavior.
```
services.AddIdentity<User, IdentityRole>();
```

6. You must also install the **Entity Framework Stores** services that handle creation and validation of users against the database. You need to provide the **VideoDbContext** to it, so that it knows which context to use when communicating with the database. You can use the fluent API to call the **AddEntityFrameworkStores** method on the **AddIdentity** method.
```
services.AddIdentity<User, IdentityRole>()
    .AddEntityFrameworkStores<VideoDbContext>();
```

7. Next you need to install the middleware components in the **Configure** method. The location of the middleware is important. If you place it too late in the pipeline, it will never be executed. Place it above the MVC middleware to make it available to the MVC framework.
```
app.UseIdentity();
```

8. Build the application with Ctrl+Shift+B to make sure that it builds correctly.

The complete **User** class:

```
public class User : IdentityUser
{
}
```

The properties in the **IdentityUser** class:

```
public class IdentityUser<TKey, TUserClaim, TUserRole, TUserLogin> where
TKey : IEquatable<TKey>
{
    public IdentityUser();
    public IdentityUser(string userName);
    public virtual ICollection<TUserRole> Roles { get; }
    public virtual int AccessFailedCount { get; set; }
    public virtual bool LockoutEnabled { get; set; }
    public virtual DateTimeOffset? LockoutEnd { get; set; }
    public virtual bool TwoFactorEnabled { get; set; }
    public virtual bool PhoneNumberConfirmed { get; set; }
    public virtual string PhoneNumber { get; set; }
    public virtual string ConcurrencyStamp { get; set; }
    public virtual string SecurityStamp { get; set; }
    public virtual string PasswordHash { get; set; }
    public virtual bool EmailConfirmed { get; set; }
    public virtual string NormalizedEmail { get; set; }
    public virtual string Email { get; set; }
    public virtual string NormalizedUserName { get; set; }
    public virtual string UserName { get; set; }
    public virtual TKey Id { get; set; }
    public virtual ICollection<TUserClaim> Claims { get; }
    public virtual ICollection<TUserLogin> Logins { get; }
    public override string ToString();
}
```

Creating the AspNet Identity Database Tables

Now that the configuration is out of the way, it is time to create a new migration that adds the necessary *AspNet* identity tables to the database.

1. Open the Package Manager Console and execute the following command to create the necessary migration file: add-migration IdentityTables

2. Execute the following command to create the identity tables in the database: update-database

3. Open the SQL Server Object Explorer and drill down to the tables in your **VideoDb** database.

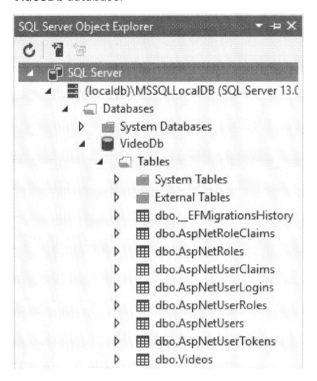

User Registration

Now that all the configuration and database table creation is done, it is time to focus on how a user can register with the site.

If you run the application as it stands right now, the **Identity** middleware will redirect to the */Account/Login* URL, which doesn't exist yet. Instead, the next piece of middleware handles the request, and the message *Hello from configuration* will be displayed in the browser.

To display a **Login** view, you must add an **AccountController** class with a **Login** action. And to log in, the user needs to register. You therefore must implement a **Register** view, and a **Register** action in the **AccountController** class.

1. Add a class named **AccountController** to the **Controllers** folder and let it inherit the **Controllers** class located in the **Microsoft.AspNetCore.Mvc** namespace.
    ```
    public class AccountController : Controller
    {
    }
    ```

2. Add an HTTP GET **Register** action to the class. The view doesn't have to receive a model with data, because the user will supply all the registration information in the view.
    ```
    [HttpGet]
    public IActionResult Register()
    {
        return View();
    }
    ```

3. Add a class called **RegisterViewModel** in the **ViewModels** folder. This will be the view model for the **Register** view.

4. Add a **string** property called **Username** that is required and has a maximum of 255 characters. The length is determined by the max number of characters that the **AspNetUser** table can store for a username.
    ```
    [Required, MaxLength(255)]
    public string Username { get; set; }
    ```

5. Add a **string** property called **Password** that is required and has the **Password** data type.
    ```
    [Required, DataType(DataType.Password)]
    public string Password { get; set; }
    ```

6. Add a **string** property called **ConfirmPassword** that has the **Password** data type and uses the **Compare** attribute to compare its value with the **Password** property. You can use the C# **nameof** operator to specify the compare property, instead of using a string literal.
    ```
    [DataType(DataType.Password), Compare(nameof(Password))]
    public string ConfirmPassword { get; set; }
    ```

7. Add a new folder called *Account* inside the *Views* folder. This folder will hold all the views related to the *Account* controller.

8. Add an **MVC View Page** view called **Register** to the *Account* folder.

9. Delete all the content in the view.

10. Add an **@model** directive for the **RegisterViewModel** class.
    ```
    @model RegisterViewModel
    ```

11. Use the **ViewBag** to add the *Register* to the **Title** property.
```
@{
    ViewBag.Title = "Register";
}
```

12. Add a <h1> heading with the text *Register*.

13. Add a <form> that posts to the **Register** action in the **Account** controller. Use Tag Helpers to create the form.
```
<form method="post" asp-controller="Account" asp-
action="Register">
</form>
```

14. Add a validation summary that only displays errors related to the model.
```
<div asp-validation-summary="ModelOnly"></div>
```

15. Add a <div> that holds a <label> and an <input> for the **Username** model property and a <span> for the validation.
```
<div>
    <label asp-for="Username"></label>
    <input asp-for="Username" />
    <span asp-validation-for="Username" ></span>
</div>
```

16. Repeat step 15 for the **Password** and **ConfirmPassword** properties in the model.

17. Add a **submit** button inside a <div> to the form. Assign the text *Register* to the **value** attribute.
```
<div>
    <input type="submit" value="Register" />
</div>
```

18. Open the **AccountController** class.

19. Add an HTTP POST **Register** action that will be called by the form when the **submit** button is clicked. It should return an **IActionResult** and take a **RegisterViewModel** parameter called **model**. The action must be asynchronous to **await** the result from the **UserManager** and **SingInManager**, which you will inject into the controller later.
```
[HttpPost]
public async Task<IActionResult> Register(RegisterViewModel model)
{
}
```

20. The first thing to do in any HTTP POST action is to check if the model state is valid; if it's not, then the view should be re-rendered.

```
if (!ModelState.IsValid) return View();
```

21. Create a new instance of the **User** entity class and assign its **Username** property value from the passed-in model, below the if-statement.
```
var user = new User { UserName = model.Username };
```

22. To work with the user entity, you need to bring in the **UserManager** and the **SignInManager** via the constructor, using dependency injection. Add a constructor to the controller and inject the two classes mentioned above.
```
private UserManager<User> _userManager;
private SignInManager<User> _signInManager;

public AccountController(UserManager<User> userManager,
SignInManager<User> signInManager)
{
    _userManager = userManager;
    _signInManager = signInManager;
}
```

23. Next you want to use the **UserManager** in the HTTP POST **Register** action to create a new user. Save the result in a variable called **result**.
```
var result = await _userManager.CreateAsync(user, model.Password);
```

24. If the user was created successfully you want to sign in that user automatically. Use the **Succeeded** property on the **result** variable to check if the user was created successfully, and the **SignInAsync** method on the **SignInManager** to sign in the user. The second parameter of the method determines if the cookie should be persisted beyond the session or not.
```
if (result.Succeeded)
{
    await _signInManager.SignInAsync(user, false);
    return RedirectToAction("Index", "Home");
}
```

25. If the user wasn't created, you want to add the errors to the **ModelState** object, so that they are sent to the client as model errors, displayed in the validation summary.
```
else
{
    foreach (var error in result.Errors)
        ModelState.AddModelError("", error.Description);
}
```

26. Return the view below the else-block.

    ```
    return View();
    ```

27. Save all the files and navigate to the */Account/Register* URL. The **Register** View should be displayed. Fill out the form with a three-letter password and click the **Register** button. The validation summary should display the errors that were looped into the **ModelState** object, in the **Register** action method.

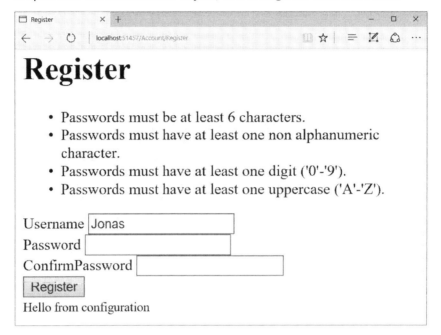

28. Fill out the form (with correct information this time). You should be redirected to the **Index** view through the **RedirectToAction** method in the **Register** action.

29. View the data in the **AspNetUsers** table in the SQL Server Object Explorer to verify that the user was registered.

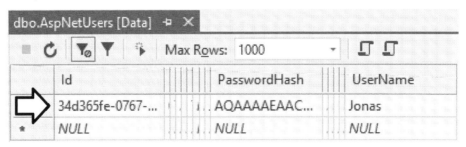

Login and Logout

In this section, you will implement login and logout in your application. The links will be added to a partial view called **_LoginLinks** that you will add to the *Views/Shared* folder. The partial view will then be rendered from the **_Layout** view using the **@Partial** or **@PartialAsync** method.

When an anonymous user arrives at the site, **Login** and **Register** links should be available. When a user has logged in or registered, the username and a **Logout** link should be visible.

You must also create a new view called **Login** in the *Views/Account* folder, a view that the **Login** link opens by calling a **Login** action in the **Account** controller.

To work with users and sign-in information in views, you inject the **SignInManager** and **UserManager**, similar to the way you use dependency injection in methods and constructors in classes.

When an anonymous user clicks a restricted link, like the **Edit** link, a **ReturnUrl** parameter is sent with the URL, so that the user will end up on that view when a successful login has been made. When creating the **LoginViewModel** you must add a property for the return URL, so that the application can redirect to it. Below is an example URL with the **ReturnUrl** parameter.

http://localhost:51457/Account/Login?**ReturnUrl=%2FHome%2FEdit%2F1**

Adding the _Login Partial View

This partial view will contain the **Login** and **Register** links that will be visible when an anonymous user visits the site, and a **Logout** link and the username when the user is logged in.

1. Add a **MVC View Page** called **_LoginLinks** to the *Views/Shared* folder.
2. Delete all the code in the view.
3. Add a **using** statement to the **Microsoft.AspNetCore.Identity** namespace to get access to the **SignInManager** and **UserManager**.
   ```
   @using Microsoft.AspNetCore.Identity
   ```
4. Inject the **SignInManager** and **UserManager** to the view, below the **using** statement.
   ```
   @inject SignInManager<User> SignInManager
   @inject UserManager<User> UserManager
   ```

5. Add if/else-blocks that check if the user is signed in, using the **IsSignedIn** method on the **SignInManager** passing it the **User** object.

```
@if (SignInManager.IsSignedIn(User))
{
    // Signed in user
}
else
{
    // Anonymous user
}
```

6. Add a <div> that displays the username to the *Signed in user*-block. Use the **User** object's **Identity** property.

```
<div>@User.Identity.Name</div>
```

7. Add a form to the *Signed in user*-block that posts to the */Account/Logout* action when a **submit** button is clicked.

```
<form method="post" asp-controller="Account" asp-action="Logout">
    <input type="submit" value="Logout" />
</form>
```

8. Add two anchor tags to the *Anonymous user* block that navigates to the **Login** and **Register** actions in the **Account** controller.

```
<a asp-controller="Account" asp-action="Login">Login</a>
<a asp-controller="Account" asp-action="Register">Register</a>
```

9. Open the **_Layout** view and add a <div> above the **@RenderBody** method in the <body> element.

10. Call the **@Html.PartialAsync** method to render the **_LoginLinks** partial view in the <div>.

```
<div>
    @await Html.PartialAsync("_LoginLinks")
</div>
```

11. Start the application without debugging (Ctrl+F5). If you are an anonymous user, the **Login** and **Register** links should be visible at the top of the view, otherwise the username and a **Logout** button should be visible.

The complete code for the **_LoginLinks** partial view:

```
@using Microsoft.AspNetCore.Identity

@inject SignInManager<User> SignInManager
@inject UserManager<User> UserManager
```

```
@if (SignInManager.IsSignedIn(User))
{
    <div>@User.Identity.Name</div>
    <form method="post" asp-controller="Account" asp-action="Logout">
        <input type="submit" value="Logout" />
    </form>
}
else
{
    <a asp-controller="Account" asp-action="Login">Login</a>
    <a asp-controller="Account" asp-action="Register">Register</a>
}
```

Adding the Logout Action

The **SignOutAsync** method on the **SignInManager** must be called to logout a user when the **Logout** button is clicked. The **Logout** action in the **Account** controller must be asynchronous because the **SignOutAsync** method is asynchronous.

1. Open the **AccountController** class.
2. Add an **async** HTTP POST action called **Logout** that returns a **Task<IActionResult>**. This action will be called when the **Logout** link is clicked.
    ```
    [HttpPost]
    public async Task<IActionResult> Logout()
    {
    }
    ```
3. Call the **SignOutAsync** method on the **_signInManager** object inside the **Logout** action.
    ```
    await _signInManager.SignOutAsync();
    ```
4. Because the user is logging out, you want the user to end up on a safe view after the logout process has completed. Add a redirect to the **Index** action in the **Home** controller.
    ```
    return RedirectToAction("Index", "Home");
    ```

The complete code for the **Logout** action:

```
[HttpPost]
public async Task<IActionResult> Logout()
{
    await _signInManager.SignOutAsync();
    return RedirectToAction("Index", "Home");
```

}

Adding the LoginViewModel Class

This model is responsible for passing the login information provided by the user, and the **ReturnUrl** URL parameter value, to the HTTP POST **Login** action.

The model needs four properties: **Username**, **Password**, **RememberMe**, and **ReturnUrl**. The **RememberMe** property determines if the cookie should be a session cookie or if a more persistent cookie should be used.

1. Add a new class called **LoginViewModel** to the *ViewModels* folder.
2. Add three **string** properties called **Username**, **Password**, and **ReturnUrl**, and a **bool** property called **RememberMe**.
3. Add the **Required** attribute to the **Username** property.
   [Required]

4. Add the **DataType.Password** and **Required** attributes to the **Password** property.
   [DataType(DataType.Password), Required]

5. Use the **Display** attribute to change the label text to *Remember Me* for the **ReturnUrl** property.
   [Display(Name = "Remember Me")]

The complete code for the **LoginViewModel** class:

```
public class LoginViewModel
{
    [Required]
    public string Username { get; set; }
    [DataType(DataType.Password), Required]
    public string Password { get; set; }
    public string ReturnUrl { get; set; }
    [Display(Name = "Remember Me")]
    public bool RememberMe { get; set; }
}
```

Adding the HTTP GET Login Action

This action will be called when the user clicks the **Login** link. You will need to create an instance of the **LoginViewModel** and assign the return URL, passed into the action, to its **ReturnUrl** property. Then pass the model to the view.

1. Open the **AccountController** class.
2. Add an HTTP GET action called **Login** that takes a string parameter called **returnUrl** and returns an **IActionResult**.
   ```
   [HttpGet]
   public IActionResult Login(string returnUrl ="")
   {
   }
   ```
3. Create an instance of the **LoginViewModel** and assign the return URL passed into the action to its **ReturnUrl** property.
   ```
   var model = new LoginViewModel { ReturnUrl = returnUrl };
   ```
4. Return the model with the view.
   ```
   return View(model);
   ```

The complete code for the HTTP GET **Login** action:

```
[HttpGet]
public IActionResult Login(string returnUrl ="")
{
    var model = new LoginViewModel { ReturnUrl = returnUrl };
    return View(model);
}
```

Adding the HTTP POST Login Action

The HTTP POST **Login** action will be called when the user clicks the **Login** button in the **Login** view. The view's login form will send the user data to this action; it therefore must have a **LoginViewModel** as a parameter. The action must be asynchronous because the **PasswordSignInAsync** method provided by the **SignInManager** is asynchronous.

1. Open the **AccountController** class.
2. Add an **async** HTTP POST action called **Login** that takes an instance of the **LoginViewModel** as a parameter and returns a **Task<IActionResult>**.
   ```
   [HttpPost]
   public async Task<IActionResult> Login(LoginViewModel model)
   {
   }
   ```
3. The first thing to do in any HTTP POST action is to check if the model state is valid; if it's not, then the view should be re-rendered.
   ```
   if (!ModelState.IsValid) return View(model);
   ```

4. Sign in the user by calling the **PasswordSignInAsync** method, passing in the username, password, and remember me values. Store the result in a variable called **result**. The last parameter determines if the user should be locked out, if providing wrong credentials.

```
var result = await
_signInManager.PasswordSignInAsync(model.Username, model.Password,
model.RememberMe, false);
```

5. Add an if-statement checking if the sign-in succeeded.

```
if (result.Succeeded)
{
}
```

6. Add another if-statement, inside the previous one, that checks that the URL isn't null or empty and that it is a local URL. It is important to check if it is a local URL, for security reasons. If you don't do that your application is vulnerable to attacks.

```
if (!string.IsNullOrEmpty(model.ReturnUrl) &&
Url.IsLocalUrl(model.ReturnUrl))
{
}
else
{
}
```

7. If the return URL exists and is safe, then redirect to it in the if-block.

```
return Redirect(model.ReturnUrl);
```

8. If the URL is empty or isn't local, then redirect to the **Index** action in the **Home** controller.

```
return RedirectToAction("Index", "Home");
```

9. Add a **ModelState** error and return the view with the model below it. Place the code below the if-statement, to be certain that it only is called if the login is unsuccessful.

```
ModelState.AddModelError("", "Login failed");
return View(model);
```

The complete code for the HTTP POST **Login** action:

```
[HttpPost]
public async Task<IActionResult> Login(LoginViewModel model)
{
    if (!ModelState.IsValid) return View();

    var result = await _signInManager.PasswordSignInAsync(
        model.Username, model.Password, model.RememberMe, false);
    if (result.Succeeded)
    {
        if (!string.IsNullOrEmpty(model.ReturnUrl) &&
            Url.IsLocalUrl(model.ReturnUrl))
        {
            return Redirect(model.ReturnUrl);
        }
        else
        {
            return RedirectToAction("Index", "Home");
        }
    }
    ModelState.AddModelError("", "Login failed");
    return View(model);
}
```

Adding the Login View

You need to add a view called **Login** to the **Account** folder, to enable visitors to log in.

1. Add an **MVC View Page** view called **Login** to the *Account* folder.
2. Delete all the content in the view.
3. Add an **@model** directive for the **LoginViewModel** class.
   ```
   @model LoginViewModel
   ```

4. Use the **ViewBag** to add a title with the text *login*.
   ```
   @{
       ViewBag.Title = "Login";
   }
   ```

5. Add a <h2> heading with the text *Login*.
6. Add a <form> that posts to the **Login** action in the **Account** controller. Use Tag Helpers to create the form, and to return the return URL.
   ```
   <form method="post" asp-controller="Account" asp-action="Login"
       asp-route-returnurl="@Model.ReturnUrl">
   </form>
   ```

7. Add a validation summary that only displays errors related to the model.
```
<div asp-validation-summary="ModelOnly"></div>
```

8. Add a `<div>` that holds a `<label>` and an `<input>` for the **Username** model property, and a `<span>` for the validation.
```
<div>
    <label asp-for="Username"></label>
    <input asp-for="Username" />
    <span asp-validation-for="Username" ></span>
</div>
```

9. Repeat step 8 for the **Password** and **RememberMe** properties in the model.

10. Add a **submit** button with the text **Login** to the form; place it inside a `<div>`.
```
<div>
    <input type="submit" value="Login" />
</div>
```

11. Start the application without debugging (Ctrl+F5). Logout if you are signed in.

12. Click the **Edit** link for one of the videos. The **Login** view should be displayed because you are an anonymous user. Note the **ReturnUrl** parameter in the URL.

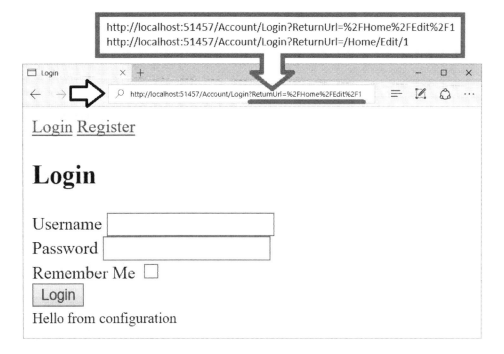

138

13. Log in as a registered user. The **Edit** view, for the video you tried to edit before, should open. Note the username and the **Logout** button at the top of the view.

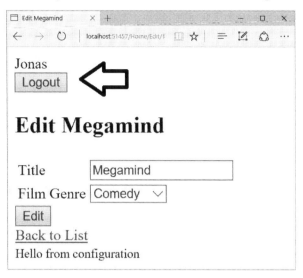

14. Click the **Logout** button to logout the current user. You should be taken to the **Index** view. Note the **Login** and **Register** links at the top of the view.

The complete markup for the **Login** view:

```
@model LoginViewModel

@{
    ViewBag.Title = "Login";
}
<h2>Login</h2>

<form method="post" asp-controller="Account" asp-action="Login"
        asp-route-returnurl="@Model.ReturnUrl">
    <div asp-validation-summary="ModelOnly"></div>
    <div>
        <label asp-for="Username"></label>
        <input asp-for="Username" />
        <span asp-validation-for="Username"></span>
    </div>
    <div>
        <label asp-for="Password"></label>
        <input asp-for=" Password" />
        <span asp-validation-for=" Password"></span>
```

```
    </div>
    <div>
        <label asp-for="RememberMe"></label>
        <input asp-for="RememberMe" />
        <span asp-validation-for="RememberMe"></span>
    </div>
    <div>
        <input type="submit" value="Login" />
    </div>
</form>
```

Summary

In this chapter, you used ASP.NET Identity to secure your application, implementing registration and login from scratch.

The first thing you did was to add a **User** entity class that inherited the **IdentityUser** base class. This gave you access to properties such as **Username**, **PasswordHash**, and **Email**.

Then you plugged the **User** entity into a **UserStore** and a **IdentityDb** class. This made it possible to create and validate a user, which then was stored in the database.

The **UserManager** and **SignInManager** were then used to implement registration and login for users, with a cookie that handles the Forms Authentication.

The **[Authorize]** and **[AllowAnonymous]** attributes were used to restrict user access to controller actions.

8. Front-End Frameworks

In this chapter, you will learn how to install front-end libraries using Bower. The two types of libraries you will install are for styling and client-side validation.

Bootstrap: Is the most popular library for styling and responsive design. You will use some Bootstrap CSS classes to style the video list and the navigation links. You can find out more about Bootstrap on their site: http://getbootstrap.com

JQuery: You will use JQuery and JQuery Validation to perform client-side validation. This will make sure that the user input is conforming to the validation rules before the data is sent to the server action. Some validation rules are added by the framework; others you have added yourself to the entity and view model classes as attributes. Examples of validation rules are: password restrictions set by the framework (can be changed), the **Required**, **MaxLength**, and **DataType** attributes.

Installing Bower and the Frameworks

Bower is the preferred way to install front-end frameworks in ASP.NET Core 1.1. When the libraries have been installed, they must be referenced from the **_Layout** view for global access, or in individual views for local access. You can use the environment tag to specify the environment the libraries should be accessible from. You usually want the un-minified libraries in the **Development** environment for easy debugging, and the minified versions in the **Staging** and **Production** environments for faster load times.

Many times, you can achieve even faster load times if you use Content Delivery Networks (CDNs), servers that have cached versions of the libraries that can be called. You can find information about the Microsoft's CDNs at:
https://docs.microsoft.com/en-us/aspnet/ajax/cdn/overview.

Four attributes are used to check that the JavaScript libraries have been installed:

asp-fallback-test-class, asp-fallback-test-property, asp-fallback-test-value and **asp-fallback-test**.

Two of the attributes are used to load an alternative source if the JavaScript libraries haven't been installed: **asp-fallback-src** and **asp-fallback-href**.

1. Add a **Bower Configuration File** to the project node. It's important that it is named *bower.json*. You can search for *bower* in the **New Item** dialog.

2. Install Bootstrap by using the **Manage Bower Packages** guide, or by typing it directly into the *dependencies* section of the *bower.json* file. Bootstrap has a dependency on JQuery, so that library will be automatically installed.
   `"bootstrap": "^3.3.7"`

3. Install the **JQuery-Validation** and **JQuery-Validation-Unobtrusive** libraries using Bower.
   ```
   "jquery-validation": "^1.16.0",
   "jquery-validation-unobtrusive": "^3.2.6"
   ```

4. Expand the *Dependencies/Bower* node in the Solution Explorer to verify that the libraries have been installed.

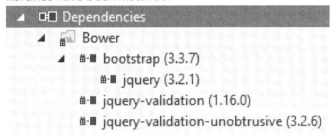

5. Expand the *wwwroot* node in the Solution Explorer. It should now have a folder named *lib*, under which the installed libraries reside.

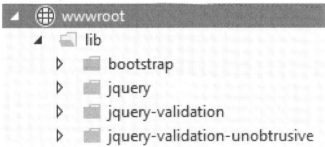

6. Open the **_Layout** view and add two <environment> Tag Helpers below the <title> element inside the <head> element. Name the first **Development** and the second **Staging, Production**. You can change environment in the project settings. In these two Tag Helpers, you specify CSS libraries you want to load when the view loads.
   ```
   <environment names="Development">
   </environment>
   ```

```
<environment names="Staging,Production">
</environment>
```

7. Add the un-minified Bootstrap library to the **Development** environment and the CDN version with a fallback in the **Staging, Production** environments.

```
<environment names="Development">
    <link rel="stylesheet"
        href="~/lib/bootstrap/dist/css/bootstrap.css" />
</environment>
<environment names="Staging,Production">
    <link rel="stylesheet"
        href="https://ajax.aspnetcdn.com/ajax/bootstrap/3.3.7/
            css/bootstrap.min.css"
        asp-fallback-href=
            "~/lib/bootstrap/dist/css/bootstrap.min.css"
        asp-fallback-test-class="sr-only"
        asp-fallback-test-property="position"
        asp-fallback-test-value="absolute" />
</environment>
```

8. Repeat step 6 at the bottom of the <body> element. In these two Tag Helpers, you specify JavaScript libraries you want to load when the HTML has finished loading.

9. Add the *bootstrap.js*, *jquery.js*, *jquery.validation.js*, and *jquery.validation.unobtrusive.js* libraries and their CDN scripts to the <environment> Tag Helper you added in the <body> element.

```
<environment names="Development">
    <script src="~/lib/jquery/dist/jquery.js"></script>
    <script src="~/lib/jquery-validation/dist/jquery.validate.js">
    </script>
    <script src="~/lib/jquery-validation-unobtrusive/
        jquery.validate.unobtrusive.js"></script>
</environment>
<environment names="Staging,Production">
    <script src="https://ajax.aspnetcdn.com/ajax/jquery/
        jquery-3.2.1.min.js"
        asp-fallback-src="~/lib/jquery/dist/jquery.js"
        asp-fallback-test="window.jQuery">
    </script>
    <script src="http://ajax.aspnetcdn.com/ajax/jquery.validate/
        1.16.0/jquery.validate.min.js"
        asp-fallback-src=
            "~/lib/jquery-validation/dist/jquery.validate.js"
        asp-fallback-test="window.jQuery && window.jQuery.validator">
```

```
        </script>
        <script src="http://ajax.aspnetcdn.com/ajax/mvc/5.2.3/
            jquery.validate.unobtrusive.min.js"
            asp-fallback-src="~/lib/jquery-validation-unobtrusive/
                jquery.validate.unobtrusive.js"
            asp-fallback-test="window.jQuery && window.jQuery.validator
                && window.jQuery.validator.unobtrusive">
        </script>
    </environment>
```

The complete dependency list in the *bower.json* file:

```
"dependencies": {
    "bootstrap": "^3.3.7",
    "jquery-validation": "^1.16.0",
    "jquery-validation-unobtrusive": "^3.2.6"
}
```

Styling with Bootstrap

Let's add a navigation bar in the **_Layout** view, and style it and the video list in the **Index** view, using Bootstrap.

The navigation bar for an anonymous user:

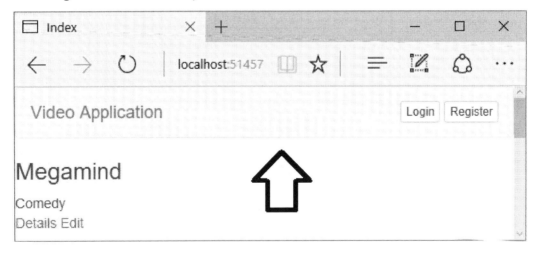

The navigation bar for a logged in user:

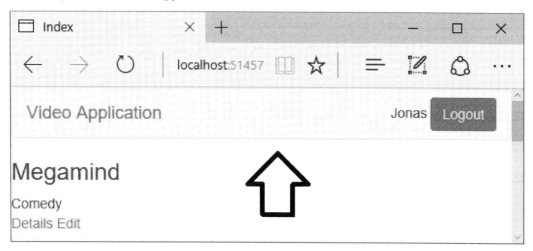

Adding a Navigation Bar

1. Open the **_Layout** view.
2. Add a <nav> element at the top of the <body> element and decorate it with the **navbar** and **navbar-default** Bootstrap classes, to create the navigation bar placeholder.
   ```
   <nav class="navbar navbar-default">
   </nav>
   ```
3. Add a <div> that will act as the navigation bar container. Add the **container-fluid** Bootstrap class to it, to make it stretch across the whole screen.
   ```
   <div class="container-fluid">
   </div>
   ```
4. Add a <div> inside the fluid container <div>; it will act as the navigation bar header. Add the **navbar-header** Bootstrap class to it.
   ```
   <div class="navbar-header">
   </div>
   ```
5. Add an anchor tag to the navigation bar header. This link will take the user back to the application root (the **Index** view) if clicked. Add the Bootstrap class **navbar-brand** and the text *Video Application* to it.
   ```
   <a class="navbar-brand" href="/">Video Application</a>
   ```
6. Cut out the <div> containing the call to the **_LoginLinks** partial view and paste it below the navbar brand <div>. Add the Bootstrap classes **navbar**, **nabar-nav**, and

pull-right to the <div> to turn the links into buttons and right align them in the navigation bar.

```
<div class="nav navbar-nav pull-right">
    @await Html.PartialAsync("_LoginLinks")
</div>
```

7. Open the **_LoginLinks** partial view.

8. Cut out the Razor expression that fetches the user's name, and paste it at the top of the form. Delete the <div>.

```
<form method="post" asp-controller="Account" asp-action="Logout">
    @User.Identity.Name
    <input type="submit" value="Logout" />
</form>
```

9. Add the Bootstrap classes **navbar-btn**, **btn**, and **btn-danger** to the **submit** button to style it.

```
<input type="submit" value="Logout" class="navbar-btn btn btn-danger"
/>
```

10. Add the Bootstrap classes **btn**, **btn-xs**, **btn-default**, and **navbar-btn** to the <a> elements to turn the links into buttons.

11. Save all files and start the application without debugging (Ctrl+F5). A navigation bar with the brand name and the links should be visible at the top of the view.

The complete markup for the **_LoginLinks** partial view:

```
@using Microsoft.AspNetCore.Identity

@inject SignInManager<User> SignInManager
@inject UserManager<User> UserManager

@if (SignInManager.IsSignedIn(User))
{
    <form method="post" asp-controller="Account" asp-action="Logout">
        @User.Identity.Name
        <input type="submit" value="Logout"
            class="navbar-btn btn btn-danger" />
    </form>
}
else
{
    <a class="btn btn-xs btn-default navbar-btn"
        asp-controller="Account" asp-action="Login">Login</a>
    <a class="btn btn-xs btn-default navbar-btn"
```

```
                asp-controller="Account" asp-action="Register">Register</a>
}
```

The navigation bar markup in the **_Layout** view:

```
<nav class="navbar navbar-default">
    <div class="container-fluid">
        <div class="navbar-header">
            <a class="navbar-brand" href="/">Video Application</a>
        </div>

        <div class="nav navbar-nav pull-right">
            @await Html.PartialAsync("_LoginLinks")
        </div>
    </div>
</nav>
```

Styling the Index View

Let's make the video list a bit more appealing by adding Bootstrap classes to make them appear like panels. The image below shows the end result.

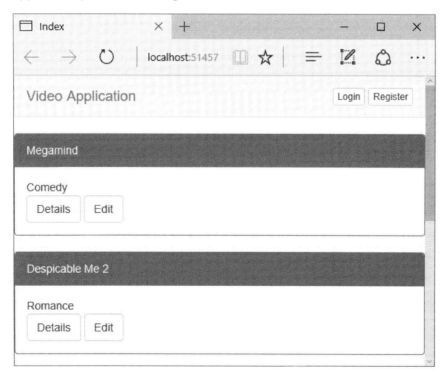

1. Open the **Index** view.
2. Add the Bootstrap classes **btn** and **btn-success** to the **Create** link in the **Index** view. This should turn the button green, with the default Bootstrap theme.
   ```
   <a class="btn btn-success" asp-action="Create">Create</a>
   ```
3. Open the **_Video** view.
4. Add the **panel** and **panel-primary** Bootstrap classes to the <section> element, to turn it into a panel with blue heading background.
   ```
   <section class="panel panel-primary">
   ```
5. Replace the <h3> heading with a <div> decorated with the **panel-heading** Bootstrap class, for the title.
   ```
   <div class="panel-heading">@Model.Title</div>
   ```
6. Move the ending </div> for the genre, below the ending </div> for the anchor tags. Add the **panel-body** Bootstrap class to the <div> surrounding the genre and anchor tags. Add the **btn** and **btn-default** Bootstrap classes to the anchor tags to turn them into buttons.
   ```
   <div class="panel-body">
       @Model.Genre
       <div>
           <a class="btn btn-default" asp-action="Details"
               asp-route-id="@Model.Id">Details</a>
           <a class="btn btn-default" asp-action="Edit"
               asp-route-id="@Model.Id">Edit</a>
       </div>
   </div>
   ```
7. Save all files and start the application without debugging (Ctrl+F5). The videos should be displayed in panels.

The complete markup for the **_Video** view:

```
@model VideoViewModel

<section class="panel panel-primary">
    <div class="panel-heading">@Model.Title</div>
    <div class="panel-body">
        @Model.Genre
        <div>
            <a class="btn btn-default" asp-action="Details"
                asp-route-id="@Model.Id">Details</a>
            <a class="btn btn-default" asp-action="Edit"
```

```
            asp-route-id="@Model.Id">Edit</a>
        </div>
    </div>
</section>
```

Adding Client-Side Validation

To take advantage of client-side validation, you only have to add the **jquery, jquery. validate**, and **jquery.validate.unobtrusive** JavaScript libraries. You have already added the libraries in a previous section, so now you only have to check that the validation works.

Pay attention to the URL field in the browser as you click the **Login**, **Edit**, and **Create** buttons when you try to enter invalid data (you can for instance leave one of the text fields empty). The URL should not refresh, because no round-trip is made to the server.

1. Run the application without debugging (Ctrl+F5).
2. Click the **Edit** button in the **Index** view; this should display the **Login** view. If you're already logged in then click the **Logout** button and repeat this step.
3. Leave the **Username** field empty and click the **Login** button. Pay attention to the URL; it should not refresh. An error message should be displayed in the form.

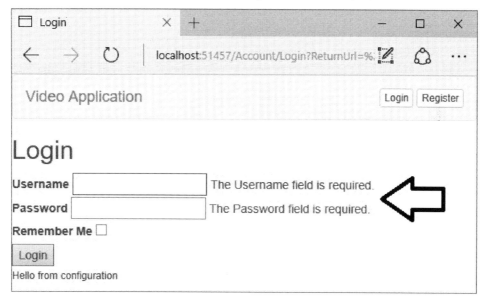

4. Login with correct credentials.

5. Clear the **Title** field and click the **Edit** button. Pay attention to the URL; it should not refresh. Two error messages should be displayed, one for the validation summary, above the controls, and one beside the text field.

6. Click the **Back to List** link to return to the **Index** view.
7. Click the **Create** link below the video list.
8. Try to add a video with an empty title. Pay attention to the URL; it should not refresh. The same type of error displayed for the **Edit** view should be displayed.

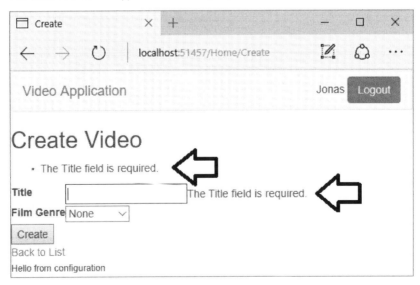

Summary

In this chapter, you used Bower to add JQuery libraries to enforce client-side validation, and Bootstrap to style the **Index** view with CSS classes.

Next, you will start implementing the video course website.

Part 2:
ASP.NET Core 1.1 MVC
How to Build a Video Course Website

9. The Use Case

Introduction

In this this part of the book you will learn how to build an ASP.NET Core 1.1 Web Application using MVC, Entity Framework Core 1.1, custom Tag Helpers, HTML, CSS, AutoMapper, and JW Player.

The Use Case

The customer has ordered a Video on Demand (VOD) application and has requested that the newest technologies be used when developing the solution. The application should run in the cloud, be web based, and run on any device. They have specifically asked that Microsoft technologies be used as the core of the solution. Any deviations from that path should be kept to a minimum.

As a first step, they would like a demo version using dummy data to get a feel for the application. The dummy data source must be interchangeable with the final SQL database storage, with minimal extra cost.

YouTube should be used to store the videos, to keep costs down. No API or functionality for uploading videos is necessary in the final application. It is sufficient for the administrator to be able to paste in a link to a video stored in a YouTube account when adding a new video with the admin user interface.

The User Interface

Users should be able to register and Login to the web application. Upon successful login or registration, the user should be automatically redirected to the membership site.

The first view after login should be a dashboard, displaying the courses available to the user. When clicking on a course, the course curriculum should be displayed in a list below a marquee and some information about the course. Each course can have multiple modules, which can have multiple videos and downloadable content. Downloadable content should open in a separate browser tab.

When the user clicks on a video listing, a new view is opened, where a video player is preloaded with the video but displays an image (no auto play). Information about the course, and a description of the video, should be displayed below the video player. To the right of the video player, a thumbnail image for the next video in the module should be displayed, as well as buttons to the previous and next video. The buttons should be disabled if no video is available.

An instructor bio should be displayed in the **Course**, **Detail**, and **Video** views.

The menu should have a logo on the far left and a settings menu to the far right. If the logged in user is an administrator, a second drop-down menu should appear to the right of the logo, containing links to views for CRUD operations on the database connected to the site.

The database entity classes should not be used as view models; instead, each view should use a view model, which contains the necessary Data Transfer Objects (DTOs) and other properties. Auto Mapper should be used to convert entities to DTO objects, which are sent to the views.

Login and Register User

When an anonymous user visits the site, the **Login** view should be displayed. From that view, the visitor will be able to register with the site by clicking on a **Register as a new user** link. The link opens a **Create** view where a new user account can be created.

When these views are displayed, a menu with the standard options should be available, like **Home** (takes the visitor to the login view), **About**, and **Contact**. The two latter views don't have to be implemented since the company will do that themselves; just leave them with their default content.

The Administrator Views

Each table should have five views for performing CRUD operations: **Index**, **Create**, **Edit**, **Delete**, and **Details**. One thing to keep in mind is that the scaffolded view won't display the name or title in a form's drop-downs. You will have to change that manually in the controller action method and the corresponding view. In some cases there will be a text field instead of a drop-down; you will have to change that as well. In a couple of instances there will be a text field displaying an id; just remove it and alter the action method accordingly.

Conclusion

After careful consideration, these are the views and controls necessary for the application to work properly.

Login and Register

It is clear that the default views can be reused; they only need some styling. The default links for registering and logging in a user in the navigation bar has to be removed, and the **Home** controller's **Index** action will reroute to the **Login** view instead of displaying the **Index** view. This will ensure that the login panel is displayed when the application starts.

Below is a mock-up image of the **Login** and **Create** views. Note the icons in the textboxes; they will be represented by Glyphicons.

The application will collect the user's email and password when registering with the site, and that information will be requested of the visitor when logging in. There will also be a checkbox asking if the user wants to remain logged in when visiting the site the next time.

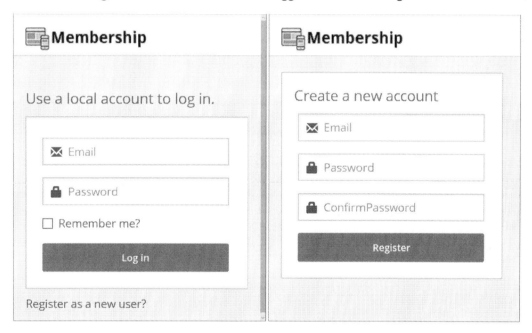

The Dashboard View

By analyzing the use case you can surmise that the dashboard's course panels should be loaded dynamically, based on the number of courses the user has access to. The courses will be displayed three to a row, to make them large enough. This means that the view model has to contain a collection of collections, defined by a course DTO.

Each course DTO should contain properties for the course id, course title, description, a course image, and a marquee image. Each course should be displayed as a panel with the course image, title, description, and a button leading to the course view.

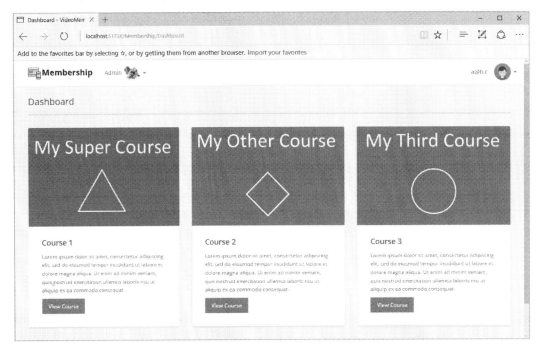

The Course View

The course view should have a button at the top, leading back to the dashboard. Below the button, there should be three sections: an overview, the course modules, and an instructor bio.

The marquee image, the course image (as a thumbnail in the marquee), the title, and description should be in the top panel.

Below the top panel to the left, the course modules and their content should be listed. Note that there are two possible types of content in a module, videos and downloads. Each video should display a thumbnail, title, description, and the length of the video (duration). Downloads are listed as links with a descriptive title.

To the right of the module list is the instructor bio, which contain a thumbnail, name, and description of the instructor.

To pull this off, the course view model needs to have a Course DTO, an Instructor DTO, and a list of Module DTOs. Each Instructor DTO should contain the avatar, name, and description of the instructor teaching a course. The Module DTO should contain the module id, title, and lists of Video DTOs and Download DTOs.

A Video DTO should contain the video id, title, description, duration, a thumbnail, and the URL to the video. When a video is clicked, the video should be loaded into, and displayed by, the **Video** view. Auto play should be disabled.

A Download DTO should contain a title and the URL to the content. When the link is clicked, the content should open in a new browser tab.

The Video View

There should be three sections in the **Video** view, below the button leading back to the **Course** view. To the left, a large video panel containing the video, course, and video information is displayed. To the top right is a panel displaying the image and title of the next video in the current module, along with **Previous** and **Next** buttons.

Below the *next video* panel is the *Instructor* panel.

To pull this off, the video view model must contain a Video DTO, an Instructor DTO, a Course DTO, and a LessonInfo DTO. The LessonInfo DTO contains properties for lesson number, number of lessons, video id, title, and thumbnail properties for the previous and next videos in the module.

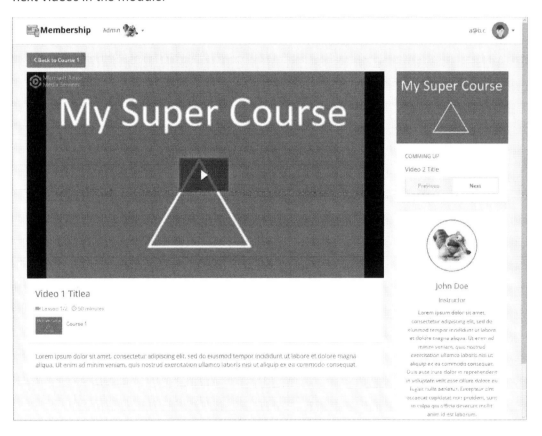

A Typical Administrator Index View

A typical **Index** view contains a title and a **Create** button at the top, a table with information about the entity, and three more buttons for editing, deleting, and displaying information about the entity.

A custom Tag Helper will be used to render the buttons, for easy reuse.

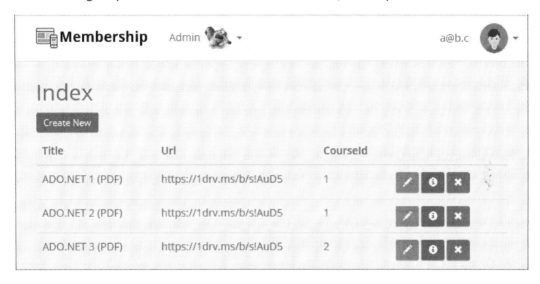

A Typical Administrator Create View

A typical **Create** view has labels and input fields for data needed to create a new record in the database. Be aware that the auto generated drop-downs will display a list of ids for the related entities; you will have to change them to display a name or title instead. The **UserCourse** views are even more complex, because they involve the **AspNet_User** table.

The view should have a **Create** button that posts the data to the server, and a **Back to List** button that takes the user back to the **Index** view.

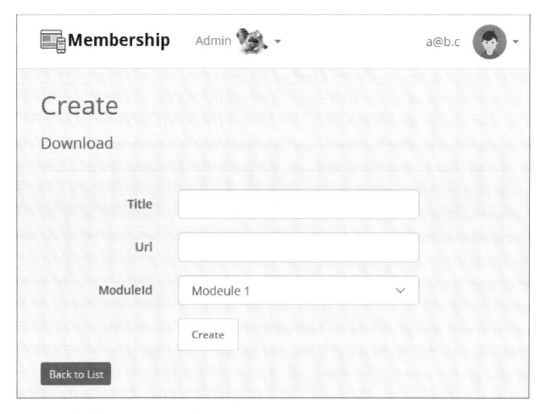

A Typical Administrator Edit View

A typical **Edit** view has labels and input fields for the data needed to update a record in the database. Be aware that the auto generated drop-downs will display a list of ids for the related entities; you will have to change them to display a name or title instead.

The view also has a **Save** button that posts the data to the server, and a **Back to List** button that takes the user back to the **Index** view.

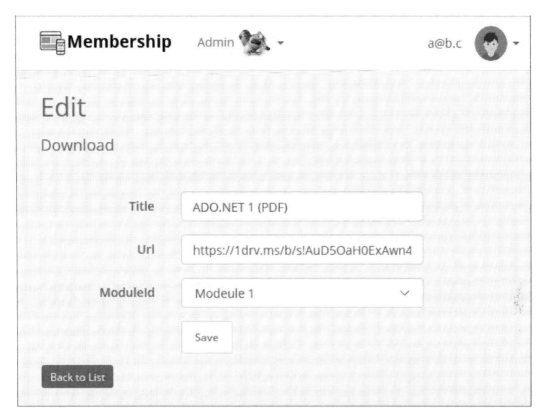

A Typical Administrator Delete View

A typical **Delete** view has labels for the entity data, a **Delete** button prompting the server to delete the entity from the database, and a **Back to List** button that takes the user back to the **Index** view.

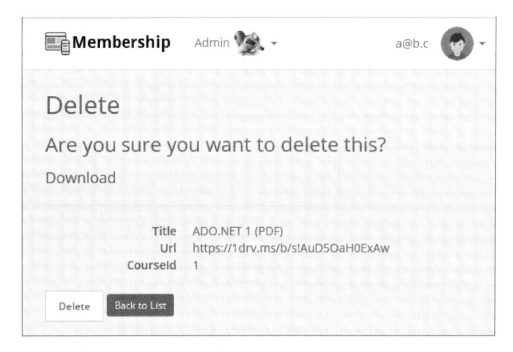

A Typical Administrator Details View

A typical **Details** view has labels for the entity data, an **Edit** button taking the user to the **Edit** view, and a **Back to List** button that takes the user back to the **Index** view.

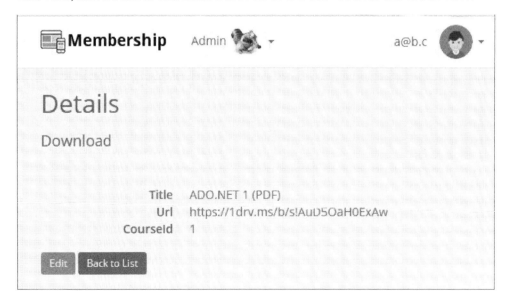

10. Setting Up the Solution

Introduction

In this chapter, you will create the solution and install the necessary NuGet packages in Visual Studio 2017.

Technologies Used in This Chapter

- **ASP.NET Core Web Application** – The project template used to create the MVC application.
- **MVC** – To structure the application.
- **AutoMapper** – A NuGet package that, when installed, will map objects from one type to another. Will be used to map entity objects to DTOs.

Overview

The customer wants you to build the web application using Visual Studio 2017 and an **ASP.NET Core Web Application** template. The first step will be to create the solution and install all the necessary NuGet packages that aren't installed with the default project template. The template will install the basic MVC plumbing and a **Home** controller with **Index**, **About**, and **Contact** action methods, and their corresponding views.

Creating the Solution

If you haven't already installed Visual Studio 2017, do so now. You can download a free version here: www.visualstudio.com/downloads.

1. Open Visual Studio 2017 and select **File-New Project** in the main menu.
2. Click on the **Web** tab and then select **ASP.NET Core Web Application** in the template list.
3. Give the project a name. You can call it *VideoOnDemand*.
4. Make sure that the **Create directory for solution** is checked. This will create a containing folder for the entire solution.
5. Click the **OK** button.
6. Select **.NET Core** and **ASP.NET Core 1.1** in the drop-downs.
7. Select **Web Application (Model-View-Controller)** in the dialog.

8. Click the **Change Authentication** button and select **Individual User Accounts** in the pop-up dialog. This will make it possible for visitors to register and Login with your site using an email and a password.
9. Click the **OK** button in the pop-up dialog.
10. Click the **OK** button in the wizard dialog.

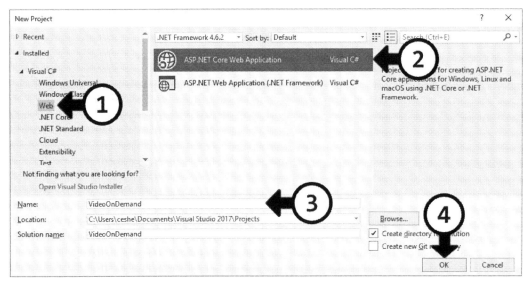

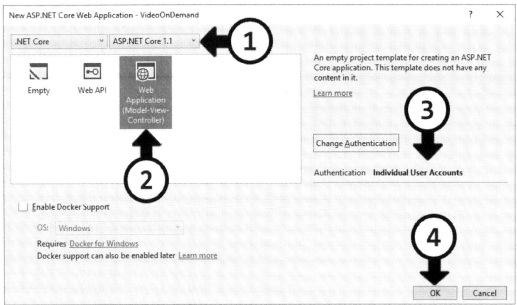

It is no longer possible to manage NuGet packages with a *project.json* file. Instead, the NuGet packages are listed in the *.csproj* file, which can be edited directly from the IDE.

It is also important to understand the concept of Dependency Injection, since it is used to make object instances available throughout the application. If a resource is needed, it can be injected into the constructor and saved to a private local variable. No objects are created in the class itself; any objects needed can be requested through DI.

Installing AutoMapper

AutoMapper will be used to map entity (database table) objects to Data Transfer Objects (DTOs), which are used to transport data to the views. You can either add the following row to the <ItemGroup> node in the *.csproj* file manually and save the file or use the NuGet manager to add AutoMapper.

```
<PackageReference Include="AutoMapper" Version="6.0.2" />
```

The following listing shows you how to use the NuGet manager to install packages.

1. Right click on the **Dependencies** node in the Solution Explorer and select **Manage NuGet Packages** in the context menu.

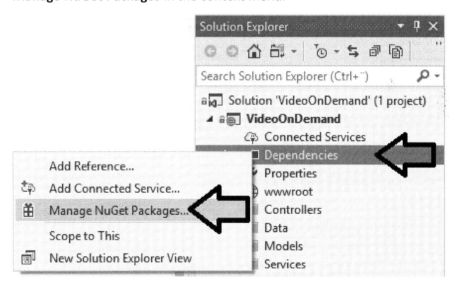

2. Click on the **Browse** link at the top of the dialog.
3. Select **nuget.org** in the drop-down to the far right in the dialog.
4. Type *AutoMapper* in the textbox.

5. Select the **AutoMapper** package in the list; it will probably be the first package in the list.
6. Make sure that you use the latest stable version (6.0.2).
7. Click the **Install** button.

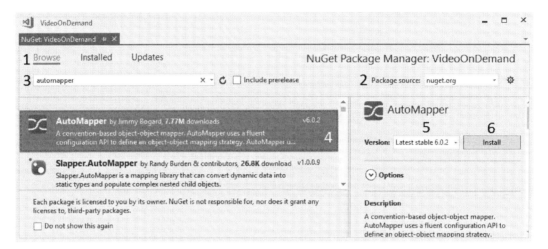

To verify that the package has been installed, you can open the *.csproj* file by right clicking on the project node and selecting **Edit VideoOnDemand.csproj**, or you can expand the *Dependencies-NuGet* folder in the Solution Explorer.

Summary

In this chapter, you created the solution and project that will be used throughout the remainder of this book. You also installed the AutoMapper NuGet package, which later will be used to map database entity objects to Data Transfer Objects (DTOs), which provide the views with data.

Next, you will redirect the **Home/Index** action to display the **Account/Login** view. This will display the login form when the application starts. Then you will style the login form, making it look more professional.

11. Login

Introduction

In this chapter, you will make the login view available as soon as a visitor navigates to the web application. To achieve this, you will redirect from the **Home/Index** action to the **Account/Login** action.

Because the login view only should be displayed to visitors who haven't already logged in, you will use Dependency Injection to make the **SignInManager** available from the controller, making it possible to check if the user is logged in.

To enable visitors to register and Login, you have to enable migrations and create a database using Entity Framework Core 1.1.

Technologies Used in This Chapter

1. **Dependency Injection** – To inject objects into a controller's constructor.
2. **C#** – For writing code in the controller's actions and constructor.
3. **Razor** – To incorporate C# in the views where necessary.
4. **HTML 5** – To build the views.
5. **Bootstrap and CSS** – To style the HTML 5 elements.
6. **Database Migration** – To create a SQL Server Database.

Creating the Database

There are only a few steps to creating the database that will enable users to register and Login. In a later chapter, you will expand the database by adding tables to store application data.

To create the database, you have to create an initial migration to tell Entity Framework how the database should be set up. You do this by executing the **add-migration** command in the Package Manager Console.

After the migration has been successfully created, you execute the **update-database** command in the same console to create the database. After the database has been created, you can view it in the *SQL Server Object Explorer*, which can be opened from the **View** menu.

1. Open the *Package Manager Console* by selecting **View-Other Windows-Package Manager Console** in the main menu.
2. Type in *add-migration Initial* and press **Enter** on the keyboard to create the first migration for the database.
3. Open the *application.json* file to change the database name in the connection string to a more readable name. Remove the *aspnet-* prefix and the *guid* suffix from the **Database** attribute in the connection string; leave only *VideoOnDemand* as the database name.
   ```
   "DefaultConnection":
       "Server=(localdb)\\mssqllocaldb;Database=VideoOnDemand;
       Trusted_Connection=True;MultipleActiveResultSets=true"
   ```
4. Type in *update-database* and press **Enter** to create the database.
5. Open the *SQL Server Object Explorer* from the **View** menu and make sure that the database was successfully created.

It may take a second or two for the SQL Server node to populate in the SQL Server Object Explorer. When it has, expand the server named **MSSQLLocalDB** and then the **VideoOn-Demand** database. Several tables should have been added to the database. The tables prefixed with AspNet are the tables used for storing user account information, and they are used when a user registers and logs in. In this course, you will use the **AspNetUsers**, **AspNetRoles**, and **AspNetUserRoles** tables when implementing registration and login for your users, and to determine if a user is an administrator.

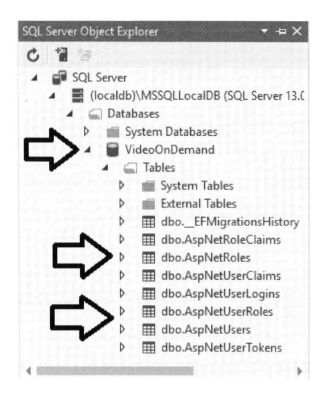

Redirecting to the Login View

ASP.NET Core is designed from the ground up to support and leverage Dependency Injection (DI). Dependency Injection is a way to let the framework automatically create instances of services (classes) and inject them into constructors. Why is this important? Well, it creates loose couplings between objects and their collaborators. This mean that no hard-coded instances need to be created in the collaborator itself; they are sent into it.

Not only can built-in framework services be injected, objects from your own classes can also be configured for DI in the **Startup** class.

Now, you will use DI to pass in the **SignInManager** to a constructor in the **HomeController** class and store it in a private variable. The **SignInManager** and its **ApplicationUser** type need two **using** statements: **Microsoft.AspNetCore.Identity** and **VideoOnDemand. Models**.

1. Open the **HomeController** class located in the *Controllers* folder.
2. Add the following two **using** statements.
   ```
   using Microsoft.AspNetCore.Identity;
   using VideoOnDemand.Models;
   ```
3. Add a constructor that receives the **SignInManager** through dependency injection and stores it in a private class level variable.
   ```
   private SignInManager<ApplicationUser> _signInManager;

   public HomeController(SignInManager<ApplicationUser> signInMgr)
   {
       _signInManager = signInMgr;
   }
   ```
4. Check if the user is signed in using the class level variable you just added, and redirect to the **Login** action in the **AccountController** class if it's an anonymous user. Otherwise open the default **Index** view, for now. You will change this in a later chapter.
   ```
   public IActionResult Index()
   {
       if (!_signInManager.IsSignedIn(User))
           return RedirectToAction("Login", "Account");

       return View();
   }
   ```
5. Run the application by pressing F5 or Ctrl+F5 (without debugging) on the keyboard.
6. The login view should be displayed. If you look at the URL, it should point to /Account/login on the localhost (your local IIS server) because of the **RedirectToAction** method call.

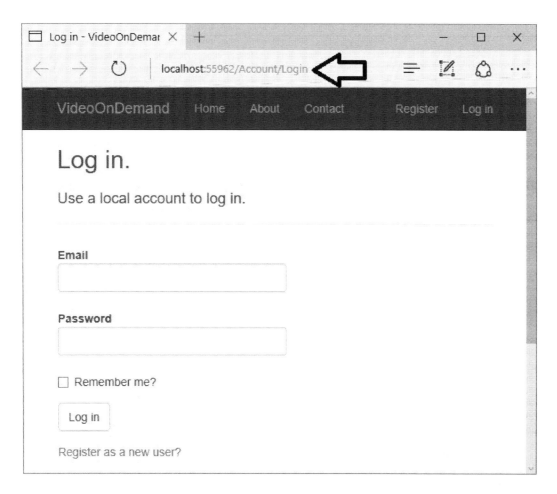

Styling the Login View

As you can see in the image above, the **Login** view isn't very pleasing to the eye. Let's change that by styling it with CSS, Bootstrap, and Glyphicons. After it has been styled, the view should look something like this.

Adding the login.css Stylesheet

1. Stop the application in Visual Studio.
2. Add a new style sheet file called *login.css* to the *wwwroot/css* folder in the Solution Explorer. Right click on the folder and select **Add-New Item**.
3. Select the **Style Sheet** template in the list, name it *login.css*, and click the **Add** button.
4. Remove the **Body** selector from the file.
5. Open the **_Layout** view in the *Views/Shared* folder.
6. Add a link to the *login.css* file in the **Development** <environment> tag. You can copy an existing link and alter it or drag the file from the Solution Explorer.
   ```
   <environment names="Development">
       ...
       <link rel="stylesheet" href="~/css/login.css" />
   </environment>
   ```
7. Add a link to the *login.css* file in the *bundleconfig.json* file.
   ```
   "inputFiles": [
       "wwwroot/css/site.css",
       "wwwroot/css/login.css"
   ]
   ```
8. Save the files.

174

Changing the Layout of the View

These changes will prepare the form for its much needed styling.

1. Open the **Login** view located in the *Views/Account* folder.
2. Remove the <h2> title element.
3. Change the Bootstrap class on the <div> with the **col-md-8** class to **col-md-4**.
4. Change the Bootstrap class on the <div> further down, from **col-md-4** to **col-md-8** and remove its content.
5. Cut out the <h4> heading at the top of the <form> element and paste it in above the <section> element. Add the class **login-panel-heading** to the <h4> element.
   ```
   <div class="col-md-4">
       <h4 class="login-panel-heading">Use a local account to
   Login.</h4>
   ```
6. Add two <div> elements below the <h4> heading and use Bootstrap classes to turn them into a panel and a panel body. This will make it easier to style the login form and to give it the nice border. Don't forget to add the ending </div> tags outside the </section> end tag.
   ```
   <div class="panel login-panel">
       <div class="panel-body login-panel-body">
           <section>
   ```
7. Add the class **login-form** to the <form> element.
8. Remove the horizontal rule <hr/> element from the form.
9. Remove the <label> and <span> elements from the email **form-group**.
10. Replace the **col-md-10** class with the **icon-addon** Bootstrap class in the email **form-group**.
11. Add a new <label> element targeting the **Email** model property below the email <input> element, and add the **envelope** glyphicon.
12. Add the **placeholder** attribute with the text *Email* to the email <input> element.
    ```
    <div class="form-group">
        <div class="icon-addon">
            <input asp-for="Email" placeholder="Email"
                class="form-control" />
            <label for="Email" class="glyphicon glyphicon-envelope" />
        </div>
    </div>
    ```
13. Repeat steps 7-10 for the **Password** model property, but use the **glyphicon-lock** class instead.

14. Remove the <div> with the **col-md-10** class and its closing element from the checkbox **form-group**.

15. Add the class **login-form-checkbox** to the <div> decorated with the **form-group** class. You will use this class later to style the checkbox with CSS.

```
<div class="form-group login-form-checkbox">
    <div class="checkbox">
        <label asp-for="RememberMe">
            <input asp-for="RememberMe" />
            @Html.DisplayNameFor(m => m.RememberMe)
        </label>
    </div>
</div>
```

16. Add the class **login-form-submit** to the submit **form-group**.

17. Replace the **col-md-offset-2 col-md-10** classes with **col-md-12** to let the button occupy the full width of the row.

18. Change the Bootstrap button type from **default** to **primary**.

```
<div class="form-group login-form-submit">
    <div class="col-md-12">
        <button type="submit" class="btn btn-primary">
            Login
        </button>
    </div>
</div>
```

19. Move the two *Register a new user* and *Forgot your Password?* <p> elements immediately above the closing **col-md-4** column </div>.

The form should look like this after the layout change.

Use a local account to log in.

Email

Password

☐ Remember me?

Log in

The complete code for the **Login** View:

```
@using System.Collections.Generic
@using Microsoft.AspNetCore.Http
@using Microsoft.AspNetCore.Http.Authentication
@model LoginViewModel
@inject SignInManager<ApplicationUser> SignInManager

@{
    ViewData["Title"] = "Login";
}

<div class="row">
    <div class="col-md-4">
        <h4 class="login-panel-heading">
            Use a local account to Login.</h4>
        <div class="panel login-panel">
            <div class="panel-body login-panel-body">
                <section>
                    <form asp-controller="Account" asp-action="Login"
                     asp-route-returnurl="@ViewData["ReturnUrl"]"
                     method="post" class="form-horizontal login-form">
                        <div asp-validation-summary="All"
                            class="text-danger">
                        </div>

                        <div class="form-group">
                            <div class="icon-addon">
                                <input asp-for="Email"
                                    placeholder="Email"
                                    class="form-control" />
                                <label for="Email" class="glyphicon
                                    glyphicon-envelope" />
                            </div>
                        </div>

                        <div class="form-group">
                            <div class="icon-addon">
                                <input asp-for="Password"
                                    placeholder="Password"
                                    class="form-control" />
                                <label for="Password" class="glyphicon
                                    glyphicon-lock"></label>
                            </div>
                        </div>
```

```
                        <div class="form-group login-form-checkbox">
                            <div class="checkbox">
                                <label asp-for="RememberMe">
                                    <input asp-for="RememberMe" />
                                    @Html.DisplayNameFor(m =>
                                        m.RememberMe)
                                </label>
                            </div>
                        </div>

                        <div class="form-group login-form-submit">
                            <div class="col-md-12">
                                <button type="submit"
                                    class="btn btn-primary">
                                    Login
                                </button>
                            </div>
                        </div>
                    </form>
                </section>
            </div>
        </div>
        <p>
            <a asp-action="Register"
                asp-route-returnurl="@ViewData["ReturnUrl"]">
                Register as a new user?
            </a>
        </p>
        <p><a asp-action="ForgotPassword">Forgot your password?</a></p>
    </div>
    <div class="col-md-8">
    </div>
</div>

@section Scripts {
    @{ await Html.RenderPartialAsync("_ValidationScriptsPartial"); }
}
```

Styling the Login View

Now that you have altered the Login view's layout, it's time to style it using CSS in the *login.css* file. Add the CSS selector one at a time, save the file, and observe the changes in the browser.

Add a 40px top margin to the heading, pushing it down a little from the navigation bar.

```
.login-panel-heading
{
    margin-top: 40px;
}
```

Next, make the panel width 280px, and remove the border.

```
.login-panel
{
    width: 280px;
    border: none;
}
```

Next, add a darker gray color to the panel border and make it 1px wide, and add 20px padding to the panel body.

```
.login-panel-body
{
    border: 1px solid #cecece !important;
    padding: 20px;
}
```

The form has bottom padding and margin that needs to be removed.

```
.login-form-submit {
    margin-bottom: 0px;
    padding-bottom: 0px;
}
```

The GlyphiconsGlyphicons should be displayed inside the textboxes, and the textboxes should have a max width of 225px.

```
.icon-addon {
    position: relative;
    color: #555;
    display: block;
}
```

```
    .icon-addon .glyphicon {
        position: absolute;
        left: 30px;
        padding: 10px 0;
    }

    .icon-addon .form-control {
        padding-left: 30px;
        border-radius: 0;
    }

    .icon-addon:hover .glyphicon {
        color: #2580db;
    }

.login-form input {
    max-width: 225px;
    margin-left: 20px;
}
```

Position the checkbox in relation to the textboxes; align it with their left sides.

```
.login-form .checkbox {
    margin-left: 20px;
    margin-top: -10px;
}
```

The **submit** button should be aligned with the textboxes and have the same width as them.

```
.login-form button {
    width: 100%;
}
```

The last thing to style is the padding around the error messages to align them with the textboxes, and make them the same width.

```
.login-form .validation-summary-errors ul {
    padding-left: 20px;
}
```

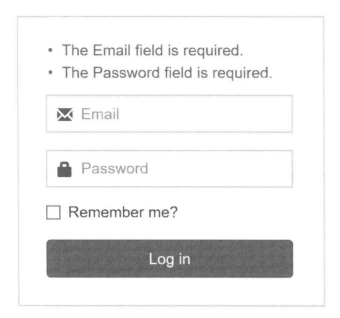

Summary

In this chapter, you changed the layout of the **Login** view, and applied CSS and Bootstrap classes to its elements, to make it look nicer to the user. You also created the database and tables needed to handle registration and login.

Next, you will change the layout of the **Account/Register** view and apply CSS and Bootstrap classes to its elements.

12. Register User

Introduction

In this chapter, you will alter the layout of the **Account/Register** view and style it using CSS and Bootstrap. The view can be reached from a link on the **Account/Login** view, which is available as soon as a visitor navigates to the web application.

Technologies Used in This Chapter

1. **Razor** – To incorporate C# in the views where necessary.
2. **HTML 5** – To build the views.
3. **Bootstrap and CSS** – To style the HTML 5 elements.

Overview

The task appointed to you by the company is to make sure that visitors have a nice user experience when registering with the site, using the **Account/register** view. The finished **Register** view should look like the image below.

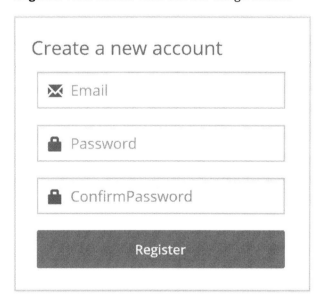

Changing the Layout of the View

These changes will prepare the form for its much needed styling.

1. Open the **Register** view in the *Views/Account* folder.
2. Remove the <h2> heading.
3. Create a panel above the <form> element by adding a <div> element and decorate it with the **panel** class. Add another class called **register-panel**; it will be used to style the panel and its intrinsic elements.
4. Add another <div> below the panel <div> and decorate it with the **panel-body** class. Add another class called **register-panel-body**; it will be used to style its intrinsic elements. Don't forget to add the closing </div> elements below the closing </form> element.
    ```
    <div class="panel register-panel">
        <div class="panel-body register-panel-body">
    ```
5. Add a class called **register-form** to the <form> element.
6. Remove the <hr/> element from the form.
7. Remove the <label> and <span> elements from the email **form-group**.
8. Replace the **col-md-10** class with the **icon-addon** Bootstrap class in the email **form-group**.
9. Add a new <label> element targeting the **Email** model property below the email <input> element, and add the **envelope** glyphicon.
10. Add the **placeholder** attribute with the text *Email* to the email <input> element.
    ```
    <div class="form-group">
        <div class="icon-addon">
            <input asp-for="Email" placeholder="Email"
                class="form-control" />
            <label for="Email" class="glyphicon glyphicon-envelope"/>
        </div>
    </div>
    ```
11. Repeat steps 7-10 for the **Password** model property. Use the **glyphicon-lock** class.
12. Repeat steps 7-10 for the **ConfirmPassword** model property. Use the **glyphicon-lock** class.
13. Add the class **register-form-submit** to the submit **form-group**.

14. Replace the **col-md-offset-2 col-md-10** classes with **col-md-12** to let the button occupy the full width of the row.

15. Change the Bootstrap button type from **default** to **primary**.

```
<div class="form-group register-form-submit">
    <div class="col-md-12">
        <button type="submit" class="btn btn-primary">
            Register</button>
    </div>
</div>
```

The complete markup for the **Register** view:

```
@model RegisterViewModel
@{ ViewData["Title"] = "Register"; }

<div class="panel register-panel">
    <div class="panel-body register-panel-body">
        <form asp-controller="Account" asp-action="Register"
         asp-route-returnurl="@ViewData["ReturnUrl"]" method="post"
         class="form-horizontal register-form">
            <h4>Create a new account.</h4>
            <div asp-validation-summary="All" class="text-danger"></div>

            <div class="form-group">
                <div class="icon-addon">
                    <input asp-for="Email" placeholder="Email"
                        class="form-control" />
                    <label for="Email" class="glyphicon
                        glyphicon-envelope"></label>
                </div>
            </div>
            <div class="form-group">
                <div class="icon-addon">
                    <input asp-for="Password" placeholder="Password"
                     class="form-control" />
                    <label for="Password" class="glyphicon
                        glyphicon-lock"></label>
                </div>
            </div>
            <div class="form-group">
                <div class="icon-addon">
                    <input asp-for="ConfirmPassword"
                        placeholder="Confirm Password"
                        class="form-control" />
                    <label for="ConfirmPassword" class="glyphicon
```

185

```
                        glyphicon-lock" />
                </div>
            </div>

            <div class="form-group register-form-submit">
                <div class="col-md-12">
                    <button type="submit" class="btn btn-primary">
                    Register</button>
                </div>
            </div>
        </form>
    </div>
</div>

@section Scripts {
    @{ await Html.RenderPartialAsync("_ValidationScriptsPartial"); }
}
```

Styling the Register View

Because the same styles already have been applied to elements in the **Login** view, the selectors and properties in the *login.css* file can be reused. Instead of adding a new style-sheet for the **Register** view, you can add its CSS selectors to the existing selectors in the *login.css* file.

Add a 40px top margin to the panel by appending the **.register-panel** selector to the **.login-panel-heading** selector in the *login.css* file.

```
.login-panel-heading, .register-panel {
    margin-top: 40px;
}
```

Next, add 20px padding, a 1px dark gray border to the panel, and give the panel a fixed width of 280px.

```
.login-panel-body, .register-panel-body {
    border: 1px solid #cecece !important;
    padding: 20px;
}
```

```
.login-panel, .register-panel {
    width: 280px;
    border: none;
}
```

The textboxes are next. Let's make them the same width as the ones in the **Login** view.

```
.login-form input, .register-form input {
    margin-left: 20px;
    max-width: 225px;
}
```

Make the button the same width as the textboxes.

```
.login-form button, .register-form button {
    width: 100%;
}
```

The last thing to alter is the error message element. Make it the same width as the textboxes.

```
.login-form .validation-summary-errors ul,
.register-form .validation-summary-errors ul {
    padding-left: 20px;
}
```

The styled **Register** view should look like the image below.

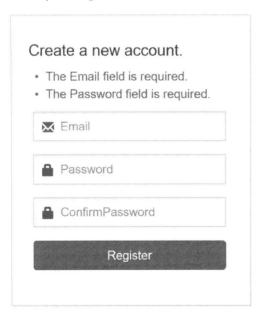

Testing the Registration Form

1. Start the application.
2. Click the **Register as new user?** link below the login form.
3. Fill in an email address and a password and click the **Register** button. It can be a fake email address if you like.
4. If the registration succeeded, the **Home/Index** view should be displayed, and the email should be visible to the right in the navigation bar.
5. Click the **Logout** link to the far right in the navigation bar. The login form should be displayed.
6. Try to Login to the site with the email you just registered with. This should take you back to the **Home/Index** view.
7. Close the application from Visual Studio.
8. Open the *SQL Server Object Explorer* from the **View** menu.
9. Expand the **MSSQLLocalDB** node, and then your database.
10. Expand the **Tables** node and right click on the **AspNetUsers** table. See image below.
11. Select the **View Data** option to open the table in Visual Studio.
12. The table should contain the user you added. See image below.

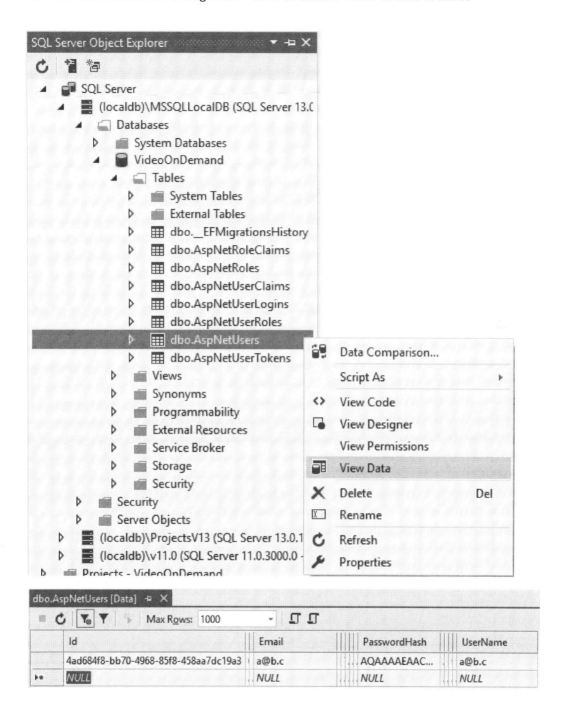

Summary

In this chapter, you changed the layout of the **Register** view and applied CSS and Bootstrap classes to spruce up its elements. You also registered a user and logged in using the account.

Next, you will change the layout of the navigation bar, and style it with CSS and Bootstrap classes. You will also create a drop-down menu for the logout and settings options, and remove their links from the navigation bar.

Then you will hide the **Home**, **About**, and **Contact** links whenever the user is logged in.

Lastly you will add a logotype to the navigation bar.

13. Modifying the Navigation Bar

Introduction

The default layout and styling of the navigation bar leaves a bit to be desired. In this chapter, you will alter the layout of the navigation bar, only displaying certain links when the user is logged out, and creating a drop-down menu for the Logout and Settings options. You will also add a logo to the navigation bar, making it look more professional.

Technologies Used in This Chapter

1. **Razor** – To incorporate C# in the views where necessary.
2. **HTML 5** – To build the views.
3. **Bootstrap and CSS** – To style the HTML 5 elements.

Overview

Your task is to change the appearance of the navigation bar. It should be white with a logo to the far left. The **Home**, **About**, and **Contact** links should only be visible to users before they have logged in to the site. No other links should be visible in the navigation bar, except for a drop-down menu at the far right, which should be visible when the user has logged in.

To control when the links are displayed you need to inject the **SignInManager** and **User-Manager** to the **_Layout** view.

```
@inject SignInManager<ApplicationUser> SignInManager
@inject UserManager<ApplicationUser> UserManager
```

To achieve this you will have to alter the **_Layout** and **_LoginPartial** views.

Current navigation bar when logged out

Current navigation bar when logged in

191

Altered navigation bar when logged out

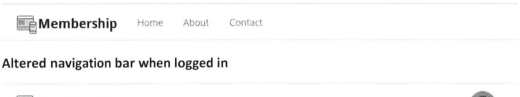

Altered navigation bar when logged in

Styling the Navigation Bar

You will change the navigation bar color to white, add a stylesheet called *menu.css*, add a logo to the navigation bar, position the links, and hide them when logged in.

1. Right click on the *wwwroot/css* folder and select **Add-New Item** in the context menu.
2. Select the **Style Sheet** template and name the file *menu.css*.
3. Remove the **body** selector.
4. Add a link to the *menu.css* file in the *bundleconfig.json* file.
   ```
   "inputFiles": [
       "wwwroot/css/site.css",
       "wwwroot/css/login.css",
       "wwwroot/css/menu.css"
   ]
   ```
5. Open the **_Layout** view in the *Views/Shared* folder.
6. Add a <link> to the *menu.css* file in the **_Layout** view.
7. Locate the <nav> element inside the <body> element. Remove the **navbar-inverse** class. This should make the navigation bar white.
8. To control when the links are displayed, you need to inject the **SignInManager** and **UserManager** into the **_Layout** view.
   ```
   @inject SignInManager<ApplicationUser> SignInManager
   @inject UserManager<ApplicationUser> UserManager
   ```
9. Use the **SignInManager** and the logged in user to hide the **Home**, **About**, and **Contact** links when the user is logged in.
   ```
   @if (!SignInManager.IsSignedIn(User)) {
       <ul class="nav navbar-nav">
           <li><a asp-area="" asp-controller="Home"
   ```

```
                asp-action="Index">Home</a></li>
        <li><a asp-area="" asp-controller="Home"
                asp-action="About">About</a></li>
        <li><a asp-area="" asp-controller-"Home"
                asp-action="Contact">Contact</a></li>
    </ul>
}
```

10. To replace the brand text (*VideoOnDemand*) with a logo, you delete the text in the <a> tag decorated with the **navbar-brand** class, and add the logo image in its place. You can drag the image from the *wwwroot/images* folder.

11. Add the **alt** tag with the text *Brand* to the <img> element you added to the <a> tag.

```
<a asp-area="" asp-controller="Home" asp-action="Index"
    class="navbar-brand">
    <img alt="Brand"
        src="~/images/Logos/membership-icon-30x152.png" />
</a>
```

12. Add a light gray horizontal bottom border to the navigation bar, and make the background color white. Add the CSS selector to the *menu.css* file.

```
.navbar {
    border-bottom: 1px solid #dadada;
    background-color: #fff;
}
```

13. Run the application and log out to verify that the **Home**, **About**, and **Contact** links are visible. Login to the application and verify that the links no longer are visible.

Remove the Register and Login links

The **Register** and **Login** links are redundant since the Login form is visible, and a register link is available below the Login form. Remove the links from the **_LoginPartial** view.

1. Open the **_LoginPartial** view located in the *Views/Shared* folder.
2. Delete the else-block from the view.
3. Save the file and run the application.
4. Verify that the links no longer appear when logged out.
5. Close the application in Visual Studio.

Add the Drop-Down Menu

To give the navigation bar a cleaner look, you will remove the **Logout** and **Manage** links (the email greeting link) and add a drop-down link with an avatar and the email address.

1. Open the **_LoginPartial** view located in the *Views/Shared* folder.
2. Remove the **navbar-right** class from the <form> element.
3. Add an <li> element displaying the user's name (which by default is the email address) immediately inside the <ul> element decorated with the **navbar-right** class.
   ```
   <li>@User.Identity.Name</li>
   ```
4. Add another <li> element below the one you just added, and decorate it with the **dropdown** and **pull-right** Bootstrap classes. This will create the drop-down menu item, to which you will add options.
   ```
   <li class="dropdown pull-right"></li>
   ```
5. Add an <a> element inside the previous <li> element. This will be the link to open the menu. Decorate it with the **dropdown-toggle** and **user-dropdown** classes, and give it the id **user-dropdown**. Also add the **data-toggle** attribute set to **dropdown**, the attribute **role** set to **button**, and the **aria-expanded** attribute set to **false**. These settings will ensure that the anchor tag will act as the menu's open/close button, and that the menu is closed by default.
   a. Add the avatar image inside the <a> tag and decorate the <img> element with the classes **img-circle** and **avatar**. Set the image height to 40.
   b. Add a caret symbol by decorating a <span> element with the **caret**, **text-light**, and **hidden-xs** Bootstrap classes. The second class gives the caret a lighter gray color, and the last class hides the caret on portable devices, or when the browser has a very small size.
   ```
   <a href="#" id="user-dropdown"
       class="dropdown-toggle user-dropdown"
       data-toggle="dropdown" role="button" aria-expanded="false">
       <img src-"~/images/avatar.png" class="img-circle avatar"
           alt="" height="40">
       <span class="caret text-light hidden-xs"></span>
   </a>
   ```
6. Add a <ul> element around the two original <li> elements and assign the **dropdown-menu** class and the **role="menu"** attribute to it.

a. Replace the text and the method call in the <a> element of the first <li> with the text *Settings*.

b. Replace the <button> element in the second <li> element with an <a> element calling the **submit** method.

```
<ul class="dropdown-menu" role="menu">
    <li><a asp-area="" asp-controller="Manage" asp-action="Index"
        title="Manage">Settings</a></li>
    <li><a href="javascript:document.getElementById(
            'logoutForm').submit()">Log off</a></li>
</ul>
```

The complete code in the **_LoginPartial** view

```
@using Microsoft.AspNetCore.Identity
@using VideoMembershipTemp.Models

@inject SignInManager<ApplicationUser> SignInManager
@inject UserManager<ApplicationUser> UserManager

@if (SignInManager.IsSignedIn(User))
{
    <form asp-area="" asp-controller="Account" asp-action="Logout"
        method="post" id="logoutForm">
        <ul class="nav navbar-nav navbar-right">
            <li style="padding-top:20px;color:#555;">
                @User.Identity.Name</li>
            <li class="dropdown pull-right">
                <a href="#" id="user-dropdown" class="dropdown-toggle
                  user-dropdown" data-toggle="dropdown" role="button"
                  aria-expanded="false">
                    <img src="~/images/avatar.png"
                        class="img-circle avatar" alt="" height="40">
                    <span class="caret text-light hidden-xs"></span>
                </a>
                <ul class="dropdown-menu" role="menu">
                    <li><a asp-area="" asp-controller="Manage"
                        asp-action="Index"
                        title="Manage">Settings</a></li>
                    <li><a href="javascript:document.getElementById(
                        'logoutForm').submit()">Log off</a></li>
                </ul>
            </li>
        </ul>
```

```
        </form>
}
```

Style the Drop-Down Menu

As it stands right now, the drop-down menu leaves a lot to be desired when it comes to styling. You will therefore apply CSS to its elements, to make it look crisp to the user.

When you have finished styling the drop-down menu in the *menu.css* file, it should look like this.

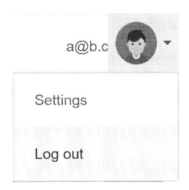

To make the drop-down fit in better with the navigation bar, it has to be positioned 7px from the top and bottom, using padding. Note that the id has to be used for specificity.

```
.dropdown.pull-right {
    padding-top: 0px;
}

#user-dropdown {
    padding: 7px;
}
```

The email has to be pushed down to be aligned to the avatar. Add a 20px top padding and make the text gray.

```
.navbar-right > li {
    padding-top: 20px;
    color: #555;
}
```

Make the drop-down menu's corners more square and give it a more defined border without a drop shadow and padding.

```
.dropdown-menu {
    padding: 0;
    border: 1px solid #dadada;
    border-radius: 2px;
    box-shadow: none;
}
```

The menu items could be a bit larger. Add some padding and change the text color.

```
.dropdown-menu li > a {
    color: #666c74;
    padding: 15px 40px 15px 20px;
}
```

Summary

In this chapter, you modified the navigation bar and added a drop-down menu, all in an effort to make it look more professional and appealing to the user.

Next, you will figure out what Data Transfer Objects are needed to display the data in the *Membership* views.

14. Data Transfer Objects

Introduction

In this chapter, you will begin the creation of the *Membership* views, by figuring out what objects are needed to transfer the necessary data from the server to the client. These objects are referred to as Data Transfer Objects, or DTOs.

In some solutions the DTOs are the same as the entities used to create the database. In this solution you will create DTOs for data transfer only, and entities for database CRUD (Create, Read, Update, Delete) operations. The objects are then transformed from one to the other using AutoMapper.

Technologies Used in This Chapter

1. **C#** – To create the DTOs.

Overview

Your task is to figure out what DTOs are needed to display the necessary data in the three *Membership* views: **Dashboard**, **Course**, and **Video**.

The DTOs

The best way to figure out what data is needed is to go back and review the use case and look at the mock-view images. Here they are again for easy reference.

Dashboard view

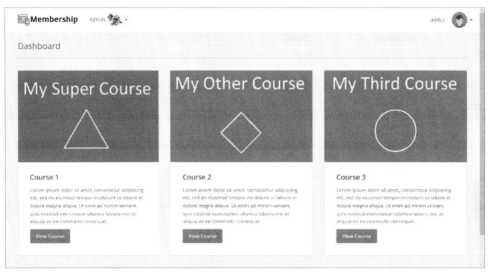

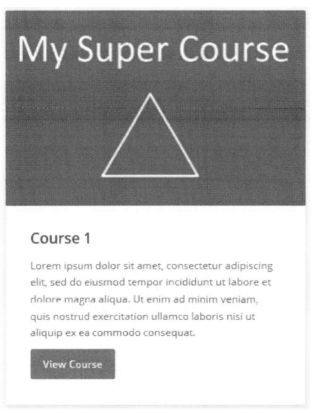

Course View

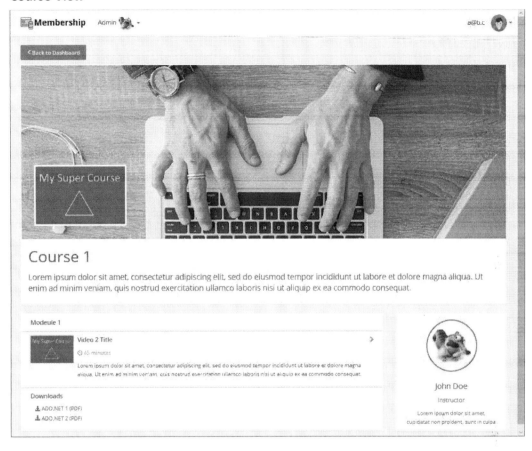

Video View

By studying the **Dashboard** view image you can surmise that the following data is needed for a single course panel: course image, title, description, and a button leading to the course view (course id). But if you examine the **Course** view image, you can see that the course also has a marquee image.

How do you translate this into a class? Let's do it together, property by property.

The class will be called **CourseDTO**, and have the following properties:

Property	Type
CourseId	int
CourseTitle	string
CourseDescription	string
MarqueeImageUrl	string
CourseImageUrl	string

Looking at the **Course** and **Video** view images, you can see that they are more complex. They both have three distinct areas. The **Course** view has a description area with a marquee image, a list of modules, and an instructor bio. Each module also has lists of videos and downloads. The **Video** view has a video area with a description and video information, an area for navigating to previous and next videos, and an instructor bio.

Let's begin with the smallest DTOs and work our way up to the largest.

The second class is the **DownloadDTO**, which has the following properties:

Property	Type
DownloadUrl	int
DownloadTitle	string

The third class is the **VideoDTO**, which has the following properties:

Property	Type
Id	int
Title	string
Description	string
Duration	string (how long the video is)
Thumbnail	string
Url	string (link to the video)

The fourth class is the **InstructorDTO**, which has the following properties:

Property	Type
InstructorName	string
InstructorDescription	string
InstructorAvatar	string

The fifth class is the **ModuleDTO**, which has the following properties:

Property	Type
Id	int
ModuleTitle	string
Videos	List<VideoDto>
Downloads	List<DownloadDto>

The sixth class is the **LessonInfoDTO**, which is used in the *Coming Up* section of the **Video** view.

Property	Type
LessonNumber	int
NumberOfLessons	int
PreviousVideoId	int (used for the **Previous** button link)
NextVideoId	int (used for the **Next** button link)
NextVideoTitle	string
NextVideoThumbnail	string (the next video's image)

But there's one more DTO, the **UserCourseDTO**, which is used when matching a user with a course. Note that the **DisplayName** attribute is used to change the descriptive text displayed in the form labels for this model.

Property	Type
UserId	string
CourseId	int
Email	string
CourseTitle	string

Adding the DTOs

Now it's time to add all the DTOs to the project. Let's do it together for one of them, then you can add the rest yourself.

1. Open the project in Visual Studio.
2. Right click on the *Modules* folder in the Solution Explorer and select **Add-New Folder**. Name the folder *DTOModels*.
3. Right click on the *DTOModels* folder and select **Add-Class**.
4. Select the **Class** template.
5. Name the class *CourseDTO* and click the **Add** button.
6. Add the properties from the **CourseDTO** list above.
7. Repeat the steps 3-6 for all other DTOs.

The complete code in the **CourseDTO** class:

```
public class CourseDTO
{
    public int CourseId { get; set; }
    public string CourseTitle { get; set; }
    public string CourseDescription { get; set; }
    public string MarqueeImageUrl { get; set; }
    public string CourseImageUrl { get; set; }
}
```

The complete code in the **DownloadDTO** class:

```
public class DownloadDTO
{
    public string DownloadUrl { get; set; }
    public string DownloadTitle { get; set; }
}
```

The complete code in the **VideoDTO** class:

```
public class VideoDTO
{
    public int Id { get; set; }
    public string Title { get; set; }
    public string Description { get; set; }
    public string Duration { get; set; }
    public string Thumbnail { get; set; }
    public string Url { get; set; }
}
```

The complete code in the **InstructorDTO** class:

```
public class InstructorDTO
{
    public string InstructorName { get; set; }
    public string InstructorDescription { get; set; }
    public string InstructorAvatar { get; set; }
}
```

The complete code in the **ModuleDTO** class:

```
public class ModuleDTO {
    public int Id { get; set; }
    public string ModuleTitle { get; set; }
    public List<VideoDTO> Videos { get; set; }
    public List<DownloadDTO> Downloads { get; set; }
}
```

The complete code in the **LessonInfoDTO** class:

```
public class LessonInfoDTO
{
    public int LessonNumber { get; set; }
    public int NumberOfLessons { get; set; }
    public int PreviousVideoId { get; set; }
    public int NextVideoId { get; set; }
    public string NextVideoTitle { get; set; }
    public string NextVideoThumbnail { get; set; }
}
```

The complete code in the **UserCourseDTO** class:

Note that the **DisplayName** attribute is used to change the descriptive text displayed in the form labels for this model.

```
public class UserCourseDTO
{
    [DisplayName("User Id")]
    public string UserId { get; set; }
    [DisplayName("Course Id")]
    public int CourseId { get; set; }
    [DisplayName("Email")]
    public string UserEmail { get; set; }
    [DisplayName("Title")]
    public string CourseTitle { get; set; }
}
```

The View Models

That's great, now you know what the individual DTOs contain, but how do you get the information to the views? With the more complex views, there's no easy way to pass multiple DTOs at the same time. You could use Tuples, but that is hard to implement. A better choice is to use a view model.

A view model is exactly what it sounds like, a model that can contain other objects as references, and is sent to the view.

There will be three view models, although you could argue that the first one isn't strictly necessary, because it contains only one property. I beg to differ, however, because it will be easier to update the view with more data, if the need should arise.

The first view model is the **DashboardViewModel**, which has only one property. The property data type is somewhat complex; it is a list containing a list. The reason for using a list in a list is that you want to display three course panels on each row. An easy way to make sure that is possible is to add a list containing a maximum of three **CourseDTOs**, one for each row, to the outer list.

Property	Type
Courses	List<List<CourseDTO>>

The second view model is the **CourseViewModel**, which contains a **CourseDTO**, an **InstructorDTO**, and a list of **ModuleDTOs**.

Property	Type
Course	CourseDTO
Instructor	InstructorDTO
Modules	IEnumerable<ModuleDTO>

The third view model is the **VideoViewModel**, which contains a **VideoDTO**, an **Instructor-DTO**, a **CourseDTO**, and a **LessonInfoDTO**.

Property	Type
Video	VideoDTO
Instructor	InstructorDTO
Course	CourseDTO
LessonInfo	LessonInfoDTO

Adding the View Models

Now, it's time to add all the view models to the project. Let's do it together for one of them, then you can add the rest yourself.

1. Open the project in Visual Studio.
2. Right click on the *Modules* folder in the Solution Explorer and select **Add-New Folder**. Name the folder *MembershipViewModels*.

3. Right click on the *MembershipViewModels* folder and select **Add-Class**.
4. Select the **Class** template.
5. Name the class *CourseViewModel* and click the **Add** button.
6. Add the properties from the **CourseViewModel** list above. Don't forget to add a using statement to the **DTOModels** namespace.
7. Repeat steps 3-6 for all the other view models.

The complete **CourseViewModel** class:

```
public class CourseViewModel
{
    public CourseDTO Course { get; set; }
    public InstructorDTO Instructor { get; set; }
    public IEnumerable<ModuleDTO> Modules { get; set; }
}
```

The complete **DashboardViewModel** class:

```
public class DashboardViewModel
{
    public List<List<CourseDTO>> Courses { get; set; }
}
```

The complete **VideoViewModel** class:

```
public class VideoViewModel
{
    public VideoDTO Video { get; set; }
    public InstructorDTO Instructor { get; set; }
    public CourseDTO Course { get; set; }
    public LessonInfoDTO LessonInfo { get; set; }
}
```

Summary

In this chapter, you figured out the Data Transfer Objects (DTOs) needed to display the data in the views. You also figured out how to transport multiple DTOs to the view with one model, a view model.

Next, you will figure out how the data will be stored in a data source using entity classes.

15. Entity Classes

Introduction

In this chapter, you will add the entity classes needed to store data in the data sources. In the next chapter you will implement a mock data repository using the entities you define in this chapter, and later on you will create database tables from the entities.

Now that you have defined the DTOs, you can figure out what the data objects, the entities, should contain. There will not always be a 1-1 match between a DTO and an entity; that's where an object mapper comes into the picture. In a later chapter you will use AutoMapper to convert an entity to a DTO.

Technologies Used in This Chapter
1. **C#** – Creating entity classes.
2. **Attributes** – To define behaviors of entity properties.

Overview

You task it to use your knowledge about the DTOs to create a set of entity classes that will make up the data sources. Remember that an entity doesn't have to contain all properties of a DTO, and that sometimes it will contain more properties.

The Entities

Let's go back and review the DTOs one at a time, and decide which of their properties should be duplicated in the entities. Some of the entity properties need restrictions, like maximum length, required, and if it's a primary key in the table.

The Video Entity

Properties of the **VideoDTO**: Id, Title, Description, Duration, Thumbnail, and Url.

The **Video** entity needs the same properties that the DTO has, but it could use a few more. You might want to keep track of the entity's position relative to other entities, so a **Position** property could be added to the class. Then the **Video** entity needs to know what module it belongs to, which can be solved by adding a **ModuleId** navigation property.

A video can only belong to one module in this scenario. If you want a video to be used in multiple modules, you need to implement a many-to-many relationship entity between the **Video** and **Module** entities. In this application it is sufficient that a video only can belong to one module and that a module can have multiple videos associated with it.

You could also add a **CourseId** navigation property, to avoid lengthy joins.

Properties in the **Video** entity class:

Property	Type	Attribute
Id	int	Key (primary key in Entity Framework table)
Title	string	MaxLength(80) and Required
Description	string	MaxLength(1024)
Thumbnail	string	MaxLength(1024)
Url	string	MaxLength(1024)
Position	int	
Duration	int	
ModuleId	int	Navigation property
CourseId	int	Navigation property

The Download Entity

Properties in the **DownloadDTO**: DownloadUrl and DownloadTitle.

Looking back at the **Video** entity, you can surmise that more properties are needed in the **Download** entity than are defined in its DTO class. It needs a unique id, and the same navigation properties as the **Video** entity.

Note that the property names don't have to be the same in the DTO and the entity. Auto-Mapper can be configured to map between properties with different names. It can, however, use auto-mapping between properties with identical names.

Properties in the **Download** entity class:

Property	Type	Attribute
Id	int	Key (will make it the primary key)
Title	string	MaxLength(80) and Required
Url	string	MaxLength(1024)
ModuleId	int	Navigation property
CourseId	int	Navigation property

The Instructor Entity

Properties in the **InstructorDTO**: InstructorName, InstructorDescription, and Instructor-Avatar.

Apart from the name, description, and avatar properties, the **Instructor** entity needs a unique id and a property that ties it to the **Course** entity. This makes it possible to assign the same instructor to many courses, but each course can only have one instructor. This is implemented by a 1-many relationship, where the many-part is located in the **Instructor** entity. Entity framework knows that it should implement a 1-many relationship if one entity has a collection of the other entity, and the other has a corresponding id.

Properties in the **Instructor** entity class:

Property	Type	Attribute
Id	int	Key (will make it the primary key)
Name	string	MaxLength(80) and Required
Description	string	MaxLength(1024)
Thumbnail	string	MaxLength(1024)
Courses	List<Course>	Navigation property

The Course Entity

Properties in the **CourseDTO**: CourseId, CourseTitle, CourseDescription, CourseImageUrl, and MarqueeImageUrl.

Apart from the DTO properties, the **Course** entity needs a unique id, an instructor id and a single **Instructor** entity, and a list of **Module** entities.

The single **Instructor** property is the 1 in the 1-many relationship between the **Course** and **Instructor** entities.

The list of **Module** entities is the many in a 1-many relationship between the **Course** entity and the **Module** entities. A course can have many modules, but a module can only belong to one course.

You could change this behavior by implementing another entity that connects the **Course** and the **Module** entities, creating a many-many relationship. Here you'll implement the 1-many relationship.

Property	Type	Attribute
Id	int	Key (will make it the primary key)
ImageUrl	string	MaxLength(255)
MarqueeImageUrl	string	MaxLength(255)
Title	string	MaxLength(80), Required
Description	string	MaxLength(1024)
InstructorId	int	Navigation property
Instructor	Instructor	Navigation property
Modules	List<Module>	Navigation property

The Module Entity

Properties in the **ModuleDTO**: Id, ModuleTitle, Videos, and Downloads.

Apart from the DTO properties, the **Module** entity needs a unique id, and needs a navigation property to the **Course** entity it belongs to.

The single **Course** entity is the 1 in a 1-many relationship between the **Course** entity and the **Module** entity. A module can only belong to one course, but a course can have many modules.

The lists of **Video** and **Download** entities are the many part of the 1-many relationships between them and a **Module** entity. A module can have many videos and downloads, and a download and a video can only belong to one module.

Property	Type	Attribute
Id	int	Key (will make it the primary key)
Title	string	MaxLength(80), Required
CourseId	int	Navigation property
Course	Course	Navigation property
Videos	List<Video>	Navigation property
Downloads	List<Download>	Navigation property

The UserCourse Entity

Properties in the **UserCourseDTO**: UserId, CourseId, CourseTitle, and UserEmail.

Apart from the DTO properties, the **UserCourse** entity needs a navigation property to the **Course** entity. Note that the **UserEmail** property in the DTO isn't persisted to the database; you get that info from the logged in user information.

This is the most complex of the entities because it connects a **Course** to a user with the system's **AspNetUser** entity, which isn't readily available. This will become apparent when you create the SQL Server database and implement the administrator user interface in upcoming chapters.

In earlier versions of Entity Framework a composite primary key, a primary key made up of more than one property, could be defined using attributes in the entity class. In Entity Framework Core, they are defined in the **DbContext** class. You will do this in a later chapter.

Property	Type	Attribute
UserId	string	Part of a composite primary key
CourseId	int	Part of a composite primary key
Course	Course	Navigation property

Adding the Entity Classes

With the entity properties defined, you can create their classes. Let's implement one together, then you can add the rest yourself.

Depending on the order you implement the entity classes, you might end up with properties that aren't fully implemented until other entity classes have been added. For instance, the **Instructor** entity has a property called **Courses**, which is dependent on the **Course** class.

1. Open Visual Studio.
2. Right click on the project node and select **Add-New Folder** in the context menu.
3. Name the folder *Entities*.
4. Right click on the *Entities* folder and select **Add-Class**.
5. Name the class *Video* and click the **Add** button.
6. Add a public property named **Id** of type **int**.
7. Add the **[Key]** attribute to it, to make it the primary key. You will have to resolve the namespace **System.ComponentModel.DataAnnotations**.
   ```
   public class Video
   {
       [Key]
       public int Id { get; set; }
   }
   ```

8. Add another property named **Title** and restrict it to 80 characters. The title should also be required, because the video needs a title.
    ```
    [MaxLength(80), Required]
    public string Title { get; set; }
    ```

9. Add a property of type **string** named **Description** and restrict it to 1024 characters.

10. Add a property of type **string** named **Thumbnail** and restrict it to 1024 characters.

11. Add a property of type **string** named **Url** and restrict it to 1024 characters.

12. Add a property of type **int** named **Duration**.

13. Add a property of type **int** named **Position**.

14. Add a property of type **int** named **ModuleId**.

15. Add a property of type **int** named **CourseId**.

16. Repeat steps 4-7 to add the necessary properties for the other entity classes listed above.

The complete code for the **Video** entity class:

```
public class Video
{
    [Key]
    public int Id { get; set; }
    [MaxLength(80), Required]
    public string Title { get; set; }
    [MaxLength(1024)]
    public string Description { get; set; }
    [MaxLength(1024)]
    public string Thumbnail { get; set; }
    [MaxLength(1024)]
    public string Url { get; set; }

    public int Duration { get; set; }
    public int Position { get; set; }
    public int ModuleId { get; set; }
    // Side-step from 3rd normal form for
    // easier access to a video's course
    public int CourseId { get; set; }
}
```

The complete code for the **Download** entity class:

```
public class Download
{
    [Key]
    public int Id { get; set; }
    [MaxLength(80), Required]
    public string Title { get; set; }
    [MaxLength(1024)]
    public string Url { get; set; }

    public int ModuleId { get; set; }
    // Side-step from 3rd normal form for
    // easier access to a video's course
    public int CourseId { get; set; }
}
```

The complete code for the **Instructor** entity class:

```
public class Instructor
{
    [Key]
    public int Id { get; set; }
    [MaxLength(80), Required]
    public string Name { get; set; }
    [MaxLength(1024)]
    public string Description { get; set; }
    [MaxLength(1024)]
    public string Thumbnail { get; set; }

    public List<Course> Courses { get; set; }
}
```

The complete code for the **Course** entity class:

```
public class Course
{
    [Key]
    public int Id { get; set; }
    [MaxLength(255)]
    public string ImageUrl { get; set; }
    [MaxLength(255)]
    public string MarqueeImageUrl { get; set; }
    [MaxLength(80), Required]
    public string Title { get; set; }
```

```
    [MaxLength(1024)]
    public string Description { get; set; }

    public int InstructorId { get; set; }
    public Instructor Instructor { get; set; }
    public List<Module> Modules { get; set; }
}
```

The complete code for the **Module** entity class:

```
public class Module
{
    [Key]
    public int Id { get; set; }
    [MaxLength(80), Required]
    public string Title { get; set; }

    public int CourseId { get; set; }
    public Course Course { get; set; }
    public List<Video> Videos { get; set; }
    public List<Download> Downloads { get; set; }
}
```

The complete code for the **UserCourse** entity class:

```
public class UserCourse
{
    public string UserId { get; set; }
    public int CourseId { get; set; }
    public Course Course { get; set; }
}
```

Summary

In this chapter, you discovered and implemented the entity classes, and their properties and restrictions.

Next, you will create a repository interface, and implement it in a class with mock data.

16. Mock Data Repository

Introduction

In this chapter, you will create an interface called **IReadRepository**, which will be a contract that any data source repository will implement for easy reuse, and to make dependency injection possible. This is crucial because it makes it possible to switch one repository for another without breaking the application; it is also a requirement from the customer.

You will implement the interface in a class called **MockReadRepository**, which will be used when building the user interface. Once the UI is working, you will switch to another repository called **SQLReadRepository**, which targets the database you will create in a later chapter.

You will add some dummy data in the **MockReadRepository** class that will act as an in-memory database, containing the same "tables" as the finished database. They use the same entity classes when storing the data.

Technologies Used in This Chapter
1. **C#** – To create the interface, repository class, and dummy data.
2. **LINQ** – To query the data in the in-memory database.

Overview

You will create a reusable interface, which will be used by all repositories that communicate with the user interface. You will also create an in-memory database, and fill it with data. Then you will call repository methods from a controller to make sure that the correct data is returned.

Add the IReadRepository Interface and MockReadRepository Class

First you will add the **IReadRepository** interface, and then implement it in the **MockReadRepository** class. The interface will be empty to start with, but you will add methods to it throughout this chapter. Once it has been completed, it can be reused by the **SQLReadRepository** later in the book.

1. Right click on the project node in the Solution Explorer and select **Add-New Folder**.
2. Name the folder *Repositories*.
3. Right click on the *Repositories* folder and select **Add-New Item**.
4. Select the **Interface** template.
5. Name it *IReadRepository* and click the **Add** button.
6. Add the **public** access modifier to the class, to make it accessible in the whole application.
7. Right click on the *Repositories* folder and select **Add-Class**.
8. Name the class *MockReadRepository* and click the **Add** button.
9. Implement the interface in the class.
   ```
   public class MockReadRepository : IReadRepository
   ```
10. Add a region called **Mock Data** to the class.
11. Save the files.

Add Data to the MockReadRepository Class

To build the UI, you need to add dummy data to the **MockReadRepository** class. The data can then be queried from the methods implemented through the **IReadRepository** interface, and used in the views. Add the following data in the **Mock Data** region. You can of course modify the data as you see fit.

The Course List

```
List<Course> _courses = new List<Course> {
    new Course { Id = 1, InstructorId = 1,
        MarqueeImageUrl = "/images/laptop.jpg",
        ImageUrl = "/images/course.jpg", Title = "C# For Beginners",
        Description = "Course 1 Description."
    },
    new Course { Id = 2, InstructorId = 1,
        MarqueeImageUrl = "/images/laptop.jpg",
        ImageUrl = "/images/course2.jpg", Title = "Programming C#",
        Description = "Course 2 Description."
    },
    new Course { Id = 3, InstructorId = 2,
        MarqueeImageUrl = "/images/laptop.jpg",
        ImageUrl = "/images/course3.jpg", Title = "MVC 5 For Beginners",
        Description = "Course 3 Description."
    } };
```

The UserCourses List

You can copy the user id from the **AspNetUsers** table and use it as the user id in the data.

```
List<UserCourse> _userCourses = new List<UserCourse>
{
    new UserCourse { UserId = "4ad684f8-bb70-4968-85f8-458aa7dc19a3",
        CourseId = 1 },
    new UserCourse { UserId = "00000000-0000-0000-0000-000000000000",
        CourseId = 2 },
    new UserCourse { UserId = "4ad684f8-bb70-4968-85f8-458aa7dc19a3",
        CourseId = 3 },
    new UserCourse { UserId = "00000000-0000-0000-0000-000000000000",
        CourseId = 1 }
};
```

The Modules List

```
List<Module> _modules = new List<Module>
{
    new Module { Id = 1, Title = "Module 1", CourseId = 1 },
    new Module { Id = 2, Title = "Module 2", CourseId = 1 },
    new Module { Id = 3, Title = "Module 3", CourseId = 2 }
};
```

The Downloads List

```
List<Download> _downloads = new List<Download>
{
    new Download{Id = 1, ModuleId = 1, CourseId = 1,
        Title = "ADO.NET 1 (PDF)",
        Url = "https://1drv.ms/b/s!AuD5OaH0ExAwn48rX9TZZ3kAOX6Peg" },
    new Download{Id = 2, ModuleId = 1, CourseId = 1,
        Title = "ADO.NET 2 (PDF)",
        Url = "https://1drv.ms/b/s!AuD5OaH0ExAwn48rX9TZZ3kAOX6Peg" },
    new Download{Id = 3, ModuleId = 3, CourseId = 2,
        Title = "ADO.NET 1 (PDF)",
        Url = "https://1drv.ms/b/s!AuD5OaH0ExAwn48rX9TZZ3kAOX6Peg" }
};
```

The Instructors List

```
List<Instructor> _instructors = new List<Instructor>
{
    new Instructor{ Id = 1, Name = "John Doe",
        Thumbnail = "/images/Ice-Age-Scrat-icon.png",
        Description = "Lorem ipsum dolor sit amet, consectetur elit."
    },
     new Instructor{ Id = 2, Name = "Jane Doe",
        Thumbnail = "/images/Ice-Age-Scrat-icon.png",
        Description = "Lorem ipsum dolor sit, consectetur adipiscing."
    }
};
```

The Videos List

```
List<Video> _videos = new List<Video>
{
    new Video { Id = 1, ModuleId = 1, CourseId = 1, Position = 1,
        Title = "Video 1 Title", Description = "Video 1 Description:
        A very very long description.", Duration = 50,
        Thumbnail = "/images/video1.jpg",
        Url = "www.youtube.com/watch?v=by2FMc9Srsg"
    },
    new Video { Id = 2, ModuleId = 1, CourseId = 1, Position = 2,
        Title = "Video 2 Title", Description = "Video 2 Description:
        A very very long description.", Duration = 45,
        Thumbnail = "/images/video2.jpg",
        Url = "www.youtube.com/watch?v=by2FMc9Srsg"
    },
    new Video { Id = 3, ModuleId = 3, CourseId = 2, Position = 1,
        Title = "Video 3 Title", Description = "Video 3 Description:
        A very very long description.", Duration = 41,
        Thumbnail = "/images/video3.jpg",
        Url = "www.youtube.com/watch?v=by2FMc9Srsg"
    },
    new Video { Id = 4, ModuleId = 2, CourseId = 1, Position = 1,
        Title = "Video 4 Title", Description = "Video 4 Description:
        A very very long description.", Duration = 42,
        Thumbnail = "/images/video4.jpg",
        Url = "www.youtube.com/watch?v=by2FMc9Srsg"
    }
};
```

The GetCourses Method

The first method you will add to the **IReadRepository** interface and implement in the **MockReadRepository** class is called **GetCourses**. It takes the user id as a parameter and returns an **IEnumerable** of **Course** objects.

The purpose of this method is to return a list with all courses available for the logged in user.

1. Open the **IReadRepository** interface.
2. Add a method description for the **GetCourses** class. It should return an **IEnumerable** of **Customer** entities. Resolve any missing **using** statements.
   ```
   IEnumerable<Course> GetCourses(string userId);
   ```
3. Open the **MockReadRepository** class and add the method. You can do it manually, or point to the squiggly line under the interface name and add it by clicking on the quick actions button; select **Implement interface**. Resolve any missing **using** statements.
   ```
   public IEnumerable<Course> GetCourses(string userId)
   {
   }
   ```
4. Now you need to write a LINQ query that targets the **_userCourses** list for the logged in user, and join in the **_courses** list to get to the courses.
   ```
   var courses = _userCourses.Where(uc => uc.UserId.Equals(userId))
       .Join(_courses, uc => uc.CourseId, c => c.Id,
           (uc, c) => new { Course = c })
       .Select(s => s.Course);
   ```
5. With the user's courses in a list, you can add the instructor and modules by looping through it and using LINQ to fetch the appropriate data. The course objects have an instructor id, and the modules have a course id assigned to them.
   ```
   foreach (var course in courses)
   {
       course.Instructor = _instructors.SingleOrDefault(
           s => s.Id.Equals(course.InstructorId));
       course.Modules = _modules.Where(
           m => m.CourseId.Equals(course.Id)).ToList();
   }
   ```
6. Return the courses list from the method.

Testing the GetCourses Method

1. Open the **HomeController** class and find the **Index** action method. This is the action that is executed when a user navigates to the site.
2. Create an instance of the **MockReadRepository** class called **rep** before any other code inside the **Index** method. Resolve any missing **using** statements.
   ```
   var rep = new MockReadRepository();
   ```
3. Call the **GetCourses** method on the **rep** instance variable and store the result in a variable called **courses**. Don't forget to pass in a valid user id from the **_userCourses** list in the mock data.
   ```
   var courses = rep.GetCourses(
       "4ad684f8-bb70-4968-85f8-458aa7dc19a3");
   ```
4. Place a breakpoint on the next code line in the **Index** action.
5. Press F5 on the keyboard to debug the application. When the breakpoint is hit, examine the content of the **courses** variable. It should contain a list of all courses available to the logged in user.
6. Stop the application in Visual Studio.

The complete code in the **Index** action:

```
public IActionResult Index()
{
    var rep = new MockReadRepository();
    var courses = rep.GetCourses(
        "4ad684f8-bb70-4968-85f8-458aa7dc19a3");

    if (!_signInManager.IsSignedIn(User))
        return RedirectToAction("Login", "Account");

    return View();
}
```

The GetCourse Method

The next method you will add to the **IReadRepository** interface and implement in the **MockReadRepository** class is called **GetCourse**. It takes a user id and a course id as parameters, and returns a **Course** object.

The purpose of this method is to return a specific course for a user when the button in the course panel is clicked.

1. Open the **IReadRepository** interface.
2. Add a method description for the **GetCourse** class. It should return an instance of the **Customer** entity. Resolve any missing **using** statements.
   ```
   Course GetCourse(string userId, int courseId);
   ```
3. Open the **MockReadRepository** class and add the method. Resolve any missing **using** statements.
   ```
   public Course GetCourse(string userId, int courseId)
   {
   }
   ```
4. Now you need to write a LINQ query that fetches a single course, using the **_userCourses** and **_courses** lists. Store the result in a variable called **course**.
   ```
   var course = _userCourses.Where(uc => uc.UserId.Equals(userId))
       .Join(_courses, uc => uc.CourseId, c => c.Id,
           (uc, c) => new { Course = c })
       .SingleOrDefault(s => s.Course.Id.Equals(courseId)).Course;
   ```
5. You need to fetch the instructor and assign the result to the **Instructor** property. Use the **InstructorId** property in the **course** object.
   ```
   course.Instructor = _instructors.SingleOrDefault(
       s => s.Id.Equals(course.InstructorId));
   ```
6. You need to fetch the course modules and assign the result to the **Modules** property.
   ```
   course.Modules = _modules.Where(
       m => m.CourseId.Equals(course.Id)).ToList();
   ```
7. Next, you'll need to fetch the downloads and videos for each module, and assign the results to the **Downloads** and **Videos** properties respectively on each module instance.
   ```
   foreach (var module in course.Modules)
   {
       module.Downloads = _downloads.Where(
           d => d.ModuleId.Equals(module.Id)).ToList();
       module.Videos = _videos.Where(
           v => v.ModuleId.Equals(module.Id)).ToList();
   }
   ```

8. Return the course.

Testing the GetCourse Method

1. Open the **HomeController** class and find the **Index** action method. This is the action that is executed when a user navigates to the site.
2. Locate the call to the **GetCourses** method in the **Index** action.
3. Call the **GetCourse** method on the **rep** instance variable below the previous method call. Store the result in a variable called **course**. Don't forget to pass in a valid user id from the **_userCourses** list and a valid course id from the **_courses** list in the mock data.

    ```
    var course = rep.GetCourse(
        "4ad684f8-bb70-4968-85f8-458aa7dc19a3", 1);
    ```

4. Place a breakpoint on the next code line in the **Index** action.
5. Press F5 on the keyboard to debug the application. When the breakpoint is hit, examine the content of the **course** variable. The **course** object's properties should have data, including the **Videos**, **Downloads**, and **Modules** collections.
6. Stop the application in Visual Studio.

The complete code in the **Index** action:

```
public IActionResult Index()
{
    var rep = new MockReadRepository();
    var courses = rep.GetCourses(
        "4ad684f8-bb70-4968-85f8-458aa7dc19a3");
    var course = rep.GetCourse(
        "4ad684f8-bb70-4968-85f8-458aa7dc19a3", 1);


    if (!_signInManager.IsSignedIn(User))
        return RedirectToAction("Login", "Account");

    return View();
}
```

The GetVideo Method

The next method you will add to the **IReadRepository** interface and implement in the **MockReadRepository** class is called **GetVideo**. It takes a user id and a video id as parameters, and returns a **Video** object.

The purpose of this method is to return a specific video that the user requests by clicking on a video in one of the **Course** view's module lists.

1. Open the **IReadRepository** interface.
2. Add a method description for the **GetVideo** class. It should return an instance of the **Video** entity. Resolve any missing **using** statements.
   ```
   Video GetVideo(string userId, int videoId);
   ```
3. Open the **MockReadRepository** class and add the method. Resolve any missing **using** statements.
   ```
   public Video GetVideo(string userId, int videoId) { ... }
   ```
4. Now you need to write a LINQ query that fetches a single video using the **_videos** and **_userCourses** lists. Store the result in a variable called **video**.
   ```
   var video = _videos
       .Where(v => v.Id.Equals(videoId))
       .Join(_userCourses, v => v.CourseId, uc => uc.CourseId,
           (v, uc) => new { Video = v, UserCourse = uc })
       .Where(vuc => vuc.UserCourse.UserId.Equals(userId))
       .FirstOrDefault().Video;
   ```
5. Return the video.

Testing the GetVideo Method

1. Open the **HomeController** class and find the **Index** action method.
2. Locate the call to the **GetCourse** method in the **Index** action.
3. Call the **GetVideo** method on the **rep** instance variable below the previous method call. Store the result in a variable called **video**. Don't forget to pass in a valid user id from the **_userCourses** list and a valid video id from the **_videos** list in the mock data.
   ```
   var video = rep.GetVideo(
       "4ad684f8-bb70-4968-85f8-458aa7dc19a3", 1);
   ```
4. Place a breakpoint on the next code line in the **Index** action.

5. Press F5 on the keyboard to debug the application. When the breakpoint is hit, examine the content of the **video** variable.

6. Stop the application in Visual Studio.

The complete code in the **Index** action:

```
public IActionResult Index()
{
    var rep = new MockReadRepository();
    var courses = rep.GetCourses(
        "4ad684f8-bb70-4968-85f8-458aa7dc19a3");
    var course = rep.GetCourse(
        "4ad684f8-bb70-4968-85f8-458aa7dc19a3", 1);
    var video = rep.GetVideo(
        "4ad684f8-bb70-4968-85f8-458aa7dc19a3", 1);

    if (!_signInManager.IsSignedIn(User))
        return RedirectToAction("Login", "Account");

    return View();
}
```

The GetVideos Method

The next method you will add to the **IReadRepository** interface and implement in the **MockReadRepository** class is called **GetVideos**. It takes a user id and an optional module id as parameters, and returns a list of **Video** objects.

The purpose of this method is to return all videos for the logged in user, and display them in the **Course** view. If a module id is passed in, only the videos for that module will be returned.

1. Open the **IReadRepository** interface.

2. Add a method description for the **GetVideos** class. It should return an **IEnumerable** of the **Video** entity. Resolve any missing **using** statements.
```
IEnumerable<Video> GetVideos(string userId, int moduleId =
default(int));
```

3. Open the **MockReadRepository** class and add the method. Resolve any missing **using** statements.
```
public IEnumerable<Video> GetVideos(string userId,
int moduleId = default(int)) { }
```

4. Now you need to write a LINQ query that fetches all videos for the logged in user, using the **_videos** and **_userCourses** lists. Store the result in a variable called **videos**.

```
var videos = _videos
    .Join(_userCourses, v => v.CourseId, uc => uc.CourseId,
        (v, uc) => new { Video = v, UserCourse = uc })
    .Where(vuc => vuc.UserCourse.UserId.Equals(userId));
```

5. Return all the videos in the **videos** collection if the module id is 0, otherwise return only the videos in the **videos** collection that match the module id.

```
return moduleId.Equals(0) ?
    videos.Select(s => s.Video) :
    videos.Where(v => v.Video.ModuleId.Equals(moduleId))
        .Select(s => s.Video);
```

Testing the GetVideos Method

1. Open the **HomeController** class and find the **Index** action method.
2. Locate the call to the **GetVideo** method in the **Index** action.
3. Call the **GetVideos** method on the **rep** instance variable below the previous method call. Store the result in a variable called **videos**. Don't forget to pass in a valid user id from the **_userCourses** list in the mock data.

```
var videos = rep.GetVideos(
    "4ad684f8-bb70-4968-85f8-458aa7dc19a3");
```

4. Call the **GetVideos** method on the **rep** instance variable below the previous method call. Store the result in a variable called **videosForModule**. Don't forget to pass in a valid user id from the **_userCourses** list and a valid module id from the **_modules** list in the mock data.

```
var videosForModule = rep.GetVideos(
    "4ad684f8-bb70-4968-85f8-458aa7dc19a3", 1);
```

5. Place a breakpoint on the next code line in the **Index** action.
6. Press F5 on the keyboard to debug the application. When the breakpoint is hit, examine the content of the **videos** and **videosForModule** variables.
7. Stop the application in Visual Studio.
8. Delete all the test variables and the **rep** instance from the **Index** action when you have verified that the correct data is returned.

The complete code in the **Index** action before deleting the variables:

```
public IActionResult Index()
{
    var rep = new MockReadRepository();
    var courses = rep.GetCourses(
        "4ad684f8-bb70-4968-85f8-458aa7dc19a3");
    var course = rep.GetCourse(
        "4ad684f8-bb70-4968-85f8-458aa7dc19a3", 1);
    var video = rep.GetVideo("4ad684f8-bb70-4968-85f8-458aa7dc19a3", 1);
    var videos = rep.GetVideos("4ad684f8-bb70-4968-85f8-458aa7dc19a3");
    var videosForModule = rep.GetVideos(
        "4ad684f8-bb70-4968-85f8-458aa7dc19a3", 1);

    if (!_signInManager.IsSignedIn(User))
        return RedirectToAction("Login", "Account");

    return View();
}
```

The complete code in the **Index** action after deleting the variables:

```
public IActionResult Index()
{
    if (!_signInManager.IsSignedIn(User))
        return RedirectToAction("Login", "Account");

    return View();
}
```

The complete code in the **IReadRepository** interface:

```
public interface IReadRepository
{
    IEnumerable<Course> GetCourses(string userId);
    Course GetCourse(string userId, int courseId);

    Video GetVideo(string userId, int videoId);
    IEnumerable<Video> GetVideos(string userId,
        int moduleId = default(int));
}
```

The complete code in the **MockReadRepository** class (without the mock data):

```
public class MockReadRepository : IReadRepository
{
    public IEnumerable<Course> GetCourses(string userId)
    {
        var courses = _userCourses.Where(uc =>
            uc.UserId.Equals(userId))
            .Join(_courses, uc => uc.CourseId, c => c.Id,
                (uc, c) => new { Course = c })
            .Select(s => s.Course);

        foreach (var course in courses)
        {
            course.Instructor = _instructors.SingleOrDefault(
                s => s.Id.Equals(course.InstructorId));
            course.Modules = _modules.Where(
                m => m.CourseId.Equals(course.Id)).ToList();
        }

        return courses;
    }

    public Course GetCourse(string userId, int courseId)
    {
        var course = _userCourses.Where(uc =>
            uc.UserId.Equals(userId))
            .Join(_courses, uc => uc.CourseId, c => c.Id,
                (uc, c) => new { Course = c })
            .SingleOrDefault(s => s.Course.Id.Equals(courseId)).Course;

        course.Instructor = _instructors.SingleOrDefault(
            s => s.Id.Equals(course.InstructorId));

        course.Modules = _modules.Where(
            m => m.CourseId.Equals(course.Id)).ToList();

        foreach (var module in course.Modules)
        {
            module.Downloads = _downloads.Where(
                d => d.ModuleId.Equals(module.Id)).ToList();
            module.Videos = _videos.Where(
                v => v.ModuleId.Equals(module.Id)).ToList();
        }
```

```
        return course;
    }

    public Video GetVideo(string userId, int videoId)
    {
        var video = _videos
            .Where(v => v.Id.Equals(videoId))
            .Join(_userCourses, v => v.CourseId, uc => uc.CourseId,
                (v, uc) => new { Video = v, UserCourse = uc })
            .Where(vuc => vuc.UserCourse.UserId.Equals(userId))
            .FirstOrDefault().Video;

        return video;
    }

    public IEnumerable<Video> GetVideos(string userId,
    int moduleId = default(int))
    {
        var videos = _videos
            .Join(_userCourses, v => v.CourseId, uc => uc.CourseId,
                (v, uc) => new { Video = v, UserCourse = uc })
            .Where(vuc => vuc.UserCourse.UserId.Equals(userId));

        return moduleId.Equals(0) ?
            videos.Select(s => s.Video) :
            videos.Where(v => v.Video.ModuleId.Equals(moduleId))
                .Select(s => s.Video);
    }
}
```

Summary

In this chapter, you added mock test data to a repository class, created the **IReadReposi-tory** interface, and implemented it in the **MockReadRepository** class. Then you tested the repository class from the **Index** action in the **Home** controller.

Next, you will create the **Membership** controller and add three actions: **Dashboard**, **Course**, and **Video**. These actions will be used when serving up the view to the user. Auto-Mapper and **IReadRepository** instances will be injected into the **Membership** controller. AutoMapper will be used to convert entity objects into DTO objects that can be sent to the UI views, when you add the views in later chapters.

17. The Membership Controller and AutoMapper

Introduction

In this chapter you will create a new **Membership** controller and add its three actions: **Dashboard**, **Course**, and **Video**. For now, they won't be serving up any views, you will use them to implement the mapping between entity objects and DTO objects with Auto-Mapper, and to fetch the data for each action from the **MockReadRepository** you implemented in the previous chapter.

AutoMapper and **IReadRepository** will be injected to a constructor you add to the **Membership** controller. Two other objects are injected to the constructor with Dependency Injection. The first is the **UserManager**, which is used to get the user id from the logged in user, and the second is the **IHttpContextAccessor**, which contains information about the logged in user.

Using AutoMapper removes tedious and boring work, code that you otherwise would have to implement manually to convert one object to another.

Technologies Used in This Chapter
1. **C#** – Creating controller actions, view models, and mapping objects.
2. **AutoMapper** – To map entity objects to DTO objects.

Overview

You will begin with adding the **Membership** controller and its action methods. Then you will use dependency injection to inject the four previously mentioned objects into the controller's constructor and save them in private class level variables.

Then you will set up AutoMapper's configuration in the *Startup.cs* file. With that setup complete, you can proceed with the actual mappings in the action methods.

Adding the Membership Controller

You want to keep the membership actions separate from the **HomeController**, which handles the login and registration. To achieve this, you create the **MembershipController** class, and add the membership actions to it.

Three action methods are needed to serve up the views. The first is the **Dashboard** action, which displays the courses the user has access to. From each course panel in the **Dashboard** view, the user can click a button to open the course, using the second action method called **Course**. The **Course** view lists the content for that course. When a user clicks a video item, the video is opened in the **Video** view, which is generated by the **Video** action method.

Adding the Controller

1. Right click on the *Controllers* folder in the Solution Explorer and select **Add-Controller**.
2. Select the **MVC Controller – Empty** template, and click the **Add** button.
3. Name the controller *MembershipController* and click the **Add** button.
4. Rename the **Index** action **Dashboard** and add the **[HttpGet]** attribute to it.
```
[HttpGet]
public IActionResult Dashboard()
{
}
```
5. Copy the **Dashboard** action method and the attribute.
6. Paste it in twice and rename the methods **Course** and **Video**. Also add an **int** parameter called **id** to them.
```
[HttpGet]
public IActionResult Course(int id)
{
}

[HttpGet]
public IActionResult Video(int id)
{
}
```
7. Add a constructor to the controller.
```
public MembershipController()
{
}
```

8. Inject **IHttpContextAccesor** into the constructor and save the user from it to a variable called **user**. Resolve any missing **using** statements.

```
public MembershipController(IHttpContextAccessor
httpContextAccessor)
{
    var user = httpContextAccessor.HttpContext.User;
}
```

9. Inject the **UserManager** into the constructor and call its **GetUserId** method. Save the user id in a private class level variable called **_userId**. Resolve any missing **using** statements.

```
private string _userId;
public MembershipController(IHttpContextAccessor
httpContextAccessor,  UserManager<ApplicationUser> userManager)
{
    var user = httpContextAccessor.HttpContext.User;
    _userId = userManager.GetUserId(user);
}
```

10. Inject **IMapper** into the constructor to get access to AutoMapper in the controller. Save the instance to a private, read-only, class level variable called **_mapper**.

11. To be able to inject objects from classes that you create, you have to add a service mapping to the **ConfigureServices** method in the *Startup.cs* file. Because you are injecting the **IReadRepository** interface into the constructor, you have to specify what class will be used to serve up the objects. Without the mapping an exception will be thrown.

    a. Open the *Startup.cs* file, and locate the **ConfigureServices** method and go to the end of the method.

    b. Use the **AddSingleton** method to add the connection between **IReadRepository** and **MockReadRepository**. This will ensure that only one instance of the class will be created when the interface is injected to constructors. It will also be very easy to switch the object class in the future. In a later chapter, you will switch the **MockReadRepsitory** class for the **SQLReadRepository** class, which also implements the **IReadRepository** interface.

```
services.AddSingleton<IReadRepository, MockReadRepository>();
```

12. Inject the **IReadRepository** interface into the constructor and save the instance to a private class level variable called **_db**.

```
public MembershipController(
    IHttpContextAccessor httpContextAccessor,
    UserManager<ApplicationUser> userManager,
    IMapper mapper, IReadRepository db)
```

The complete **MembershipController** class so far:

```
public class MembershipController : Controller
{
    private string _userId;
    private IReadRepository _db;
    private readonly IMapper _mapper;
    public MembershipController(
    IHttpContextAccessor httpContextAccessor,
    UserManager<ApplicationUser> userManager,
    IMapper mapper, IReadRepository db) {
        // Get Logged in user's UserId
        var user = httpContextAccessor.HttpContext.User;
        _userId = userManager.GetUserId(user);
        _db = db;
        _mapper = mapper;
    }

    [HttpGet]
    public IActionResult Dashboard()
    {
        return View();
    }

    [HttpGet]
    public IActionResult Course(int id)
    {
        return View();
    }

    [HttpGet]
    public IActionResult Video(int id)
    {
        return View();
    }
}
```

Configuring AutoMapper

For AutoMapper to work properly, you have to add configuration to the **ConfigureServices** method in the *Startup.cs* file. The configuration tells AutoMapper how to map between objects, in this case between entities and DTOs. Default mapping can be achieved by specifying the class names of the objects to be mapped, without naming specific properties. With default matching, only properties with the same name in both classes will be matched.

A more granular mapping can be made by specifying exactly which properties that match. In this scenario the property names can be different in the classes.

1. Open the *Startup.cs* file and locate the **ConfigureServices** method.
2. Go to the end of the method and assign a call to AutoMapper's **MapperConfiguration** method to a variable called **config**.
   ```
   var config = new AutoMapper.MapperConfiguration(cfg =>
   {
   }
   ```
3. Add a mapping for the **Video** entity and **VideoDTO** classes inside the **config** block. Since the properties of interest are named the same in both classes, no specific configuration is necessary.
   ```
   cfg.CreateMap<Video, VideoDTO>();
   ```
4. Add a mapping for the **Download** entity and the **DownloadDTO** classes inside the **config** block. Here specific configuration is necessary since the properties are named differently in the two classes.
   ```
   cfg.CreateMap<Download, DownloadDTO>()
       .ForMember(dest => dest.DownloadUrl,
           src => src.MapFrom(s => s.Url))
       .ForMember(dest => dest.DownloadTitle,
           src => src.MapFrom(s => s.Title));
   ```
5. Now do the same for the **Instructor**, **Course**, and **Module** entities and their DTOs. Note that there are no mappings for the **UserCourseDTO** and **LessonInfoDTO** because we don't need any.
6. Create a variable called **mapper** below the **config** block. Assign the result from a call to the **CreateMapper** method to a variable named **mapper**.
   ```
   var mapper = config.CreateMapper();
   ```

7. Add the mapper as singleton instance to the **services** collection, like you did with the **IReadRepository**.
   ```
   services.AddSingleton(mapper);
   ```

8. Place a breakpoint at the end of the **Membership** constructor and start the application. Navigate to *http://localhost:xxxxx/Membership/Dashboard* to hit the constructor.

9. Inspect the class level variables and verify that the **_db** variable has correct data for all entities.

The complete AutoMapper configuration in the **ConfigurationServices** method:

```
var config = new AutoMapper.MapperConfiguration(cfg =>
{
    cfg.CreateMap<Video, VideoDTO>();

    cfg.CreateMap<Instructor, InstructorDTO>()
        .ForMember(dest => dest.InstructorName,
            src => src.MapFrom(s => s.Name))
        .ForMember(dest => dest.InstructorDescription,
            src => src.MapFrom(s => s.Description))
        .ForMember(dest => dest.InstructorAvatar,
            src => src.MapFrom(s => s.Thumbnail));

    cfg.CreateMap<Download, DownloadDTO>()
        .ForMember(dest => dest.DownloadUrl,
            src => src.MapFrom(s => s.Url))
        .ForMember(dest => dest.DownloadTitle,
            src => src.MapFrom(s => s.Title));

    cfg.CreateMap<Course, CourseDTO>()
        .ForMember(dest => dest.CourseId, src =>
            src.MapFrom(s => s.Id))
        .ForMember(dest => dest.CourseTitle,
            src => src.MapFrom(s => s.Title))
        .ForMember(dest => dest.CourseDescription,
            src => src.MapFrom(s => s.Description))
        .ForMember(dest => dest.MarqueeImageUrl,
            src => src.MapFrom(s => s.MarqueeImageUrl))
        .ForMember(dest => dest.CourseImageUrl,
            src => src.MapFrom(s => s.ImageUrl));
```

```
    cfg.CreateMap<Module, ModuleDTO>()
        .ForMember(dest => dest.ModuleTitle,
            src => src.MapFrom(s => s.Title));
});

var mapper = config.CreateMapper();
services.AddSingleton(mapper);
```

Implementing the Action Methods

Now that you have set everything up for object mapping with AutoMapper, it's time to utilize that functionality in the three action methods you added to the **Memebership-Controller** class earlier.

The Dashboard Action Method

This action will serve data to the **Dashboard** view, which you will add in a later chapter. The view will be served an instance of the **DashboardViewModel** class that you created in an earlier chapter.

The purpose of the **Dashboard** action method is to fill the **DashboardViewModel** with the appropriate data, using the **_db** in-mamory database that you added to the **MockRead-Repository** class. The **MockReadRepository** object was injected to the **Membership** constructor through the **IReadRepository** parameter, using dependency injection that you configured in the **ConfigureServices** method in the *Startup.cs* class.

Your next task will be to fill the view model using AutoMapper, mapping data from the **_db** database to DTO objects that can be used in views that you will add in coming chapters.

The view will be able to display as many courses as the user has access to, but only three to a row. This means that you will have to divide the list of courses into a list of lists, with three **CourseDTO** objects each. This will make it easy to loop out the panels in the view when it is implemented.

To refresh your memory, this is the view that this action method will be serving.

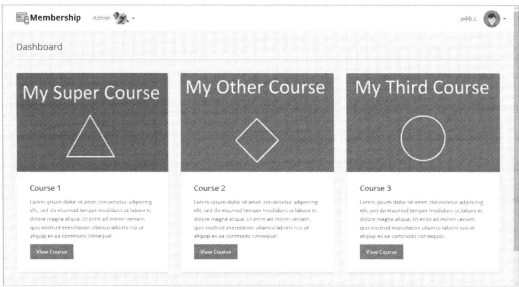

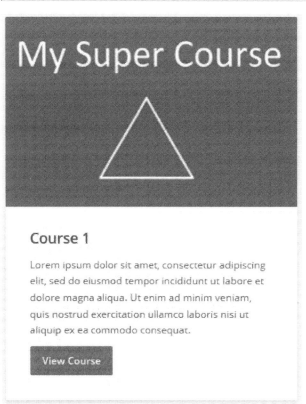

1. Open the **MembershipController** class and locate the **Dashboard** action method.
2. Call the **Map** method on the **_mapper** variable in the **Dashboard** action method to convert the result from a call to the **GetCourses** method on the **_db** variable; don't forget to pass in the logged in user's id, not a hardcoded value. This should fetch all the courses for the user and convert them into **CourseDTO** objects. Store the result in a variable named **courseDtoObjects**.

```
var courseDtoObjects = _mapper.Map<List<CourseDTO>>(
    _db.GetCourses(_userId));
```

3. Clear all breakpoints in the controller class.
4. Place a breakpoint on the return statement at the end of the **Dashboard** action method.
5. Run the application with debugging (F5).
6. Navigate to *http://localhost:xxxxx/Membership/Dashboard* to hit the breakpoint.
7. Inspect the **courseDtoObjects** variable to verify that it contains **CourseDTO** objects with data.

```
[HttpGet]
public IActionResult Dashboard()
{
    var courseDtoObjects = _mapper.Map<List<CourseDTO>>(_db.GetCourse
                        ▲ ◉ courseDtoObjects  Count = 2  ◄►
    return View();        ▷ ◉ [0]        {VideoOnDemand.Models.DTOModels.CourseDTO}
}                         ▷ ◉ [1]        {VideoOnDemand.Models.DTOModels.CourseDTO}
                          ▷ ◉ Raw View
```

8. Stop the application in Visual Studio.
9. Create an instance of the **DashboardViewModel** and the **Courses** property on the model. Note that the **Courses** property is a list of lists, where each of the inner lists will contain a maximum of three **CourseDTO** objects, to satisfy the view's needs.

```
var dashboardModel = new DashboardViewModel();
dashboardModel.Courses = new List<List<CourseDTO>>();
```

10. Divide the **CourseDTOs** in the **courseDtoObjects** collection into sets of three, and add them to new **List<CourseDTO>** instances.

```
var noOfRows = courseDtoObjects.Count <= 3 ? 1 :
    courseDtoObjects.Count / 3;
for (var i = 0; i < noOfRows; i++) {
    dashboardModel.Courses.Add(courseDtoObjects.Take(3).ToList());
}
```

11. Return the **DashboardViewModel** instance in the **View** method.
    ```
    return View(dashboardModel);
    ```

12. Make sure that the breakpoint is still on the return statement, and start the application with debugging (F5).

13. Navigate to *http://localhost:xxxxx/Membership/Dashboard* to hit the breakpoint.

14. Inspect the **dashboardModel** variable and verify that its **Courses** property contains at least one list of **CourseDTO** objects.

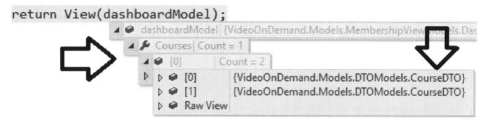

15. Stop the application in Visual Studio.

The complete code for the **Dashboard** action:

```
[HttpGet]
public IActionResult Dashboard()
{
    var courseDtoObjects = _mapper.Map<List<CourseDTO>>(
        db.GetCourses(_userId));

    var dashboardModel = new DashboardViewModel();
    dashboardModel.Courses = new List<List<CourseDTO>>();

    var noOfRows = courseDtoObjects.Count <= 3 ? 1 :
        courseDtoObjects.Count / 3;
    for (var i = 0; i < noOfRows; i++)
    {
        dashboardModel.Courses.Add(courseDtoObjects.Take(3).ToList());
    }

    return View(dashboardModel);
}
```

The Course Action Method

This action will serve data to the **Course** view, which you will add in a later chapter. The view will be served an instance of the **CourseViewModel** class that you created in a previous chapter.

The purpose of the **Course** action method is to fill that view model with the appropriate data using the **_db** in-mamory database that you added to the **MockReadRepository**. The **MockReadRepository** was injected to the **Membership** constructor through the **IRead-Repository** parameter using dependency injection, which you configured in the **Configure-Services** method in the *Startup.cs* class.

Your next task will be to fill the view model using AutoMapper, to map data from the **_db** database to DTO objects that can be used in views that you will add in coming chapters.

The view will display the selected course and its associated modules. Each module will list the videos and downloads associated with it. The instructor bio will also be displayed beside the module list.

To refresh your memory, this is the view that this action method will be serving.

John Doe

Instructor

Lorem ipsum dolor sit amet,
cupidatat non proident, sunt in culpa

1. Open the **MembershipController** class and locate the **Course** action method.
2. Fetch the course matching the id passed in to the **Course** action and the logged in user's user id, by calling the **GetCourse** method on the **_db** variable. Store the result in a variable called **course**.
   ```
   var course = _db.GetCourse(_userId, id);
   ```
3. Call the **Map** method on the **_mapper** variable to convert the course you just fetched into a **CourseDTO** object. Store the result in a variable named **mappedCourseDTOs**.
   ```
   var mappedCourseDTOs = _mapper.Map<CourseDTO>(course);
   ```
4. Call the **Map** method on the **_mapper** variable to convert the **Instructor** object in **course** object into a **InstructorDTO** object. Store the result in a variable named **mappedInstructorDTO**.
   ```
   var mappedInstructorDTO =
   _mapper.Map<InstructorDTO>(course.Instructor);
   ```

5. Call the **Map** method on the **_mapper** variable to convert the **Modules** collection in the **course** object into a **List<ModuleDTO>**. Store the result in a variable named **mappedModuleDTOs**.

```
var mappedModuleDTOs =
_mapper.Map<List<ModuleDTO>>(course.Modules);
```

6. Loop over the **mappedModuleDTOs** collection to fetch the videos and downloads associated with the modules. Use AutoMapper to convert videos and downloads in the **course** object's **Modules** collection to **List<VideoDTO>** and **List<DownloadDTO>** collections. Assign the collections to their respective properties in the loop's current **ModuleDTO**.

```
for (var i = 0; i < mappedModuleDTOs.Count; i++)
{
    mappedModuleDTOs[i].Downloads =
        course.Modules[i].Downloads.Count.Equals(0) ? null :
            _mapper.Map<List<DownloadDTO>>(
                course.Modules[i].Downloads);

    mappedModuleDTOs[i].Videos =
        course.Modules[i].Videos.Count.Equals(0) ? null :
        _mapper.Map<List<VideoDTO>>(course.Modules[i].Videos);
}
```

7. Create an instance of the **CourseViewModel** class named **courseModel**.

8. Assign the three mapped collections: **mappedCourseDTOs**, **mappedInstructorDTO**, and **mappedModuleDTOs** to the **courseModel** object's **Course**, **Instructor**, and **Modules** properties.

```
var courseModel = new CourseViewModel
{
    Course = mappedCourseDTOs,
    Instructor = mappedInstructorDTO,
    Modules = mappedModuleDTOs
};
```

9. Return the **courseModel** object with the **View** method.

```
return View(courseModel);
```

10. Place a breakpoint on the return statement at the end of the **Course** action.

11. Run the application with debugging (F5).

12. Navigate to *http://localhost:xxxxx/Membership/Course/1* to hit the breakpoint.

13. Inspect the **courseModel** variable to verify that it contains a course, an instructor, and modules with videos and downloads.
14. Stop the application in Visual Studio.

The complete code for the **Course** action:

```
[HttpGet]
public IActionResult Course(int id)
{
    var course = _db.GetCourse(_userId, id);
    var mappedCourseDTOs = _mapper.Map<CourseDTO>(course);
    var mappedInstructorDTO =
        _mapper.Map<InstructorDTO>(course.Instructor);
    var mappedModuleDTOs =
        _mapper.Map<List<ModuleDTO>>(course.Modules);

    for (var i = 0; i < mappedModuleDTOs.Count; i++)
    {
        mappedModuleDTOs[i].Downloads =
            course.Modules[i].Downloads.Count.Equals(0) ? null :
            _mapper.Map<List<DownloadDTO>>(
                course.Modules[i].Downloads);

        mappedModuleDTOs[i].Videos =
            course.Modules[i].Videos.Count.Equals(0) ? null :
            _mapper.Map<List<VideoDTO>>(course.Modules[i].Videos);
    }

    var courseModel = new CourseViewModel
    {
        Course = mappedCourseDTOs,
        Instructor = mappedInstructorDTO,
        Modules = mappedModuleDTOs
    };

    return View(courseModel);
}
```

The Video Action Method

In this action, you will create an instance of the **VideoViewModel** class you added earlier. This model will then be sent to a **Video** view that you will add in an upcoming chapter.

The model will be filled with appropriate data, using the **_db** in-memory database that you added to the **MockReadRepository** class. The **MockReadRepository** was injected to the **Membership** controller's constructor though the **IReadRepository** parameter, using dependency injection. You configured the DI in the **ConfigureServices** method in the **Startup** class.

Your next task will be to fill the view model using AutoMapper, mapping data from the **_db** database to DTO objects that can be used in views in coming chapters.

The **Video** view will display the selected video, information about the video, buttons to select the next and previous videos, and an instructor bio.

To refresh your memory, this is the view the **Video** action will display.

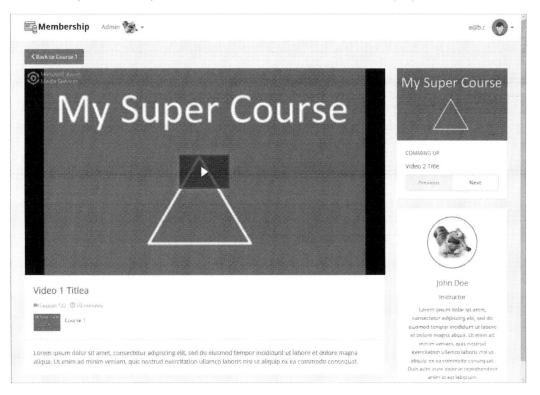

Video 1 Titlea

📹 Lesson 1/2 🕐 50 minutes

 Course 1

Lorem ipsum dolor sit amet, consectetur adipiscing elit, sed aliqua. Ut enim ad minim veniam, quis nostrud exercitation

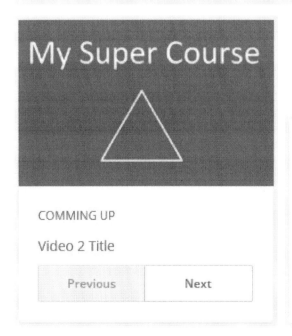

COMMING UP

Video 2 Title

Previous	Next

John Doe

Instructor

Lorem ipsum dolor sit amet, cupidatat non proident, sunt in culpa

1. Open the **MembershipController** class and locate the **Video** action method.
2. Call the **_db.GetVideo** method to fetch the video matching the id passed in to the **Video** action, and the logged in user's id. Store the result in a variable called **video**.

```
var video = _db.GetVideo(_userId, id);
```

3. Call the **_db.GetCourse** method to fetch the course matching the **CourseId** property in the **video** object, and the logged in user's id. Store the result in a variable called **course**.

```
var course = _db.GetCourse(_userId, video.CourseId);
```

4. Call the **_mapper.Map** method to convert the **Video** object into a **VideoDTO** object. Store the result in a variable named **mappedVideoDTO**.

```
var mappedVideoDTO = _mapper.Map<VideoDTO>(video);
```

5. Call the **_mapper.Map** method to convert the **course** object into a **CourseDTO** object. Store the result in a variable named **mappedCourseDTOs**.

```
var mappedCourseDTO = _mapper.Map<CourseDTO>(course);
```

6. Call the **_mapper.Map** method to convert the **Instructor** object in the **course** object into a **InstructorDTO** object. Store the result in a variable named **mappedInstructorDTO**.

```
var mappedInstructorDTO =
_mapper.Map<InstructorDTO>(course.Instructor);
```

7. Call the **_db.GetVideos** method to fetch all the videos matching the current module id. You need this data to get the number of videos in the module, and to get the index of the current video. Store the videos in a variable called **videos**.

```
var videos = _db.GetVideos(_userId, video.ModuleId).ToList();
```

8. Store the number of videos in a variable called **count**.

```
var count = videos.Count();
```

9. Find the index of the current video in the module video list. You will display the index and the video count to the user, in the view. Store the value in a variable called **index**.

```
var index = videos.IndexOf(video);
```

10. Fetch the id for the previous video in the module by calling the **ElementAtOrDefault** method on the **videos** collection. Store its id in a variable called **previousId**.

```
var previous = videos.ElementAtOrDefault(index - 1);
var previousId = previous == null ? 0 : previous.Id;
```

11. Fetch the id, title, and thumbnail for the next video in the module by calling the **ElementAtOrDefault** method on the **videos** collection. Store the values in variables called **nextId**, **nextTitle** and **nextThumb**.

```
var next = videos.ElementAtOrDefault(index + 1);
var nextId = next == null ? 0 : next.Id;
var nextTitle = next == null ? string.Empty : next.Title;
var nextThumb = next == null ? string.Empty : next.Thumbnail;
```

12. Create an instance of the **VideoViewModel** class named **videoModel**.

```
var videoModel = new VideoViewModel
{
};
```

13. Assign the three mapped collections: **mappedCourseDTOs**, **mappedInstructorDTO** and **mappedVideoDTOs** to the **videoModel** object's **Course**, **Instructor**, and **Video** properties. Create an instance of the **LessonInfoDTO** for the **LessonInfo** property in the **videoModel** object and assign the variable values to its properties. The **LessonInfoDTO** will be used with the previous and next buttons, and to display the index of the current video.

```
var videoModel = new VideoViewModel
{
    Video = mappedVideoDTO,
    Instructor = mappedInstructorDTO,
    Course = mappedCourseDTO,
    LessonInfo = new LessonInfoDTO
    {
        LessonNumber = index + 1,
        NumberOfLessons = count,
        NextVideoId = nextId,
        PreviousVideoId = previousId,
        NextVideoTitle = nextTitle,
        NextVideoThumbnail = nextThumb
    }
};
```

14. Return the **videoModel** object with the **View** method.

```
return View(videoModel);
```

15. Place a breakpoint on the return statement at the end of the **Video** action.
16. Run the application with debugging (F5).
17. Navigate to *http://localhost:xxxxx/Membership/Video/1* to hit the breakpoint.

18. Inspect the **videoModel** object to verify that it contains a video, a course, an instructor, and a lesson info object.
19. Stop the application in Visual Studio.

The complete code for the **Video** action:

```
[HttpGet]
public IActionResult Video(int id)
{
    var video = _db.GetVideo(_userId, id);
    var course = _db.GetCourse(_userId, video.CourseId);
    var mappedVideoDTO = _mapper.Map<VideoDTO>(video);
    var mappedCourseDTO = _mapper.Map<CourseDTO>(course);
    var mappedInstructorDTO =
        _mapper.Map<InstructorDTO>(course.Instructor);

    // Create a LessonInfoDto object
    var videos = _db.GetVideos(_userId, video.ModuleId).ToList();
    var count = videos.Count();
    var index = videos.IndexOf(video);
    var previous = videos.ElementAtOrDefault(index - 1);
    var previousId = previous == null ? 0 : previous.Id;
    var next = videos.ElementAtOrDefault(index + 1);
    var nextId = next == null ? 0 : next.Id;
    var nextTitle = next == null ? string.Empty : next.Title;
    var nextThumb = next == null ? string.Empty : next.Thumbnail;

    var videoModel = new VideoViewModel
    {
        Video = mappedVideoDTO,
        Instructor = mappedInstructorDTO,
        Course = mappedCourseDTO,
        LessonInfo = new LessonInfoDTO
        {
            LessonNumber = index + 1,
            NumberOfLessons = count,
            NextVideoId = nextId,
            PreviousVideoId = previousId,
            NextVideoTitle = nextTitle,
            NextVideoThumbnail = nextThumb
        }
    };
    return View(videoModel);
}
```

Summary

In this chapter, you added configuration for the entity and DTO classes to AutoMapper in the **Startup** class. You also implemented the **Membership** controller and injected the necessary objects into its constructor. Then you implemented the three actions (**Dashboard**, **Course**, and **Video**) that will be used when rendering their corresponding views in coming chapters.

Next, you will implement the **Dashboard** view, and render it from the **Dashboard** action.

18. The Dashboard View

Introduction

In this chapter, you will add a **Dashboard** view to the *Views/Membership* folder. It will be rendered by the **Dashboard** action in the **Membership** controller. This is the first view the user sees after logging in; it lists all the courses the user has access to.

The courses are displayed three to a row, to make them the optimal size.

Technologies Used in This Chapter

1. **HTML** – To create the view's layout.
2. **CSS** – To style the view.
3. **Razor –** To use C# in the view.

Overview

Your task is to use the view model in the **Dashboard** action to render a view that displays the user's courses in a list. Each course should be displayed as a panel with the course image, title, description, and a button that opens the **Course** view for that course.

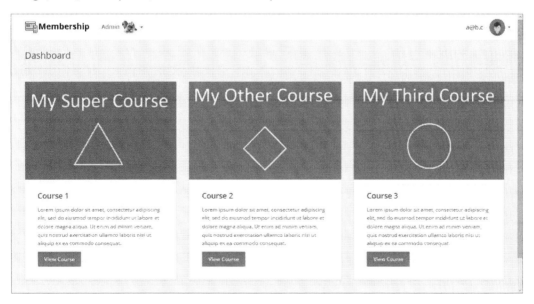

Implementing the Dashboard View

First, you will add the **Dashboard** view to the *Views/Membership* folder. Then you will add markup to the view, displaying the courses as panels. Looping over the courses in the view model, each panel will be rendered using a partial view called **_CoursePanelPartial**.

Adding the Dashboard View

To follow convention, the **Dashboard** view must reside in a folder named *Membership* located inside the *Views* folder. The convention states that a view must have the same name as the action displaying it, and it must be placed in a folder with the same name as the controller, inside the *Views* folder.

1. Open the **Membership** controller.
2. Right click on, or in, the **Dashboard** action and select **Add View** in the context menu. You might have to close the controller and open it again for the menu option to become available.
3. You can keep the preselected values and click the **Add** button. This will add the necessary *Membership* folder to the *Views* folder, and scaffold the **Dashboard** view.

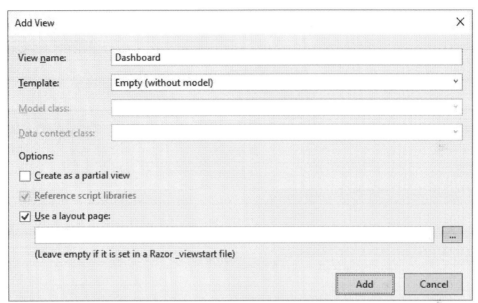

4. Open the *Views* folder and verify that the *Membership* folder and **Dashboard** view have been created.
5. Visual Studio can get confused when a view is scaffolded, and display errors that aren't real. Close the view and open it again to get rid of those errors.
6. Open the **_ViewImports** view and add a **using** statement for the **VideoOnDemand.Models.MembershipViewModels** namespace, to get access to the **DashboardViewModel** class.
   `@using VideoOnDemand.Models.MembershipViewModels`
7. Add an **@model** directive for the **DashboardViewModel** class at the beginning of the view.
   `@model DashboardViewModel`
8. Open the **HomeController** class and locate the **Index** action.

9. Replace the **View** method call in the **return** statement with a redirect to the **Dashboard** action in the **Membership** controller.
```
return RedirectToAction("Dashboard", "Membership");
```

10. Start the application without debugging (Ctrl+F5) and Login if necessary. The text *Dashboard* should be displayed in the browser if the **Dashboard** view was rendered correctly.

The markup in the **Dashboard** view:

```
@model DashboardViewModel

@{
    ViewData["Title"] = "Dashboard";
}

<h2>Dashboard</h2>
```

The complete code for the **Index** action in the **Home** controller:

```
public IActionResult Index()
{
    if (!_signInManager.IsSignedIn(User))
        return RedirectToAction("Login", "Account");

    return RedirectToAction("Dashboard", "Membership");
}
```

Iterating Over the Courses in the Dashboard View

To display the courses three to a row, you have to add two **foreach** loops to the view. The outer loop iterates over the **Courses** collection (the parent collection) to create the rows, and the inner loop iterates over the (three) courses on that row.

For now, the view will only display a view title and the course titles; later the courses will be displayed here as panels.

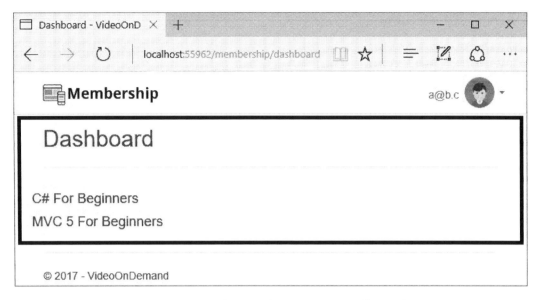

1. Add a CSS class called **text-dark** to the <h2>. You will use this class later to change the text color to a dark gray. Note that the class name isn't **dark-gray** or **gray**; If you name it text-dark, you don't have to remove or rename the class if the color or font weight is changed.

    ```
    <h2 class="text-dark">Dashboard</h2>
    ```

2. Add a <div> element around the <h2> element. Add two CSS classes called **membership** and **top-margin** to the <div>. The **membership** class is the main class for all *membership* views. The **top-margin** class will be used to add a top margin to all *membership* views.

    ```
    <div class="membership top-margin ">
        <h2 class="text-dark">Dashboard</h2>
    </div>
    ```

3. Add a horizontal line below the <h2> element. Add two CSS classes called **thick** and **margin** to the <hr> element. These classes will be used to make the line thicker and give it a margin.

    ```
    <hr class="thick margin">
    ```

4. Add a **foreach** loop, below the <hr> element that iterates over the **Course** collection in the view model. This loop represents the rows containing the course panels, where each row should have at most tree courses.

    ```
    @foreach (var dashboardRow in Model.Courses) { }
    ```

5. Add a <div> inside the loop and decorate it with the **row** Bootstrap class. The **row** class will style the <div> as a new row in the browser.
```
<div class="row">
</div>
```

6. Add a **foreach** loop inside the <div> that iterates over the (three) courses on that row. For now, add an <h4> element displaying the course title.
```
@foreach (var course in dashboardRow)
{
    <h4>@course.CourseTitle</h4>
}
```

7. Switch to the browser and refresh the **Dashboard** view (*/membership/dashboard*). The course titles should be displayed below the view's title.

The markup in the **Dashboard** view, so far:

```
@model DashboardViewModel

@{
    ViewData["Title"] = "Dashboard";
}

<div class="membership top-margin">
    <h2 class="text-dark">Dashboard</h2>
    <hr class="thick margin">
    @foreach (var dashboardRow in Model.Courses)
    {
        <div class="row">
            @foreach (var course in dashboardRow)
            {
                <h4>@course.CourseTitle</h4>
            }
        </div>
    }
</div>
```

Creating the _CoursePanelPartial Partial View

Instead of cluttering the **Dashboard** view with the course panel markup, you will create a partial view called **_CoursePanelPartial** that will be rendered for each course. A Bootstrap **panel** will be used to display the course information.

1. Right click on the *Views/Membership* folder and select **Add-View**.
2. Name the view **_CoursePanelPartial** and check the **Create as partial view** checkbox before clicking the **Add** button.

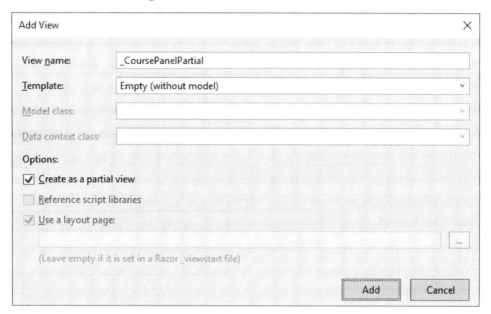

3. Delete all code in the view.
4. Open the **_ViewImports** view and add a **using** statement for the **VideoOnDemand.Models.DTOModels** namespace.
    ```
    @using VideoOnDemand.Models.DTOModels
    ```

5. Add an **@model** directive for the **CourseDTO** class. Save, close and open the partial view.
    ```
    @model CourseDTO
    ```

6. Add a <div> element and decorate it with the **col-sm-4** Bootstrap class, to give it 1/3 of the row space. The **col-sm-** classes have to add up to 12 on a row, and since 3 courses are added to each row, that is fulfilled.
    ```
    <div class="col-sm-4">
    </div>
    ```

7. Add a <div> inside the previous <div> and decorate it with the Bootstrap **panel** class to style it as a panel, the outer most container for the course information.

Also add a CSS class called **course-listing**. It will act as a main selector, for specificity, and to keep the styles separate from other styles.

```
<div class="panel course-listing">
</div>
```

8. Add an <img> element decorated with a CSS class called **thumb** to the previous <div>. The class will be used when styling the image. Add the **CourseImageUrl** property in the view model as the image source.

```
<img class="thumb" src="@Model.CourseImageUrl">
```

9. Add a <div> element below the image and decorate it with the **panel-body** Bootstrap class. This is the area where the video information is displayed.

```
<div class="panel-body">
</div>
```

10. Add an <h3> element in the previous <div> and decorate it with a CSS class named **text-dark**. Add the **CourseTitle** property in the view model to it.

```
<h3 class="text-dark">@Model.CourseTitle</h3>
```

11. Add a <p> element for the **CourseDescription** view model property below the <h3> element.

```
<p>@Model.CourseDescription</p>
```

12. Add an <a> element below the description and style it as a blue button with the **btn btn-primary** Bootstrap classes. Use the **CourseId** view model property in the **href** URL to determine which course will be fetched by the **Course** action, and displayed by the **Course** view. Add the text *View Course* to the button.

```
<a class="btn btn-primary"
href="~/Membership/Course/@Model.CourseId">View Course</a>
```

13. Open the **Dashboard** view.

14. Replace the <h4> element with a call to the **PartialAsync** method that will render the **_CoursePanelPartial** partial view for each course.

```
@foreach (var course in dashboardRow)
{
    @await Html.PartialAsync("_CoursePanelPartial", course)
}
```

15. Save all files and refresh the **Dashboard** view in the browser. As you can see, the view needs styling, which will be your next task.

258

The complete markup for the **_CoursePanelPartial** partial view:

```
@model CourseDto

<div class="col-sm-4">
    <div class="panel course-listing">
        <img class="thumb" src="@Model.CourseImageUrl">
        <div class="panel-body">
            <h3 class="title text-dark">@Model.CourseTitle</h3>
            <p class="desc">@Model.CourseDescription</p>
            <div class="bottom-aligned">
                <a class="btn btn-primary learn-more"
                    href="~/Membership/Course/@Model.CourseId">
                    View Course
                </a>
            </div>
        </div>
    </div>
</div>
```

Styling the Dashboard View and the _CoursePanelPartial Partial View

Now, you will use the CSS classes you added to the **Dashboard** view and the **_CoursePanel-Partial** partial view, to style them with CSS. To do that, you will add two CSS style sheets called *membership.css* and *course-panel.css*. The *membership.css* file will contain CSS selectors that are reused in all the *Membership* views.

1. Right click on the *wwwroot/css* folder and select **Add-New Item**.
2. Select the **Style Sheet** template.
3. Name the style sheet *membership.css* and click the **Add** button.
4. Repeat steps 1-3 for the *course-panel.css* style sheet.
5. Open the *bundleconfig.json* file and add links to the files.
   ```
   "inputFiles": [
       "wwwroot/css/site.css",
       "wwwroot/css/login.css",
       "wwwroot/css/menu.css",
       "wwwroot/css/membership.css",
       "wwwroot/css/course-panel.css"
   ]
   ```
6. Open the **_Layout** view and add a link to the files in the **Development** <environment> element inside the <head> element.
   ```
   <link rel="stylesheet" href="~/css/membership.css" />
   ```

```
<link rel="stylesheet" href="~/css/course-panel.css" />
```

Add the following CSS selectors one at a time to the *membership.css* file and save it. Refresh the browser and observe the changes.

Add a 25px top margin to the main <div> in the **Dashboard** view.

```
.membership.top-margin {
    margin-top: 25px;
}
```

Change the <h2> header color to a dark gray and make the font size smaller.

```
.membership h2 {
    font-size: 1.5em;
}
```

```
.membership .text-dark {
    color: #454c56 !important;
}
```

Change the color of the horizontal line to a light gray and make it thicker. Set its top margin to 15px and its bottom margin to 25px.

```
.membership hr {
    border-top: 1px solid #dadada;
}
```

```
.membership hr.thick {
    border-top-width: 2px;
}
```

```
.membership hr.margin {
    margin: 15px 0 25px;
}
```

Make the font size smaller and the font bold for all <h3> elements. This will affect the course title in the **Dashboard** view.

```
.membership h3 {
    font-size: 1.25em;
    font-weight: 600;
}
```

Make the font size smaller and the line height larger for all <p> and <a> elements. This will affect the course description and the buttons in the *Membership* views.

```css
.membership p, .membership a {
    font-size: 0.875em;
    font-weight: 400;
    line-height: 1.6;
}
```

Style the **btn-primary** Bootstrap buttons in the *Membership* views to have a lighter blue color, more padding, smaller border radius, larger font-weight, and no border or outline.

```css
.membership a.btn {
    font-weight: 800;
    padding: 9px 15px;
    border-radius: 2px;
}

.membership a.btn.btn-primary {
    background-color: #2d91fb;
    outline: none;
    border: none;
}

.membership a.btn.btn-primary:hover {
    background-color: #0577f0;
    border-color: #0577f0;
}
```

Change the font to Google's Open Sans for the entire application. If you want other font settings, you can create your own CSS link at Google.

Add a link to the Google font in the **_Layout** view's <head> element.

1. Open the **_Layout** view.
2. Add the font link to the <head> element.
   ```html
   <link href="https://fonts.googleapis.com/css?
       family=Open+Sans:400,400i,600,600i" rel="stylesheet">
   ```
3. Open the *membership.css* file in the *wwwroot/css* folder.
4. Add the **Open Sans** font family to the **body** selector.
   ```css
   body {
   ```

```
        font-family: "Open Sans", sans-serif;
        ...
    }
```

5. Add the **background-color** property to the **body** selector and change the background color to light gray.
   ```
   background-color: #f2f2f2;
   ```

6. Save the files.

Add the following CSS selectors one at a time to the *course-panel.css* file and save it. Refresh the browser and observe the changes.

Change the size of the course thumbnails in the **_CoursePanelPartial** partial view so that they fit in the panel.

```
.course-listing.panel .thumb {
    width: 100%;
    height: auto;
}
```

Add padding to the panel to make the text area look more uniform.

```
.course-listing.panel .panel-body {
    padding: 10px 30px 30px 30px;
}
```

Style the panel with a small border radius to make it look more square, and add a box shadow to lift it from the background. Remove the border to avoid displaying a thin white border around the panel.

```
.course-listing.panel {
    border: none;
    border-radius: 2px;
    box-shadow: 0 2px 5px 0 rgba(0, 0, 0, 0.1);
}
```

Summary

In this chapter, you added the **Dashboard** view and the **_CoursePanelPartial** partial view, and styled them with CSS and Bootstrap.

Next, you will add the **Course** view and the **_ModuleVideosPartial** and **_InstructorBio-Partial** partial views that are part of the **Course** view. Then you will style them with CSS and Bootstrap.

19. The Course View

Introduction

In this chapter, you will add the **Course** view and three partial views called **_Module-VideosPartial**, **_ModuleDownloadsPartial**, and **_InstructorBioPartial** that are part of the **Course** view. As you add view and partial view content, you style it with CSS and Bootstrap. The **Course** view is displayed when the user clicks one of the **Dashboard** view's course panel buttons. The view contains information about the selected course and has module lists containing all the videos belonging to that course. The instructor's bio is displayed beside the module lists. You will also add a button at the top of the view that takes the user back to the **Dashboard** view.

Technologies Used in This Chapter
1. **HTML** – To create the view's layout.
2. **CSS** – To style the view.
3. **Razor** – To use C# in the view.

Overview

Your task is to use the view model in the **Course** action and render a view that displays a marquee, course image, title, and description as a separate row below the *Back to Dashboard* button at the top of the view. Below that row, a second row divided into two columns should be displayed. Add rows in the left column for each module in the course, and list the videos for each module. Display the instructor's bio in the right column.

Adding the Course View

First, you will add the **Course** view to the *Views/Membership* folder.

Then, you will add a button that navigates to the **Dashboard** view, a marquee with a course image, course information, an instructor bio, and modules with videos and downloads. You will create three partial views, one called **_InstructorBioPartial** for the instructor bio, one called **_ModuleVideosPartial** for the videos, and one called **_ModuleDownloads-Partial** for downloads. The three areas will then be styled with Bootstrap and CSS.

1. Open the **Membership** controller.
2. Right click on the **Course** action and select **Add-View**.
3. Make sure that the **Create as partial view** checkbox is unchecked.
4. Click the **Add** button to create the view.

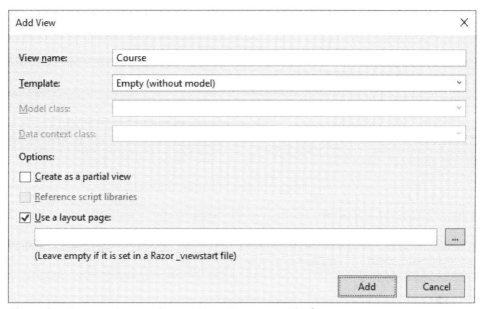

5. Close the **Course** view and open it again to get rid of any errors.
6. Add an **@model** directive for the **CourseViewModel** class at the beginning of the view.
   ```
   @model CourseViewModel
   ```
7. Save all the files. Close the **Course** view and open it again.
8. Start the application without debugging (Ctrl+F5) and navigate to *Membership/Dashboard*. Open a course by clicking on one of the panel buttons, or navigate to the *Membership/Course/1* URL. The text *Course* should be displayed in the browser if the **Course** view was rendered correctly.

The markup in the **Course** view, so far:

```
@model CourseViewModel

@{
    ViewData["Title"] = "Course";
}

<h2>Course</h2>
```

Adding the Back to Dashboard Button

Now, you will add the button that takes the user back to the **Dashboard** view. The button should be placed inside a <div> decorated with three CSS classes called **membership, top-margin**, and **course-content**, which will be used later for styling.

The button should be placed on a separate row that takes up the full page width. Add the **row** and **col-sm-12** Bootstrap classes to two nested <div> elements to add the row and the column.

1. Open the **Course** view.
2. Remove the <h2> heading.
3. Add a <div> element and decorate it with the three CSS classes: **membership, top-margin**, and **course-content**.
   ```
   <div class="membership top-margin course-content">
   </div>
   ```
4. Add the row with a <div> element, place it inside the previous <div>, and decorate it with the **row** Bootstrap class and a CSS class called **navigation-bar**. The latter class will be used to add margin to the row.
   ```
   <div class="row navigation-bar">
   </div>
   ```
5. Add the column with a <div> element, place it inside the previous <div>, and decorate it with the **col-sm-12** Bootstrap class to make it as wide as possible.
   ```
   <div class="col-sm-12">
   </div>
   ```
6. Add a blue button using an <a> element decorated with the **btn** and **btn-primary** Bootstrap classes. Add the path to the **Dashboard** view in the **href** attribute.
   ```
   <a class="btn btn-primary" href="~/Membership/Dashboard"></a>
   ```

7. Add a <span> inside the <a> element and decorate it with the Glyphicon classes to add an arrow (<) icon. Add the text *Back to Dashboard* after the <span> in the <a> element.

```
<a class="btn btn-primary" href="~/Membership/Dashboard">
    <span class="glyphicon glyphicon-menu-left"></span>
    Back to Dashboard
</a>
```

8. Save the view and refresh it in the browser. A blue button with the text < *Back to Dashboard* should be visible at the top of the view.
9. Click the button to navigate to the **Dashboard** view.
10. Click the button in one of the panels in the **Dashboard** view to get back to the **Course** view.

The markup in the **Course** view, so far:

```
@model CourseViewModel

@{
    ViewData["Title"] = "Course";
}

<div class="membership top-margin course-content">
    <div class="row navigation-bar">
        <div class="col-sm-12">
            <a class="btn btn-primary" href="~/Membership/Dashboard">
                <span class="glyphicon glyphicon-menu-left"></span>
                Back to Dashboard
            </a>
        </div>
    </div>
</div>
```

Adding the Course.css Style Sheet

To style the **Course** view and its partial views, you need to add a CSS style sheet called *course.css* to the *wwwroot/css* folder and a link to the file in the **_Layout** view.

1. Right click on the *wwwroot/css* folder and select **Add-New Item**.
2. Select the Style Sheet template and name the file *course.css*.
3. Click the **Add** button to create the file.

4. Open the **_Layout** view and add a link to the file in the **Development** <environment> element.

   ```
   <link rel="stylesheet" href="~/css/course.css" />
   ```

5. Open the *bundleconfig.json* file and add a link to the file.

   ```
   "wwwroot/css/course.css"
   ```

6. Remove the **body** selector in the *course.css* file.

7. Save the files.

Adding the Course Information to the View

Now, you will add markup for the course information panel and style it with Bootstrap and CSS.

The panel should be placed on a separate row that takes up the full page width. Add the Bootstrap **row** and **col-sm-12** classes to two nested <div> elements. This will create a row and a column. Use the **panel** and **panel-body** Bootstrap classes to style the panel <div> elements.

Use a <div> to display the marquee image as a background image inside the panel.

Add the course title as an <h1> element and the course description as an <h4> element inside the **panel-body** <div>.

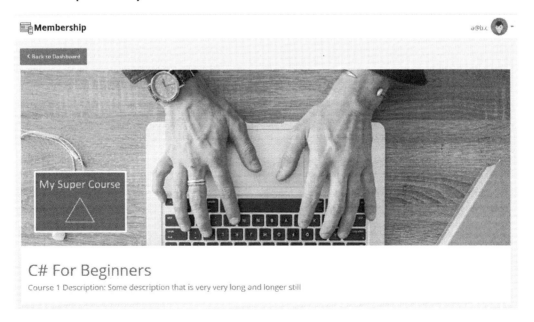

1. Open the **Course** view.
2. Add three nested <div> elements below the button <div> inside the *membership* <div>. Decorate the first with the Bootstrap **row** class, the second with the **col-sm-12** class, and the third with the **panel** class.

```
<div class="row">
    <div class="col-sm-12">
        <div class="panel course-content">
        </div>
    </div>
</div>
```

3. Add a <div> inside the **panel** <div> and decorate it with a CSS class called **marquee**. Add the **background-image** style to it and use the **Course.MarqueeImageUrl** property to get the course's marquee image. Call the **url** method to ensure a correctly formatted URL.

```
<div class="marquee" style="background-image:
    url('@Model.Course.MarqueeImageUrl');">
</div>
```

4. Add an <img> element for the **Course.CourseImageUrl** property inside the **marquee** <div>; decorate it with a CSS class called **cover-image**.

```
<div class="marquee" style="background-image:
    url('@Model.Course.MarqueeImageUrl');">
    <img src="@Model.Course.CourseImageUrl" class="cover-image">
</div>
```

5. Add a <div> below the **marquee** <div> inside the **panel** <div>. Decorate it with the **panel-body** Bootstrap class. This is the area where the course title and description are displayed.

```
<div class="panel-body">
</div>
```

6. Add an <h1> element for the **Course.CourseTitle** property and an <h4> element for the **Course.CourseDescription** property inside the **panel-body** <div>.

The markup for the course information row in the **Course** view:

```
<div class="row">
    <div class="col-sm-12">
        <div class="panel course-content">
            <div class="marquee" style="background-image:
                url('@Model.Course.MarqueeImageUrl');">
```

```
            <img src="@Model.Course.CourseImageUrl"
                class="cover-image">
        </div>
        <div class="panel-body">
            <h1>@Model.Course.CourseTitle</h1>
            <h4 class="product-desc">
                @Model.Course.CourseDescription</h4>
        </div>
    </div>
</div>
</div>
```

Styling the Course Information Section

Now, you will style the course information panel with Bootstrap and CSS.

Open the *course.css* file and add a 10px bottom margin to the button row, using the **navigation-bar** class that you added to it.

```
.navigation-bar {
    margin-bottom: 10px;
}
```

Now, style the marquee. Make it cover the entire width of its container, give it a height of 400px, and hide any overflow. The marquee position has to be relative for the course image to be positioned correctly. Make the background image cover the entire available space.

```
.course-content .marquee {
    width: 100%;
    height: 400px;
    overflow: hidden;
    position: relative; /* Is needed for the cover image's absolute
position */
    background-size: cover;
}
```

Now, style the cover image by making its width automatic and the height 140px. Use absolute positioning to place the image at the bottom of the marquee. Add a 30px margin to move the image away from the marquee borders. Add a 4px solid white border around the image and give it a subtle border radius of 2px.

```css
.course-content .marquee .cover-image {
    width: auto;
    height: 140px;
    position: absolute;
    bottom: 0;
    margin: 30px;
    border: 4px solid #FFF;
    border-radius: 2px;
}
```

Open the *membership.css* file and add the following style to override the color for the <h1> and <h4> elements in the *Membership* views.

Change the color to a light gray for the <h1> and <h4> elements in the *Membership* views.

```css
.membership h1, .membership h4 {
    color: #666c74;
}
```

Adding Columns for the Modules and the Instructor Bio

Before you can add the modules and the instructor bio, you need to create a new row divided into two columns, below the marquee. Add the **row, col-sm-9**, and **col-sm-3** Bootstrap classes to nested <div> elements, to create the row and columns.

1. Open the **Course** view and add a <div> element decorated with the **row** Bootstrap class below the previous row.

   ```html
   <div class="row">
   </div>
   ```

2. Add two <div> elements inside the **row** <div>. Decorate the first <div> with the **col-sm-9** Bootstrap class, and the second with the **col-sm-3** class. This will make the first column take up ¾ of the row width and the second column ¼ of the row width.

   ```html
   <div class="col-md-9">
       @*Add modules here*@
   </div>
   <div class="col-md-3">
       @*Add instructor bio here*@
   </div>
   ```

The markup for the row and columns in the **Course** view:

```
<div class="row">
    <div class="col-sm-9">
        @*Add modules here*@
    </div>
    <div class="col-sm-3">
        @*Add instructor bio here*@
    </div>
</div>
```

Adding the Modules

To display the videos and downloads, you first have to add the modules they are associated with. The modules should be displayed below the marquee and take up ¾ of the row width. Use Razor to add a **foreach** loop that iterates over the **Modules** collection in the view model, and adds a Bootstrap panel for each module. Display the **ModuleTitle** for each module in the **panel-body** section.

1. Open the **Course** view.
2. Locate the <div> decorated with the **col-sm-9** Bootstrap class and add a **foreach** loop, which iterates over the view model's **Modules** collection.
   ```
   @foreach (var module in Model.Modules)
   {
   }
   ```
3. Add a <div> decorated with the Bootstrap **panel** class inside the loop to create a module container for each module in the collection. Add another CSS class called **module**; it will be the parent selector for the panel's intrinsic elements.
   ```
   <div class="panel module">
   </div>
   ```
4. Add a <div> inside the **panel** <div> and decorate it with the **panel-body** Bootstrap class. Add an <h5> element containing the **ModuleTitle** property.
   ```
   <div class="panel-body">
       <h5>@module.ModuleTitle</h5>
   </div>
   ```
5. Save the files and refresh the browser. The module titles for the course you selected should be listed below the marquee.

The markup for the module panels:

```
<div class="col-sm-9">
    @foreach (var module in Model.Modules)
    {
        <div class="panel module">
            <div class="panel-body">
                <h5>@module.ModuleTitle</h5>
            </div>
        </div>
    }
</div>
```

Adding the Videos

To display the video items for the modules, you will create a partial view called **_Module-VideosPartial** that will be rendered for each video. Pass in the **Video** collection from the current module in the **Course** view's **foreach** loop, to the partial view.

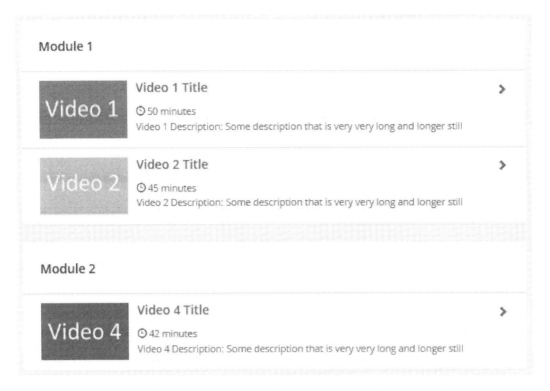

Use the Bootstrap **media** classes to display the video information in a uniform way.

1. Add a partial view called **_ModuleVideosPartial** to the *Views/Membership* folder.
2. Open the **Course** view.
3. Add an if-block that checks that the current module's **Videos** collection isn't null, below the previously added **panel-body** <div>. Pass in the **Video** collection from the current module to the **PartialAsync** method that renders the partial view, and displays the videos.

   ```
   @if (module.Videos != null)
   {
       @await Html.PartialAsync("_ModuleVideosPartial",
           module.Videos)
   }
   ```
4. Open the **_ModuleVideosPartial** view.
5. Add an **@model** directive to an **IEnumerable<VideoDTO>**.

   ```
   @model IEnumerable<VideoDTO>
   ```

6. Add a **foreach** loop that iterates over the view model.
```
@foreach (var video in Model)
{
}
```

7. Add a <div> element decorated with the **panel-body** Bootstrap class and a CSS class called **module-video**, inside the loop. The CSS class will be used for styling later. The <div> will be a container for a single video.
```
<div class="panel-body module-video">
</div>
```

8. Add an <a> element with an **href** attribute that opens a specific video to the **Video** view that you will add later. Use the current video's **Id** property to target the correct video in the **href**. Add the current video's **Title** property to the <a> element.
```
<a href="~/Membership/Video/@video.Id">
    @video.Title
</a>
```

9. Save all files and refresh the **Course** view in the browser. Each module should now have its videos listed as links. The links will not work because you haven't added the **Video** view yet.

10. Replace the **Title** property with a <div> decorated with the **media** Bootstrap class. This will format the content in a specific way, displaying an image to the left and a block of information to the right.
```
<div class="media">
</div>
```

11. Add the left (image) area to the **media** <div> by adding a <div> decorated with the **media-left** Bootstrap class. Add an additional Bootstrap class called **hidden-xs**, which will hide this <div> if the site is viewed on a smartphone or a small handheld device. You typically don't want to send large images to smartphones because they tend to take a long time to load.
```
<div class="media-left hidden-xs">
</div>
```

12. Add the video thumbnail to a <div> decorated with a CSS class called **thumb-container**. Use the image URL in the current video's **Thumbnail** property for the <img> element's **src** property.

```
<div class="thumb-container">
    <img src="@video.Thumbnail" class="thumb">
</div>
```

13. Save the files and refresh the **Course** view in the browser. Large thumbnail images will be displayed for each video; you will change that with CSS styling later.

14. Add a <div> decorated with the **media-body** Bootstrap class below the **media-left** <div>. This will be the (right) video information area.
```
<div class="media-body">
</div>
```

15. Add an <h5> element for the video title inside the **media-body** <div>. Add the view model's **Title** property to the element.
```
<h5>@video.Title</h5>
```

16. Add a <p> element decorated with a CSS class called **text-light** below the title. The CSS class will be used to display the video's length with a muted font. Add an <i> element for a watch Glyphicon; use the **glyphicon-time** class. Add the duration from the current video's **Duration** property followed by the text *minutes* after the <i> element.
```
<p class="text-light">
    <i class="glyphicon glyphicon-time"></i>
    @video.Duration minutes
</p>
```

17. Add the video description in a <p> element below the duration; use the current video's **Description** property.
```
<p>@video.Description</p>
```

18. Add a chevron icon to the right of each video item, to show that it can be opened. Add a Glyphicon inside a <div> decorated with the **media-right** and **hidden-xs** Bootstrap classes below the video description. Make the chevron muted by adding the **text-light** CSS class to it.
```
<div class="media-right hidden-xs text-light">
    <i class="glyphicon glyphicon-chevron-right"></i>
</div>
```

19. If you refresh the **Course** view in the browser, the video items would still only display one gigantic thumbnail image.

Next, you will style the partial view.

The complete markup for the **_ModuleVideosPartial** view:

```
@model IEnumerable<VideoDTO>

@foreach (var video in Model)
{
    <div class="panel-body module-video">
        <a href="~/Membership/Video/@video.Id">
            <div class="media">
                <div class="media-left hidden-xs">
                    <div class="thumb-container">
                        <img src="@video.Thumbnail" class="thumb">
                    </div>
                </div>
                <div class="media-body">
                    <h5>@video.Title</h5>
                    <p class="text-light">
                        <i class="glyphicon glyphicon-time"></i>
                        @video.Duration minutes
                    </p>
                    <p>@video.Description</p>
                </div>
                <div class="media-right hidden-xs text-light">
                    <i class="glyphicon glyphicon-chevron-right"></i>
                </div>
            </div>
        </a>
    </div>
}
```

Styling the _ModuleVideosPartial View

Before you start styling the **_ModuleVideosPartial** view, you need to add a new CSS Style Sheet called *module.css*. It will be used when styling the module section of the **Course** view.

1. Add a style sheet called *module.css* to the *wwwroot/css* folder.
2. Add a link to it in the **Development** <environment> element in the **_Layout** view.
3. Add a link to it in the *bundleconfig.json* file.

Add 10px top and bottom padding and 20px left and right padding to the modules **panel-body** elements.

```
.panel.module .panel-body {
    padding: 10px 20px;
}
```

Change the font weight to 600 for the module titles.

```
.module .panel-body h5 {
    font-weight: 600;
}
```

Add a 1px solid top border to the **module-video** <div> to separate the video items in the list.

```
.module-video {
    border-top: 1px solid #dadada;
}
```

Hide any overflow in the thumbnail image container and make it 100px wide. This means that the image can't be any wider than its container.

```
.module-video .thumb-container {
    overflow: hidden;
    width: 100px;
}
```

Make the thumbnail image as wide as it can be in its container.

```
.module-video .thumb {
    width: 100%;
}
```

Remove the top margin from the video title.

```
.module-video h5 {
    margin-top: 0;
}
```

Change the link color to gray and remove the text decoration (underlining) from the links.

```
.module-video a {
    color: #666c74;
    text-decoration: none;
}
```

Remove the bottom margin for all paragraphs in the **module-video** container.

```
.module-video p {
    margin-bottom: 0;
}
```

Adding the Downloads

To display the downloads in each module, you will create a partial view called **_Module-DownloadsPartial** that will be rendered for each download link. Pass in the **Downloads** collection from the current module in the **Course** view's **foreach** loop, to the partial view.

Use the Bootstrap **panel** classes to display the download information in a uniform way.

1. Add a partial view called **_ModuleDownloadsPartial** to the *Views/Membership* folder.
2. Open the **Course** view.
3. Add an if-block checking that the current module's **Downloads** collection isn't null, below the *videos* if-block.
   ```
   @if (module.Downloads != null)
   {
   }
   ```

4. Add a horizontal line inside the if-block for the **Downloads** collection.
```
<hr class="no-margin">
```

5. Add a <div> decorated with the **panel-body** Bootstrap class below the <hr> element inside the if-block. Add a CSS class called **download-panel** to the <div>; this class will be used as a parent selector when styling the partial view.
```
<div class="panel-body download-panel"></div>
```

6. Add an <h5> element with the text *Downloads* inside the previous <div>.
```
<h5>Downloads</h5>
```

7. Render the partial view below the <h5> element. Pass in the **Downloads** collection from the current module to the **PartialAsync** method, which renders the **_ModuleDownloadsPartial** and displays the download links.
```
@await Html.PartialAsync("_ModuleDownloadsPartial",
module.Downloads)
```

8. Open the **_ModuleDownloadsPartial** view.

9. Add an **@model** directive to an **IEnumerable<DownloadDTO>**.
```
@model IEnumerable<DownloadDTO>
```

10. Add an unordered list (<ul>) below the **@model** directive.

11. Add a **foreach** loop that iterates over the view model in the <ul> element.
```
@foreach (var download in Model)
{
}
```

12. Add listitem (<li>) inside the loop.

13. Add an <a> element that uses the current download's **DownloadUrl** property in its **href** attribute, and opens the content in a separate browser tab. The <a> element should display a download Glyphicon and the text from the current download's **DownloadTitle** property.
```
<li>
    <a href="@download.DownloadUrl" target="_blank">
        <span class="glyphicon glyphicon-download-alt"></span>
         @download.DownloadTitle
    </a>
</li>
```

14. Save the files and refresh the **Course** view in the browser. A section with download links should be displayed in the module lists, where downloadable content is available.

Next, you will style the partial view.

The complete markup for the **_ModuleDownloadsPartial** view:

```
@model IEnumerable<DownloadDTO>

<ul>
    @foreach (var download in Model)
    {
        <li>
            <a href="@download.DownloadUrl" target="_blank">
                <span class="glyphicon glyphicon-download-alt"></span>
                 @download.DownloadTitle
            </a>
        </li>
    }
</ul>
```

The markup for rendering the **_ModuleDownloadsPartial** view in the **Course** view:

```
@if (module.Downloads != null)
{
    <hr class="no-margin">
    <div class="panel-body download-panel">
        <h5>Downloads</h5>
        @await Html.PartialAsync("_ModuleDownloadsPartial",
            module.Downloads)
    </div>
}
```

The complete code for the modules, videos, and downloads in the **Course** view:

```
<div class="col-sm-9">
@foreach (var module in Model.Modules)
{
    <div class="panel module">
        <div class="panel-body">
            <h5>@module.ModuleTitle</h5>
        </div>
        @if (module.Videos != null)
        {
            @await Html.PartialAsync("_ModuleVideosPartial",
                module.Videos)
        }
        @if (module.Downloads != null)
        {
```

```
            <hr class="no-margin">
            <div class="panel-body download-panel">
                <h5>Downloads</h5>
                @await Html.PartialAsync("_ModuleDownloadsPartial",
                    module.Downloads)
            </div>
        }
    </div>
}
</div>
```

Styling the _ModuleDownloadsPartial View

Open the *membership.css* style sheet and add a selector for the **no-margin** class on <hr> elements. It should remove all margins.

```
hr.no-margin {
    margin: 0;
}
```

Open the *module.css* style sheet and add a selector for <ul> elements in the <div> decorated with the **download-panel** class. Remove all bullet styles and add a 10px left padding.

```
.download-panel ul {
    list-style-type: none;
    padding-left: 10px;
}
```

Add a selector for <li> elements in the <div> decorated with the **download-panel** class. Add a 5px top margin and make the font size smaller.

```
.download-panel li {
    margin-top: 5px;
    font-size: 0.87em;
}
```

Adding the Instructor Bio

To display the instructor bio, you will create a partial view called **_InstructorBioPartial** that will be displayed to the right of the module lists in the **Course** view. Add the **PartialAsync** method inside the <div> decorated with the **col-sm-3** Bootstrap class in the **Course** View. Pass in the **Instructor** object from the view model to the method.

John Doe

Instructor

Lorem ipsum dolor sit amet,
pariatur. Excepteur sint occaecat
cupidatat non proident, sunt in culpa
qui officia deserunt mollit anim id est
laborum.

1. Add a partial view called **_InstructorBioPartial** to the *Views/Membership* folder.
2. Open the **Course** view.
3. Add an if-block inside the <div> decorated with the **col-sm-3** Bootstrap class.
   Check that the **Instructor** object in the view model isn't null, and pass in the
   Instructor object to the **PartialAsync** method that will render the partial view.

```
@if (Model.Instructor != null)
{
    @await Html.PartialAsync("_InstructorBioPartial",
        Model.Instructor)
}
```

4. Open the **_InstructorBioPartial** partial view.
5. Add an **@model** directive to the **InstructorDTO** class.

```
@model InstructorDTO
```

6. Add a <div> decorated with the **panel** Bootstrap class and a CSS class called
   instructor-bio. It will be the parent selector for this panel.

```
<div class="instructor-bio panel">
</div>
```

7. Add a <div> decorated with the **panel-body** Bootstrap class inside the **panel** <div>.
```
<div class="panel-body">
</div>
```

8. Add an <img> element inside the **panel-body** <div> for the **InstructorThumbnail** property in the view model. Decorate the <div> with the **img-circle** Bootstrap class and a CSS class called **avatar**. The **avatar** class will style the instructor's thumbnail.
```
<img src="@Model.InstructorThumbnail" class="avatar img-circle">
```

9. Add an <h4> element for the **InstructorName** property in the view model.
```
<h4>@Model.InstructorName</h4>
```

10. Add an <h5> element with the text *Instructor*. Decorate it with the **text-primary** Bootstrap class to make the text blue.
```
<h5 class="text-primary">Instructor</h5>
```

11. Add a <p> element for the view model's **InstructorDescription** property.
```
<p>@Model.InstructorDescription</p>
```

The complete code for the **_InstructorBioPartial** partial view:

```
@model InstructorDTO

<div class="instructor-bio panel">
    <div class="panel-body">
        <img src="@Model.InstructorAvatar" class="avatar img-circle">
        <h4>@Model.InstructorName</h4>
        <h5 class="text-primary">Instructor</h5>
        <p>@Model.InstructorDescription</p>
    </div>
</div>
```

Styling the _InstructorBioPartial Partial View

Before you start styling the **_InstructorBioPartial** view, you need to add a new CSS style sheet called *instructor-bio.css*. It will be used when styling the instructor bio section in the **Course** view.

1. Add a style sheet called *instructor-bio.css* to the *wwwroot/css* folder.
2. Add a link to it in the **Development** <environment> element in the **_Layout** view.
3. Add a link to it in the *bundleconfig.json* file.

Open the *instructor-bio* style sheet and center the text in the **instructor-bio** container.

```
.instructor-bio {
    text-align: center;
}
```

Style the avatar to have a blue circle with 8px padding around it and make the image diameter 120px. The circle is created with the **img-circle** Bootstrap class, which styles the border of an element.

```
.instructor-bio .avatar {
    border: 2px solid #2d91fb;
    padding: 8px;
    height: 120px;
    width: 120px;
}
```

Summary

In this chapter, you created the **Course** view and its three partial views: **_ModuleVideos-Partial**, **_ModuleDownloadsPartial**, and **_InstructorBioPartial**. You also used Bootstrap to create rows and columns in a responsive design, and styled the views with Bootstrap and CSS.

Next, you will create the **Video** view, where the actual video can be viewed.

20. The Video View

Introduction

In this chapter, you will create the **Video** view and two partial views called **_VideoComing-UpPartial** and **_VideoPlayerPartial**. You will also reuse the already created **_InstructorBio-Partial** partial view. The content will be styled with CSS and Bootstrap as you add it. The **Video** view is displayed when the user clicks one of the video links in the **Course** view, and it contains a button that takes the user back to the **Course** view, a video player, information about the selected video, buttons to select the next and previous video, and the instructor's bio.

Technologies Used in This Chapter

1. **HTML** – To create the view's layout.
2. **CSS** – To style the view.
3. **Razor** – To use C# in the view.
4. **JavaScript** – To display the video player and load the selected video.

Overview

Your task is to use the view model in the **Video** action and render a view that displays a course image, video duration, title, and description as a separate column, on a new row, below the *Back to Course* button at the top of the view. Beside the video player column, a second column should be added. The upper part should contain the **_VideoComingUp-Partial** partial view, and the lower part the **_InstructorBioPartial** partial view.

In this exercise, the JWPlayer video player is used, but you can use any video player you like that can play YouTube videos.

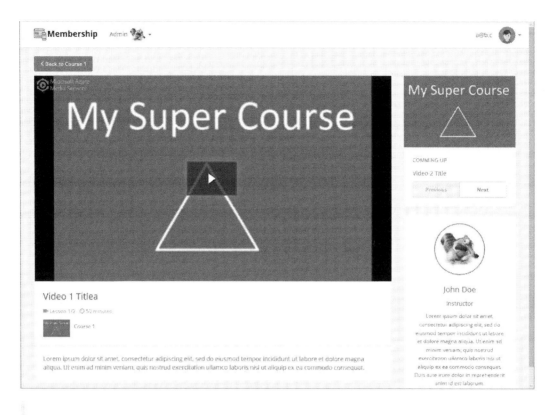

Video 1 Titlea

🎥 Lesson 1/2 🕐 50 minutes

 Course 1

Lorem ipsum dolor sit amet, consectetur adipiscing elit, sed
aliqua. Ut enim ad minim veniam, quis nostrud exercitation

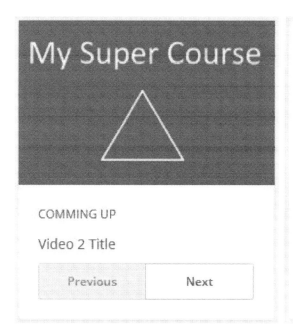

Adding the Video View

First, you will add the **Video** view to the *Views/Membership* folder.

Then, you will add a button that navigates to the **Course** view. The video player will be placed below the button, along with information about the video. To the right of the video player, in a separate column, the *Coming Up* section, with the **Previous** and **Next** buttons, will be displayed. Below that section, the instructor's bio will be displayed. You will create two partial views for the video player and the *Comin Up* section called **_VideoPlayerPartial** and **_VideoComingUpPartial**. Reuse the **_InstructorBioPartial** partial view to display the instructor's bio. The three areas will be styled with Bootstrap and CSS.

1. Open the **Membership** controller.
2. Right click on the **Video** action and select **Add-View**.
3. Make sure that the **Create as partial view** checkbox is unchecked.
4. Click the **Add** button to create the view.

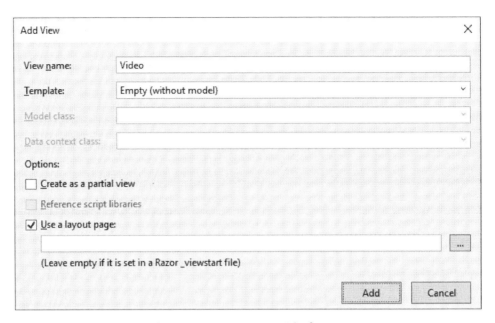

5. Close the **Video** view and open it again to get rid of any errors.
6. Add an **@model** directive for the **VideoViewModel** class at the beginning of the view.

   @model VideoViewModel

7. Save all the files.
8. Start the application without debugging (Ctrl+F5). Click on one of the courses in the **Dashboard** view and then on one of the video links in the **Course** view. The text *Video* should be displayed in the browser if the **Video** view was rendered correctly.

The markup in the **Video** view, so far:

```
@model VideoViewModel

@{
    ViewData["Title"] - "Video";
}

<h2>Video</h2>
```

Adding the Back to Course Button

Now, you will add a button that takes the user back to the **Course** view, and display the course the video belongs to.

1. Open the **Video** view.
2. Remove the <h2> element.
3. Add a <div> element decorated with three CSS classes called **membership**, **top-margin**, and **video-content**. You already have added CSS for the two first classes. The last class will act as the parent selector when styling the **Video** view and its partial views. The <div> will act as the parent container for the content in the **Video** view.
   ```
   <div class="membership top-margin video-content">
   </div>
   ```
4. Add two nested <div> elements decorated with the **row** and **col-sm-12** Bootstrap classes respectively. Add the **navigation-bar** CSS class to the **row** <div>; you added a selector for this class earlier, to add a bottom margin to the button.
   ```
   <div class="row navigation-bar">
       <div class="col-sm-12">
       </div>
   </div>
   ```
5. Add an <a> element inside the *column* <div> and decorate it with the **btn** and **btn-primary** Bootstrap classes, to turn the anchor tag into a blue button. Use the **Course.CourseId** property from the view model when creating the **href** link back to the **Course** view.
   ```
   <a class="btn btn-primary"
       href="~/Membership/Course/@Model.Course.CourseId">
   </a>
   ```
6. Add a <span> element for the **glyphicon-menu-left** Glyphicon inside the <a> element. Add the text *Back to* followed by the **Course.CourseTitle** property from the view model after the <span>.
   ```
   <span class="glyphicon glyphicon-menu-left"></span>
   Back to @Model.Course.CourseTitle
   ```
7. Start the application without debugging (Ctrl+F5). Click on a course button in the **Dashboard** view, and then on a video link in the **Course** view.

8. A blue button with the text *Back to ...* should be displayed at the top of the page. Click the button to get back to the **Course** View.
9. Click on a video link to get back to the **Video** view.

The complete code for the **Back to *Course*** button:

```
<div class="membership top-margin video-content">
    <div class="row navigation-bar">
        <div class="col-sm-12">
            <a class="btn btn-primary" href="~/Membership/Course/
                @Model.Course.CourseId">
                <span class="glyphicon glyphicon-menu-left"></span>
                Back to @Model.Course.CourseTitle
            </a>
        </div>
    </div>
</div>
```

Adding Row and Columns for the Video View Content

Now, you will use Bootstrap classes to add a row and columns that will hold the **Video** view's content.

1. Open the **Video** view.
2. Add a <div> element decorated with the **row** class, below the previous **row** <div>. Add two nested <div> elements decorated with the **col-sm-9** and **col-sm-3** classes respectively.

```
<div class="row">
    <div class="col-sm-9">
        @*Place the video player here*@
    </div>

    <div class="col-sm-3">
        @*Place the Coming Up and Instructor Bio sections here*@
    </div>
</div>
```

3. Save the file.

Adding the _VideoPlayerPartial Partial View

This partial view will display the panel containing the video player and its information.

1. Add a partial view called **_VideoPlayerPartial** to the *Views/membership* folder.

2. Delete all code in the view and save it.

3. Close and open the view to get rid of any errors.

4. Add an **@model** directive to the **VideoViewModel** class. The view needs the full view model to display all the information because the data is stored in several objects in the model.
   ```
   @model VideoViewModel
   ```

5. Add a <div> decorated with the **panel** Bootsrtap class below the **@model** directive.
   ```
   <div class="panel">
   </div>
   ```

6. Add an if-block inside the **panel** <div> that checks that the **Video.Url** property in the view model isn't null.
   ```
   @if (Model.Video.Url != null)
   {
   }
   ```

7. Add a <div> element inside the if-block with the **id** attribute set to **video**. This element will house the video player.
   ```
   <div id="video" class="video-margin"> </div>
   ```

8. Add two hidden <div> elements named **hiddenUrl** and **hiddenImageUrl** below the previous <div>. Add the **Video.Url** property to the **hiddenUrl** <div> and the **Video.Thumbnail** property to the **hiddenImageUrl** <div>. The hidden values will be read from JavaScript when the player is rendered.
   ```
   <div id="hiddenUrl" hidden="hidden">@Model.Video.Url</div>
   <div id="hiddenImageUrl" hidden="hidden">
       @Model.Video.Thumbnail</div>
   ```

9. Add a <div> decorated with the **panel-body** Bootstrap class below the if-block. This is the container for the video information.
   ```
   <div class="panel-body">
   </div>
   ```

10. Add an <h2> element for the **Video.Title** property from the view model inside the previous <div>. Decorate the element with the **text-dark** CSS class to make the title dark gray.

```
<h2 class="text-dark">@Model.Video.Title</h2>
```

11. Add a <p> element for the lesson information; decorate it with the **text-light** CSS class to make the text light gray. Add a video Glyphicon, display the video's position and the number of videos in the module, a time Glyphicon, and the video length followed by the text *minutes*. Use the **LessonInfo.LessonNumber** and **LessonInfo.NumberOfLessons** properties to display the video's position and the number of videos. Use the **Video.Duration** property to display how long the video is.

```
<p class="text-light">
    <i class="glyphicon glyphicon-facetime-video"></i>
    Lesson @Model.LessonInfo.LessonNumber/
        @Model.LessonInfo.NumberOfLessons  
    <i class="glyphicon glyphicon-time"></i>
    @Model.Video.Duration minutes
</p>
```

12. Add a <div> decorated with the **media-object** Bootstrap class. This is the container for the video thumbnail and the video title.

```
<div class="media-object">
</div>
```

13. Add an <img> element inside a <div> decorated with the **media-left** Bootstrap class. This will display the thumbnail to the left in the container. Use the **Course.CourseImageUrl** property in the **src** attribute.

```
<div class="media-left">
    <img src="@Model.Course.CourseImageUrl">
</div>
```

14. Add a <div> element decorated with the **media-body** and **media-middle** Bootstrap classes. This will be the container for the title displayed beside the thumbnail. Add the **Course.CourseTitle** property from the view model to a <p> element inside the <div>.

```
<div class="media-body media-middle">
    <p>@Model.Course.CourseTitle</p>
</div>
```

15. Add a horizontal line below the **panel-body** <div> and decorate it with the **no-margin** CSS class that you added a selector for earlier.
    ```
    <hr class="no-margin">
    ```

16. Add a <div> decorated with the **panel-body** Bootstrap class below the <hr> element. Add the **Video.Description** property from the view model to it.
    ```
    <div class="panel-body">
        @Model.Video.Description
    </div>
    ```

17. Open the **Video** view.

18. Add a call to the **PartialAsync** method to render the **_VideoPlayerPartial** partial view inside the <div> decorated with the **col-sm-9** Bootstrap class. Pass in the view model to the partial view. Surround the method call with an if-block that checks that the view model, **Video**, **LessonInfo**, and **Course** objects are not null, to ensure that the partial view only is rendered if there is sufficient data.
    ```
    <div class="col-sm-9">
        @if (Model != null && Model.Video != null &&
            Model.LessonInfo != null && Model.Course != null)
        {
            @await Html.PartialAsync("_VideoPlayerPartial", Model)
        }
    </div>
    ```

19. Save all the files and navigate to a video in the browser. You should see the video information and a huge thumbnail image.

Next, you will style the **_VideoPlayerPartial** partial view.

The complete code for the **_VideoPlayerPartial** partial view:

```
@model VideoViewModel

<div class="panel">
    @if (Model.Video.Url != null)
    {
        <div id="video" class="video-margin"> </div>
        <div id="hiddenUrl" hidden="hidden">@Model.Video.Url</div>
        <div id="hiddenImageUrl" hidden="hidden">
            @Model.Video.Thumbnail</div>
    }
```

```
    <div class="panel-body">
        <h2 class="text-dark">@Model.Video.Title</h2>
        <p class="text-light">
            <i class="glyphicon glyphicon-facetime-video"></i>
            Lesson @Model.LessonInfo.LessonNumber/
                @Model.LessonInfo.NumberOfLessons  
            <i class="glyphicon glyphicon-time"></i>
            @Model.Video.Duration minutes
        </p>
        <div class="media-object">
            <div class="media-left">
                <img src="@Model.Course.CourseImageUrl">
            </div>
            <div class="media-body media-middle">
                <p>@Model.Course.CourseTitle</p>
            </div>
        </div>
    </div>
    <hr class="no-margin">
    <div class="panel-body">
        @Model.Video.Description
    </div>
</div>
```

Styling the _VideoPlayerPartial Partial View

Before you start styling the **_VideoPlayerPartial** view, you need to add a new CSS style sheet called *video.css* that will be used when styling the **Video** view and its partial views.

1. Add a style sheet called *video.css* to the *wwwroot/css* folder.
2. Add a link to it in the **Development** <environment> element in the **_Layout** view.
3. Add a link to it in the *bundleconfig.json* file.

Open the *video.css* style sheet and make the video thumbnail's height 40px.

```
.video-content .media-left img {
    height: 40px;
}
```

Remove the video panel's border and border radius, to make it look more square.

```
.video-content .panel {
    border: none;
    border-radius: 0px;
}
```

Add JWPlayer

To play video with JWPlayer, you have to register with their site www.jwplayer.com and create a video player link that you add to the **_Layout** view. You also have to call the **jwplayer** JavaScript method in the view, to activate the video player.

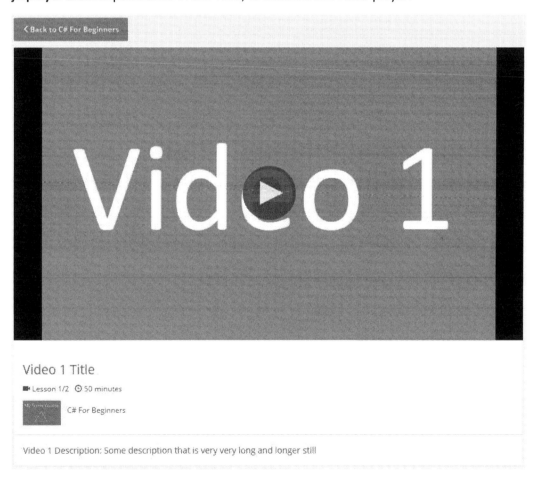

Video 1 Title

■ Lesson 1/2   ⏲ 50 minutes

   C# For Beginners

Video 1 Description: Some description that is very very long and longer still

Create a Video Player

1. Navigate to www.jwplayer.com and sign up for an account, and sign in.
2. Select the **Manage** link in the *Players* section of the menu.
3. Click the **Create New Player** button to create your video player.
4. Name the player in the text field; you can call it whatever you like.
5. Select the **Responsive** radio button in the *Basic Setup* section.
6. You can change other settings if you want, to customize the player more.
7. Click the **Save Changes** button.
8. Copy the link below the demo video player. This is the link that you will add to the **_Layout** view, to get access to the video player.

Add the Video Player to the Video View

1. Open the **_Layout** view.
2. Add the link you copied from the JWPlayer site to the two JavaScript <environment> elements at the bottom of the <body> element.
   ```
   <script src="https://content.jwplatform.com/libraries/7mEwgyci.js">
   </script>
   ```
3. Open the **Video** view.
4. Add a **Scripts** section at the bottom of the view where the **jwplayer** function is called as soon as the page has been loaded into the DOM.
   ```
   @section Scripts
   {
       <script type="text/javascript">
           $(function () {
               jwplayer("video").setup({
                   file: $("#hiddenUrl").text(),
                   image: $("#hiddenImageUrl").text()
   ```

```
            });
        });
    </script>
}
```

5. Save all files.
6. Refresh the **Video** view in the browser. The video image should be visible, and the video should start playing if you click on it.

Adding Properties to the LessonInfoDTO Class

There is one piece of information that you need to add to the **LessonInfoDTO** and the **Membership** controller. To avoid displaying an empty image container when the user navigates to the last video using the **Next** button in the *Coming Up* section, the current video's thumbnail should be displayed. You therefore have to include the current video's thumbnail and title in the **LessonInfoDTO** class and add that data to the view model in the **Video** action of the **Membership** controller.

1. Open the **LessonInfoDTO** class.
2. Add two **string** properties called **CurrentVideoTitle** and **CurrentVideoThumbnail**.
   ```
   public string CurrentVideoTitle { get; set; }
   public string CurrentVideoThumbnail { get; set; }
   ```

3. Open the **Membership** controller and locate the **Video** action.
4. Assign the thumbnail and title from the video object's **Thumbnail** and **Title** properties to the properties you just added to the **LessonInfoDTO** class.
   ```
   CurrentVideoTitle = video.Title,
   CurrentVideoThumbnail = video.Thumbnail
   ```

5. Add a video to the first module in the first course in the **MockReadRepository**. The first module should have at least three videos, so that you can use the **Previous** and **Next** buttons properly when you test the *Coming Up* section of the **Video** view.

The complete **LessonInfoDTO** class:
```
public class LessonInfoDTO {
    public int LessonNumber { get; set; }
    public int NumberOfLessons { get; set; }
    public int PreviousVideoId { get; set; }
    public int NextVideoId { get; set; }
    public string NextVideoTitle { get; set; }
```

301

```
    public string NextVideoThumbnail { get; set; }
    public string CurrentVideoTitle { get; set; }
    public string CurrentVideoThumbnail { get; set; }
}
```

The complete **LessonInfoDTO** object in the **Video** action:

```
LessonInfo = new LessonInfoDTO
{
    LessonNumber = index + 1,
    NumberOfLessons = count,
    NextVideoId = nextId,
    PreviousVideoId = previousId,
    NextVideoTitle = nextTitle,
    NextVideoThumbnail = nextThumb,
    CurrentVideoTitle = video.Title,
    CurrentVideoThumbnail = video.Thumbnail
}
```

Adding the _VideoComingUpPartial Partial View

This partial view will display the panel containing the thumbnail of the next video, its title, and the **Previous** and **Next** buttons.

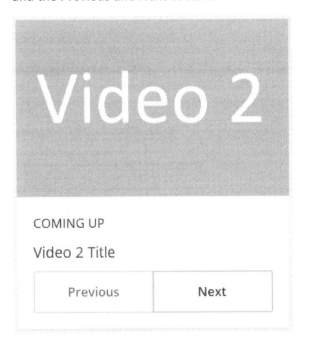

1. Add a partial view called **_VideoComingUpPartial** to the *Views/membership* folder.
2. Delete all code in the view and save it.
3. Close and open the view to get rid of any errors.
4. Add an **@model** directive to the **LessonInfoDTO** class.
   ```
   @model LessonInfoDTO
   ```
5. Add an if-block that checks that one of the **PreviousVideoId** or **NextVideoId** properties has a value greater than 0. If both are 0 then there are no other videos in the module, and the *Coming Up* section shouldn't be displayed.
   ```
   @if (Model.PreviousVideoId > 0 || Model.NextVideoId > 0)
   {
   }
   ```
6. Add a <div> element decorated with the **panel** Bootstrap class inside the if-block. Add a CSS class called **coming-up** to the <div> element; it will be the parent selector for this partial view.
   ```
   <div class="panel coming-up">
   </div>
   ```
7. Display a thumbnail for the current video, in the panel, if the **NextVideoId** property is 0; otherwise display the thumbnail for the next video. Use the **CurrentVideoThumbnail** and **NextVideoThumbnail** properties from the view model to display the correct image.
   ```
   @if (Model.NextVideoId == 0)
   {
       <img src="@Model.CurrentVideoThumbnail"
           class="img-responsive">
   }
   else
   {
       <img src="@Model.NextVideoThumbnail" class="img-responsive">
   }
   ```
8. Add a <div> decorated with the **panel-body** Bootstrap class below the <img> element. This is the container for the *Coming Up* information.
   ```
   <div class="panel-body">
   </div>
   ```

9. Add a <p> element with the text *COURSE COMPLETED* and an <h5> element for the **CurrentVideoTitle** property from the view model in the **panel-body** <div> if the **NextVideoId** property is 0. Otherwise, add a <p> element with the text *COMING UP* and an <h5> element for the **NextVideoTitle** property.

```
@if (Model.NextVideoId == 0)
{
    <p>COURSE COMPLETED</p>
    <h5>@Model.CurrentVideoTitle</h5>
}
else
{
    <p>COMING UP</p>
    <h5>@Model.NextVideoTitle</h5>
}
```

10. Add a <div> element for the **Previous** and **Next** buttons. Decorate it with the **btn-group** bootstrap class and add the **role** attribute set to **group**.

```
<div class="btn-group" role="group">
</div>
```

11. Add an if-block checking if the **PreviousVideoId** property in the view model is 0; if it is, then disable the **Previous** button. Use the **PreviousVideoId** in the <a> element's **href** attribute to target the correct video.

```
@if (Model.PreviousVideoId == 0)
{
    <a class="btn btn-default" disabled href="#">Previous</a>
}
else
{
    <a class="btn btn-default"
        href="~/Membership/Video/@Model.PreviousVideoId">
        Previous
    </a>
}
```

12. Add an if-block checking if the **NextVideoId** property in the view model is 0; if it is, then disable the **Next** button. Use the **NextVideoId** in the <a> element's **href** attribute to target the correct video.

```
@if (Model.NextVideoId == 0)
{
    <a class="btn btn-default" disabled href="#">Next</a>
}
```

```
    else
    {
        <a class="btn btn-default"
            href="~/Membership/Video/@Model.NextVideoId">Next</a>
    }
```

13. Open the **Video** view.

14. Add a call to the **PartialAsync** method to render the **_VideoComingUpPartial** partial view inside the <div> decorated with the **col-sm-3** Bootstrap class. Pass in the **LessonInfo** object from the view model to the partial view. Surround the method call with an if-block that checks that the view model and the **LessonInfo** object are not null.

```
<div class="col-sm-3">
    @if (Model != null && Model.LessonInfo != null)
    {
        @await Html.PartialAsync("_VideoComingUpPartial",
            Model.LessonInfo)
    }
</div>
```

15. Save all the files and navigate to a video in the browser. You should see the *Coming Up* section beside the video.

Next, you will style the **_VideoComingUpPartial** partial view.

The complete code for the **_VideoComingUpPartial** partial view:

```
@model LessonInfoDTO

@if (Model.PreviousVideoId > 0 || Model.NextVideoId > 0)
{
    <div class="panel coming-up">
        @if (Model.NextVideoId == 0)
        {
            <img src="@Model.CurrentVideoThumbnail"
                class="img-responsive">
        }
        else
        {
            <img src="@Model.NextVideoThumbnail"
                class="img-responsive">
        }
```

```
<div class="panel-body">
    @if (Model.NextVideoId == 0)
    {
        <p>COURSE COMPLETED</p>
        <h5>@Model.CurrentVideoTitle</h5>
    }
    else
    {
        <p>COMING UP</p>
        <h5>@Model.NextVideoTitle</h5>
    }

    <div class="btn-group" role="group">
        @if (Model.PreviousVideoId == 0)
        {
            <a class="btn btn-default" disabled href="#">
                Previous
            </a>
        }
        else
        {
            <a class="btn btn-default"
                href="~/Membership/Video/@Model.PreviousVideoId">
                Previous
            </a>
        }
        @if (Model.NextVideoId == 0)
        {
            <a class="btn btn-default" disabled href="#">
                Next
            </a>
        }
        else
        {
            <a class="btn btn-default"
                href="~/Membership/Video/@Model.NextVideoId">
                Next
            </a>
        }
    </div>
</div>
}
```

Styling the _VideoComingUpPartial Partial View

Open the *video.css* style sheet and make the button group as wide as possible.

```
.coming-up .btn-group {
    width: 100%;
}
```

Make each of the buttons take up 50% of the button group's width.

```
.coming-up .btn-group .btn {
    width: 50%;
}
```

Adding the _InstructorBioPartial Partial View

The last section you will add to the **Video** view is the **_InstructorBioPartial** partial view that displays information about the instructor.

John Doe

Instructor

Lorem ipsum dolor sit amet,
pariatur. Excepteur sint occaecat
cupidatat non proident, sunt in culpa
qui officia deserunt mollit anim id est
laborum.

1. Open the **Video** view.
2. Add a call to the **PartialAsync** method to render the **_InstructorBioPartial** partial view below the previous if-block inside the <div> decorated with the **col-sm-3**

Bootstrap class. Pass in the **instructor** object from the view model to the partial view. Surround the method call with an if-block that checks that the view model and the **Instructor** object are not null.

```
@if (Model != null && Model.Instructor != null)
{
    @await Html.PartialAsync("_InstructorBioPartial",
        Model.Instructor)
}
```

3. Save the file and refresh the **Video** view in the browser. The **_InstructorBioPartial** partial view should be displayed below the **_VideoComingUpPartial** partial view.

The complete code for the **Video** view:

```
@model VideoViewModel

@{
    ViewData["Title"] = "Video";
}

<div class="membership top-margin video-content">
    <div class="row navigation-bar">
        <div class="col-sm-12">
            <a class="btn btn-primary"
                href="~/Membership/Course/@Model.Course.CourseId">
                <span class="glyphicon glyphicon-menu-left"></span>
                Back to @Model.Course.CourseTitle
            </a>
        </div>
    </div>
    <div class="row">
        <div class="col-sm-9">
            @if (Model != null && Model.Video != null &&
                Model.LessonInfo != null && Model.Course != null)
            {
                @await Html.PartialAsync("_VideoPlayerPartial", Model)
            }
        </div>
```

```
<div class="col-sm-3">
        @if (Model != null && Model.LessonInfo != null)
        {
            @await Html.PartialAsync("_VideoComingUpPartial",
                Model.LessonInfo)
        }

        @if (Model != null && Model.Instructor != null)
        {
            @await Html.PartialAsync("_InstructorBioPartial",
                Model.Instructor)
        }
    </div>
  </div>
</div>

@section Scripts
{
    <script type="text/javascript">
        $(function () {
            jwplayer("video").setup({
                file: $("#hiddenUrl").text(),
                image: $("#hiddenImageUrl").text()
            });
        });
    </script>
}
```

Summary

In this chapter, you added the **Video** view and its partial views. You also added JWPlayer to be able to play video content in the view.

In the next part of the book, you will add the entity classes to a SQL Server Database using Entity Framework migrations. You will also add a new data repository to interact with the database. When the repository is in place, you will create a user interface for administrators.

21. SQL Data Repository

Introduction

In this chapter, you will create the database tables for storing the video data; you have already created the tables for user data in an earlier chapter. Although you could have several database contexts for interacting with the database, you will continue using the one that was provided when the application was created.

You will also seed the database with initial data when the tables are created. This makes it a little easier for you to follow along as you create the various views, because the views will already contain data that you are familiar with.

When the tables have been created and seeded, you will create a new data repository class called **SqlReadRepository**, using the same **IReadRepository** interface that you used when adding the **MockReadRepository** class. When it has been implemented, you will replace the **MockReadRepository** class with the **SqlReadRepository** class for the **IRead-Repository** service in the **ConfigureServices** method in the **Startup** class. This will make the application use the data from the database, instead of the mock data.

Technologies used in this chapter

1. **C#** – Used when seeding the database and creating the repository.
2. **Entity framework** – To create and interact with the new tables from the repository.
3. **LINQ** – To query the database tables.

Overview

Your first objective is to create the tables for storing video-related data in the database, and seed them with data. The second objective is to create a data repository that can communicate with the database tables, and use it instead of the existing mock data repository in the **Startup** class. After implementing these two steps, the application will work with live data from the database.

Adding the Tables

To tell Entity Framework that the entity classes should be added as tables in the database, you need to add them as **DbSet** properties in the **ApplicationDbContext** class. Use the same entity classes you created for the mock data repository.

You can then inject the **ApplicationDbContext** class into the constructor of the **SqlRead-Repository** class to perform CRUD (Create, Read, Update, Delete) operations on the tables. When you replace the **MockReadRepository** class with the **SqlReadRepository** class in the **IReadRepository** service, the database data will be used instead of the mock data.

Adding the Entity Classes to the ApplicationDbContext

1. Open the **ApplicationDbContext** class located in the *Data* folder.
2. Add all the entity classes as **DbSet** properties to the class.

```
public DbSet<Course> Courses { get; set; }
public DbSet<Download> Downloads { get; set; }
public DbSet<Instructor> Instructors { get; set; }
public DbSet<Module> Modules { get; set; }
public DbSet<UserCourse> UserCourses { get; set; }
public DbSet<Video> Videos { get; set; }
```

3. Because the **UserCourses** table has a composite key (**UserId** and **CourseId**), you need to specify that in the **OnModelCreating** method in the **ApplicationDbContext** class. In previous versions of ASP.NET you could do this in the entity class with attributes, but in ASP.NET Core 1.1 you pass it in as a Lambda expression to the **HasKey** method.

```
builder.Entity<UserCourse>().HasKey(uc => new { uc.UserId,
uc.CourseId });
```

4. To avoid cascading deletes when a parent record is deleted, you can add a delete behavior to the **OnModelCreating** method. A cascading delete will delete all related records to the one being deleted; for instance, if you delete an order, all its order rows will also be deleted.

```
foreach (var relationship in
builder.Model.GetEntityTypes().SelectMany(e =>
e.GetForeignKeys()))
{
    relationship.DeleteBehavior = DeleteBehavior.Restrict;
}
```

The complete code in the **ApplicationDbContext** class:

```
public class ApplicationDbContext : IdentityDbContext<ApplicationUser>
{
    public DbSet<Course> Courses { get; set; }
    public DbSet<Download> Downloads { get; set; }
    public DbSet<Instructor> Instructors { get; set; }
    public DbSet<Module> Modules { get; set; }
    public DbSet<UserCourse> UserCourses { get; set; }
    public DbSet<Video> Videos { get; set; }

    public ApplicationDbContext(
    DbContextOptions<ApplicationDbContext> options) : base(options)
    {
    }

    protected override void OnModelCreating(ModelBuilder builder)
    {
        base.OnModelCreating(builder);

        // Composite key
        builder.Entity<UserCourse>().HasKey(uc =>
            new { uc.UserId, uc.CourseId });

        // Restrict cascading deletes
        foreach (var relationship in builder.Model.GetEntityTypes()
            .SelectMany(e => e.GetForeignKeys()))
        {
            relationship.DeleteBehavior = DeleteBehavior.Restrict;
        }
    }
}
```

Adding Seed Data

To have some data to work with when the tables have been created, you will add seed data to them when they are created. You need to add a class called **DbInitializer** to the *Data* folder to add seed data.

The seed data is added using a **static** method called **Initialize**, which you will need to add to the class.

If you want the database to be recreated every time migrations are applied, you can add the following two code lines at the beginning of the **Initialize** method. This could be useful

313

in certain test scenarios where you need a clean database. You will not add them in this exercise because you want to keep the data you add between migrations.

To add data to a table, you create a list of the entity type and add instances to it. Then you add that list to the entity collection (the **DbSet** for that entity), in the **ApplicationDbClass**, using the **context** object passed into the **Initialize** method.

Note that the order in which you add the seed data is important because some tables may rely on data from other tables.

1. Add a class called **DbInitializer** to the *Data* folder.
2. Add a **public static** method called **Initialize** to the class. It should take the **ApplicationDbContext** as a parameter.
   ```
   public static void Initialize(ApplicationDbContext context)
   {
   }
   ```
3. To avoid repeating dummy data, you will add a variable with some Lorem Ipsum text that can be reused throughout the seeding process. You can generate Lorem Ipsum text at the following URL: http://loripsum.net/.
   ```
   var description = "Lorem ipsum dolor sit amet, consectetur
   adipiscing elit, sed do eiusmod tempor incididunt ut labore et
   dolore magna aliqua. Ut enim ad minim veniam, quis nostrud
   exercitation ullamco laboris nisi ut aliquip ex ea commodo
   consequat.";
   ```
4. Before seeding the tables, you must check that they haven't already been seeded. You can do that by checking if one or more tables already contain data, and if they do, you exit the method with a **return** statement. Alternatively you can check each table separately, and seed those that haven't already been seeded.
   ```
   if (context.Instructors.Any())
   {
       return;    // DB has been seeded
   }
   ```
5. Add two instructors called *John Doe* and *Jane Doe* to the **Instructor DbSet**. Use part of the text in the **description** variable for their descriptions, and add a thumbnail image. First you add the instructors to a **List** collection, then you add

that collection to the entity collection, with its **Add** method. Don't forget to call the **SaveChanges** method to persist the data.

```
var instructors = new List<Instructor>
{
    new Instructor {
        Name = "John Doe",
        Description = description.Substring(20, 50),
        Thumbnail = "/images/Ice-Age-Scrat-icon.png"
    },
    new Instructor {
        Name = "Jane Doe",
        Description = description.Substring(30, 40),
        Thumbnail = "/images/Ice-Age-Scrat-icon.png"
    }
};
context.Instructors.AddRange(instructors);
context.SaveChanges();
```

6. Add data for the other entities in the following order: **Course**, **UserCourse**, **Module**, **Video**, and **Download**. Note that the **Module** class has a conflict with a framework class, so you need to specify the namespace path for that class. You can see the complete code below. Make sure that the **UserId** property for the **UserCourse** table is assigned a user id from the **AspNetUsers** table.

7. Inject the **ApplicationDbContext** class into the **Configure** method in the **Startup** class.

```
public void Configure(IApplicationBuilder app, IHostingEnvironment
env, ILoggerFactory loggerFactory, ApplicationDbContext context)
{
    ...
}
```

8. Call the **DbInitializer.Initialize** method with the **context** object, below the **UseMvc** method call, to add the seed data.

```
DbInitializer.Initialize(context);
```

The complete code in the **DbInitializer** class:

```
public class DbInitializer
{
    public static void Initialize(ApplicationDbContext context)
    {
        #region seed data
```

```
        var description = "Lorem ipsum dolor sit amet, consectetur
            adipiscing elit, sed do eiusmod tempor incididunt ut
            labore et dolore magna aliqua. Ut enim ad minim veniam,
            quis nostrud exercitation ullamco laboris nisi ut aliquip
            ex ea commodo consequat.";
        #endregion

        // If you need to recreate the database then uncomment these
        // two code lines. All data will be deleted with the
        // database and cannot be recovered
        // context.Database.EnsureDeleted();
        // context.Database.EnsureCreated();

        // Look for any courses to check if the DB has been seeded
        if (context.Instructors.Any())
        {
            return;    // DB has been seeded
        }

        var instructors = new List<Instructor>
        {
            new Instructor { Name = "John Doe",
                Description = description.Substring(20, 50),
                Thumbnail = "/images/Ice-Age-Scrat-icon.png"
            },
            new Instructor { Name = "Jane Doe",
                Description = description.Substring(30, 40),
                Thumbnail = "/images/Ice-Age-Scrat-icon.png"
            }
        };
        context.Instructors.AddRange(instructors);
        context.SaveChanges();

        var courses = new List<Course>
        {
            new Course { InstructorId = 1, Title = "Course 1",
                Description = description,
                ImageUrl = "/images/course-small.jpg",
                MarqueeImageUrl = "/images/laptop.jpg"
            },
```

```
            new Course { InstructorId = 2, Title = "Course 2",
                Description = description,
                ImageUrl = "/images/course-small.jpg",
                MarqueeImageUrl - "/images/laptop.jpg"
            },
            new Course { InstructorId = 1, Title = "Course 3",
                Description = description,
                ImageUrl = "/images/course-small.jpg",
                MarqueeImageUrl = "/images/laptop.jpg"
            }
        };
        context.Courses.AddRange(courses);
        context.SaveChanges();

        var userCourses = new List<UserCourse>
        {
            new UserCourse {
                UserId = "58e8b22c-9243-4102-b744-a34fababb008",
                CourseId = 1
            },
            new UserCourse {
                UserId = "58e8b22c-9243-4102-b744-a34fababb008",
                CourseId = 3
            }
        };

        context.UserCourses.AddRange(userCourses);
        context.SaveChanges();

        var modules = new List<Entities.Module>
        {
            new Entities.Module { CourseId = 1, Title = "Modeule 1" },
            new Entities.Module { CourseId = 1, Title = "Modeule 2" },
            new Entities.Module { CourseId = 2, Title = "Modeule 3" }
        };

        context.Modules.AddRange(modules);
        context.SaveChanges();
```

```
            var videos = new List<Video>
            {
                new Video { ModuleId = 1, CourseId = 1,
                    Position = 1, Title = "Video 1 Title",
                    Description = description.Substring(10, 40),
                    Duration = 50,
                    Thumbnail = "/images/video1.jpg",
                    Url = "https://www.youtube.com/watch?v=BJFyzpBcaCY"
                },
                new Video { ModuleId = 1, CourseId = 1, Position = 2,
                    Title = "Video 2 Title",
                    Description = description.Substring(20, 40),
                    Duration = 45, Thumbnail = "/images/video2.jpg",
                    Url = "https://www.youtube.com/watch?v=BJFyzpBcaCY"
                },
                new Video { ModuleId = 1, CourseId = 1, Position = 3,
                    Title = "Video 3 Title",
                    Description = description.Substring(30, 40),
                    Duration = 41, Thumbnail = "/images/video3.jpg",
                    Url = "https://www.youtube.com/watch?v=BJFyzpBcaCY"
                },
                new Video { ModuleId = 3, CourseId = 2, Position = 1,
                    Title = "Video 4 Title",
                    Description = description.Substring(40, 40),
                    Duration = 41, Thumbnail = "/images/video4.jpg",
                    Url = https://www.youtube.com/watch?v=BJFyzpBcaCY
                },
                new Video { ModuleId = 2, CourseId = 1, Position = 1,
                    Title = "Video 5 Title",
                    Description = description.Substring(10, 40),
                    Duration = 42, Thumbnail = "/images/video5.jpg",
                    Url = "https://www.youtube.com/watch?v=BJFyzpBcaCY"
                }
            };
            context.Videos.AddRange(videos);
            context.SaveChanges();

            var downloads = new List<Download>
            {
                new Download{ModuleId = 1, CourseId = 1,
                    Title = "ADO.NET 1 (PDF)",
                    Url = "https://1drv.ms/b/s!AuD5OaH0ExAwn4"
                },
```

```
            new Download{ModuleId = 1, CourseId = 1,
                Title = "ADO.NET 2 (PDF)",
                Url = "https://1drv.ms/b/s!AuD5OaH0ExAwn4"
            },
            new Download{ModuleId = 3, CourseId = 2,
                Title = "ADO.NET 1 (PDF)",
                Url = "https://1drv.ms/b/s!AuD5OaH0ExAwn4"
            }
        };
        context.Downloads.AddRange(downloads);
        context.SaveChanges();
    }
}
```

The complete code for the **Configure** method in the **Startup** class:

```
public void Configure(IApplicationBuilder app, IHostingEnvironment env,
ILoggerFactory loggerFactory, ApplicationDbContext context)
{
    loggerFactory.AddConsole(Configuration.GetSection("Logging"));
    loggerFactory.AddDebug();

    if (env.IsDevelopment())
    {
        app.UseDeveloperExceptionPage();
        app.UseDatabaseErrorPage();
        app.UseBrowserLink();
    }
    else
    {
        app.UseExceptionHandler("/Home/Error");
    }

    app.UseStaticFiles();

    app.UseIdentity();

    app.UseMvc(routes =>
    {
        routes.MapRoute(
            name: "default",
            template: "{controller=Home}/{action=Index}/{id?}");
    });
```

```
    DbInitializer.Initialize(context);
}
```

Creating the Tables

To add the tables to the database, you have to create a new migration and update the database.

1. Open the Package Manager Console.
2. Execute the following command to create the migration data.
   add-migration CreateTablesWithSeedData

3. Execute the following command to make the migration changes in the database.
   update-database

4. To fill the tables with the seed data, you have to start the application (Ctrl+F5).
5. Open the *SQL Server Object Explorer* and drill down to the tables in the database. The entity tables should have been added.

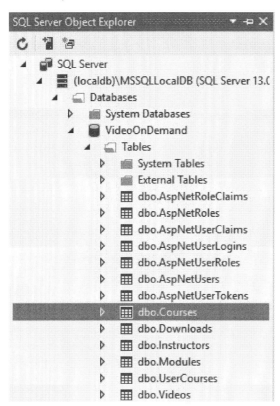

6. Right click on one of them and select **View Data** to verify that the seed data has been added.

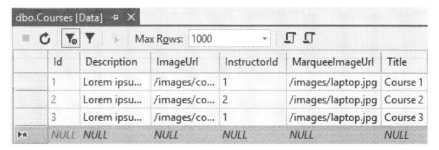

7. If for some reason the data hasn't been added, then recreate the database by adding the following two lines (temporarily) to the **Initialize** method in the **DbInitializer** method, and run the application again. Delete the two lines of code you just added. Note that all previous data, in all the tables, will be deleted when adding these lines of code, including your users and roles.

```
context.Database.EnsureDeleted();
context.Database.EnsureCreated();
```

Adding the SqlReadRepository

Now that the tables have been added to the database and seeded with data; it is time to create a new data repository that fetches data from the database. You will use the same interface that you used earlier to implement the **MockReadRepository** when implementing the **SqlReadRepository**. By doing so, you can simply replace the **MockReadRepository** class with the **SqlReadRepository** class in the **IReadRepository** service you added to the **Configuration** method in the **Startup** class. When the **SqlReadRepository** class is used to create the instances for the **IReadRepository** interface, the data will be fetched from the database.

Implementing the GetCourses method

1. Add a class called **SqlReadRepository** to the *Repositories* folder.
2. Implement the **IReadRepository** interface in the class. This will add the methods that you need to implement.

```
public class SqlReadRepository : IReadRepository
{
    ...
}
```

3. Add a constructor to the class and inject the **ApplicationDbContext** class. Store the object in a private class level variable called **_db**; this will give access to the database throughout the class.
```
private ApplicationDbContext _db;
public SqlReadRepository(ApplicationDbContext db)
{
    _db = db;
}
```

4. Copy the content from the **GetCourses** method in the **MockReadRepository** class.

5. Remove the **throw** statement from the **GetCourses** method in the **SqlReadRepository** class and paste in the code you just copied.

6. Replace **_userCourses**, which fetches mock data, with **_db.UserCourses**, which fetches data from the database. Replace **_courses** with **_db.Courses** in the **Join** method. Store the courses fetched by the LINQ expression in a variable called **courses**.
```
var courses = _db.UserCourses.Where(uc =>
uc.UserId.Equals(userId))
.Join(_db.Courses, uc => uc.CourseId, c => c.Id,
    (uc, c) => new { Course = c })
.Select(s => s.Course);
```

7. Fetch the instructor and modules associated with each course in the **foreach** loop, and assign them to the **Instructor** and **Modules** collections in the **course** variable. Replace **_instructors** with **_db.Instructors** and **_modules** with **_db.Modules**.
```
foreach (var course in courses)
{
    course.Instructor = _db.Instructors.SingleOrDefault(
        s => s.Id.Equals(course.InstructorId));
    course.Modules = _db.Modules.Where(
        m => m.CourseId.Equals(course.Id)).ToList();
}
```

8. Return the courses in the **courses** collection.

9. Open the **Startup** class and locate the **ConfigureServices** method.

10. Replace the **MockReadRepository** class with the **SqlReadRepository** class for the **IReadRepository** service. This will make the application fetch data from the database instead of the mock data.
    ```
    services.AddSingleton<IReadRepository, SqlReadRepository>();
    ```

11. Run the application and verify that the courses are displayed in the **Dashboard** view.

The complete code for the **GetCourses** method:

```
public IEnumerable<Course> GetCourses(string userId)
{
    var courses =  _db.UserCourses.Where(uc =>
        uc.UserId.Equals(userId))
        .Join(_db.Courses, uc => uc.CourseId, c => c.Id,
            (uc, c) => new { Course = c })
        .Select(s => s.Course);

    foreach (var course in courses)
    {
        course.Instructor = _db.Instructors.SingleOrDefault(
            s => s.Id.Equals(course.InstructorId));
        course.Modules = _db.Modules.Where(
            m => m.CourseId.Equals(course.Id)).ToList();
    }

    return courses;
}
```

Implementing the GetCourse Method
This method will fetch one course from the database.

1. Copy the content from the **GetCourse** method in the **MockReadRepository** class.
2. Remove the **throw** statement from the **GetCourse** method in the **SqlReadRepository** class and paste in the code you just copied.
3. Replace **_userCourses**, which fetches mock data, with **_db.UserCourses**, which fetches data from the database. Replace **_courses** with **_db.Courses** in the **Join** method. Store the course fetched by the LINQ expression in a variable called **course**.

```
var course = _db.UserCourses.Where(uc => uc.UserId.Equals(userId))
    .Join(_db.Courses, uc => uc.CourseId, c => c.Id,
        (uc, c) => new { Course = c })
    .SingleOrDefault(s => s.Course.Id.Equals(courseId)).Course;
```

4. Fetch the instructor and modules and store them in the **Instructor** and **Modules** properties of the **course** object. Replace **_instructor** with **_db.Instructor** and **_modules** with **_db.Modules**.

```
course.Instructor = _instructors.SingleOrDefault(
    s => s.Id.Equals(course.InstructorId));

course.Modules = _modules.Where(
    m => m.CourseId.Equals(course.Id)).ToList();
```

5. Fetch the videos and downloads associated with each module in the **foreach** loop, and assign them to the **Videos** and **Downloads** collections in the **course** variable. Replace **_downloads** with **_db.Downloads** and **_videos** with **_db.Videos**.

```
foreach (var module in course.Modules)
{
    module.Downloads = _db.Downloads.Where(
        d => d.ModuleId.Equals(module.Id)).ToList();
    module.Videos = _db.Videos.Where(
        v => v.ModuleId.Equals(module.Id)).ToList();
}
```

6. Return the **course** variable.
7. Run the application and click on one of the courses in the **Dashboard** view to verify that the correct course is displayed.

The complete code for the **GetCourse** method:

```
public Course GetCourse(string userId, int courseId)
{
    var course = _db.UserCourses.Where(uc => uc.UserId.Equals(userId))
        .Join(_db.Courses, uc => uc.CourseId, c => c.Id,
            (uc, c) => new { Course = c })
        .SingleOrDefault(s => s.Course.Id.Equals(courseId)).Course;

    course.Instructor = _db.Instructors.SingleOrDefault(
        s => s.Id.Equals(course.InstructorId));
    course.Modules = _db.Modules.Where(
        m => m.CourseId.Equals(course.Id)).ToList();
```

```
    foreach (var module in course.Modules)
    {
        module.Downloads = _db.Downloads.Where(
            d => d.ModuleId.Equals(module.Id)).ToList();
        module.Videos = _db.Videos.Where(
            v => v.ModuleId.Equals(module.Id)).ToList();
    }

    return course;
}
```

Implementing the GetVideo Method

This method will fetch one video from the database.

1. Copy the content from the **GetVideo** method in the **MockReadRepository** class.
2. Remove the **throw** statement from the **GetVideo** method in the **SqlReadRepository** class and paste in the code you just copied.
3. Replace **_videos** with **_db.Videos** and **_userCourses** with **_db.UserCourses**. Store the video fetched by the LINQ expression in a variable called **video**.
4. Return the video in the **video** variable.

The complete code for the **GetVideo** method:

```
public Video GetVideo(string userId, int videoId)
{
    var video = _db.Videos
        .Where(v => v.Id.Equals(videoId))
        .Join(_db.UserCourses, v => v.CourseId, uc => uc.CourseId,
            (v, uc) => new { Video = v, UserCourse = uc })
        .Where(vuc => vuc.UserCourse.UserId.Equals(userId))
        .FirstOrDefault().Video;

    return video;
}
```

Implementing the GetVideos Method

This method will fetch all videos associated with the logged in user.

1. Copy the content from the **GetVideos** method in the **MockReadRepository** class.
2. Remove the **throw** statement from the **GetVideos** method in the **SqlReadRepository** class and paste in the code you just copied.

3. Replace **_videos** with **_db.Videos** and **_userCourses** with **_db.UserCourses**. Store the videos fetched by the LINQ expression in a variable called **videos**.
4. Return all the videos in the **video** variable if the **moduleId** parameter is equal to 0, otherwise return the videos that are associated with the module id.
5. Run the application and click on one of the video items in the **Course** view to verify that the correct video is displayed.

The complete code for the **GetVideos** method:

```
public IEnumerable<Video> GetVideos(string userId, int moduleId = 0)
{
    var videos = _db.Videos
        .Join(_db.UserCourses, v => v.CourseId, uc => uc.CourseId,
            (v, uc) => new { Video = v, UserCourse = uc })
        .Where(vuc => vuc.UserCourse.UserId.Equals(userId));

    return moduleId.Equals(0) ?
        videos.Select(s => s.Video) :
        videos.Where(v => v.Video.ModuleId.Equals(moduleId))
            .Select(s => s.Video);
}
```

Summary

In this chapter, you first created the application related tables in the database and seeded them with data. Then you created a data repository that communicates with the database tables and used it instead of the existing mock data repository. After the repository swap, the application uses live data from the database.

Next, you will start building a user interface for administrators.

22. The Admin Menu

Introduction

In this chapter, you will create an **Admin** menu with links to all **Index** views associated with the controllers you will add. Since you know that a view will have the same name as its action in the controller, all the menu items can be added before the actual controllers have been created.

You will create the menu in a partial view called **_AdminMenuPartial** that is rendered in the **_Layout** view, using the **PartialAsync** method in the **Html** class.

Technologies Used in This Chapter

1. **C#** – To add authorization checks in the **_AdminMenuPartial** partial view.
2. **HTML** – To create the drop-down menu and its items

Overview

Your task is to create a menu for all the **Index** views, in a shared partial view called **_Admin-MenuPartial**, and then render it from the **_Layout** view.

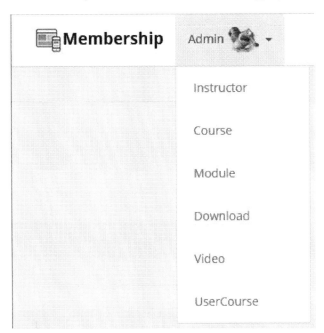

Adding the _AdminMenuPartial Partial View

Create a partial view called **_AdminMenuPartial** in the *Views/Shared* folder. Add a <ul> element styled with the **nav navbar-nav** Bootstrap classes, to make it look nice in the navigation bar. Add an <li> element styled with the **dropdown** Bootstrap class to make it a drop-down button. Add an <a> element with the text *Admin*, an avatar image, and a caret symbol, to the <li> element. Add a <ul> element styled with the **dropdown-menu** Bootstrap class that contains all the menu items as <li> elements. Use the **asp-controller** and **asp-action** Tag Helpers to target the appropriate actions in the controllers.

1. Add a partial view to the *Views/Shared* folder called **_AdminMenuPartial**.

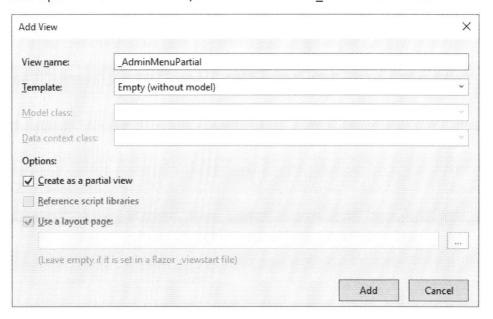

2. Delete all code in the view.
3. Inject the **SignInManager** and the **UserManager** to be able to authorize the user.
    ```
    @inject SignInManager<ApplicationUser> SignInManager
    @inject UserManager<ApplicationUser> UserManager
    ```
4. Add an if-block that checks if the user is signed in and belongs to the **Admin** role.
    ```
    @if (SignInManager.IsSignedIn(User) && User.IsInRole("Admin"))
    {
    }
    ```

5. Add a <ul> element decorated with the **nav** and **navbar-nav** Bootstrap classes inside the if-block. This is the main container for the *Admin* menu.
    ```
    <ul class="nav navbar-nav">
    </ul>
    ```

6. Add an <li> element inside the <ul> and decorate it with the **dropdown** Bootstrap class. This will be the container for the button that opens the menu.
    ```
    <li class="dropdown">
    </li>
    ```

7. Add an <a> element to the <li> element and assign # to its **href** attribute to stay on the current view when the menu item is clicked. To make it work as a toggle button for the menu, you must add the **dropdown-toggle** Bootstrap class, assign *dropdown* to the **data-toggle** attribute, and assign *button* to the **role** attribute. Assign *false* to the **aria-expanded** attribute to make the drop-down menu hidden by default.
    ```
    <a href="#" class="dropdown-toggle" data-toggle="dropdown"
    role="button" aria-expanded="false">
    </a>
    ```

8. Add the text *Admin* to the <a> element followed by the avatar image. Make the height of the image 40px, and decorate it with the **img-circle** and **avatar** Bootstrap classes. Also add a <span> for the caret symbol; decorate it with the **caret** and **text-light** classes.
    ```
    Admin
    <img src="~/images/Ice-Age-Scrat-icon.png" class="img-circle
    avatar" alt="" height="40">
    <span class="caret text-light hidden-xs"></span>
    ```

9. Create the drop-down menu section of the menu by adding a <ul> element decorated with the **dropdown-menu** Bootstrap class and the **role** attribute set to *menu*, below the <a> element.
    ```
    <ul class="dropdown-menu" role="menu">
    </ul>
    ```

10. Add <li> elements for all the **Index** actions in the different controllers. You can figure out all the controller names by looking at the entity class names; a controller should have the same name as the entity class followed by the suffix *Controller*. Assign the controller name without the suffix to the **asp-controller**

Tag Helper and the action to the **asp-action** Tag Helper. Add a suitable description in the <li> element.
```
<li><a asp-controller="Instructors" asp-
action="Index">Instructor</a></li>
```

11. Open the **_Layout** view and use the **PartialAsync** method to render the partial view. Place the call to the **PartialAsync** method above the method call that renders the **_LoginPartial** partial view.
```
@await Html.PartialAsync("_AdminMenuPartial")
```

12. Open the **AspNetUsers** table in the database and copy the id of the user that you want to be an administrator.

13. Open the **AspNetRoles** table in the database and add the **Admin** role with id 1. Values: Id = 1, ConcurrencyStamp (leave blank), Name = Admin, NormalizedName = ADMIN.

14. Open the **AspNetUserRoles** table in the database and enter the user id that you copied and the role id 1.

15. Save all the files and run the application without debugging (Ctrl+F5) log out and make sure that you are logged in as an administrator. Click the **Admin** menu to open it. Clicking any of the menu items will generate a *404 Not Found* error because you haven't added the necessary controllers, actions, and views yet.

The complete markup in the **_AdminMenuPartial** partial view:

```
@inject SignInManager<ApplicationUser> SignInManager
@inject UserManager<ApplicationUser> UserManager

@if (SignInManager.IsSignedIn(User) && User.IsInRole("Admin"))
{
    <ul class="nav navbar-nav">
        <li class="dropdown">
            <a href="#" class="dropdown-toggle" data-toggle="dropdown"
                role="button" aria-expanded="false">
                Admin
                <img src="~/images/Ice-Age-Scrat-icon.png"
                    class="img-circle avatar" alt="" height="40">
                <span class="caret text-light hidden-xs"></span>
            </a>
            <ul class="dropdown-menu" role="menu">
                <li><a asp-controller="Instructors" asp-action="Index">
```

```
                    Instructor</a></li>
              <li><a asp-controller="Courses" asp-action="Index">
                 Course</a></li>
              <li><a asp-controller="Modules" asp-action="Index">
                 Module</a></li>
              <li><a asp-controller="Downloads" asp-action="Index">
                 Download</a></li>
              <li><a asp-controller="Videos" asp-action="Index">
                 Video</a></li>
              <li><a asp-controller="UserCourses" asp-action="Index">
                 UserCourse</a></li>
          </ul>
        </li>
    </ul>
}
```

Summary

In this chapter, you added the **Admin** menu and targeted the controllers, actions, and views that you will begin adding in the next chapter.

23. Controllers and Views

Introduction

In this chapter, you will create controllers and views that are used when performing CRUD (Create, Read, Update, Delete) operations against the tables in the database. The administrator user interface doesn't have to be as well styled as the previous user interface.

In some cases drop-downs will display incorrect data in the views; this is something that you will have to correct. Instead of displaying the item indices, they should display the title or name.

Technologies used in this chapter

1. **C#** – To create controllers and their actions.
2. **HTML** – To create views.
3. **Entity framework** – To perform CRUD operations.

Overview

Your task is to create the controllers, actions, and views that enable the user to display, add, update, and delete data in the database tables. The easiest way to do this is to use Visual Studio's built-in scaffolding feature.

A typical **Index** view.

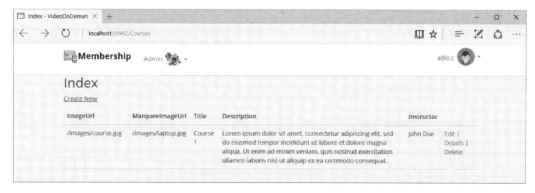

A typical **Create** view.

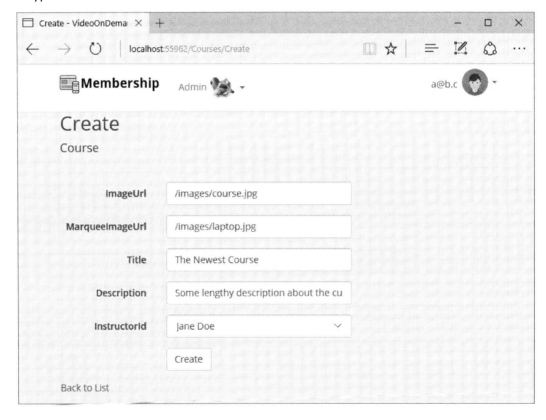

A typical **Edit** view.

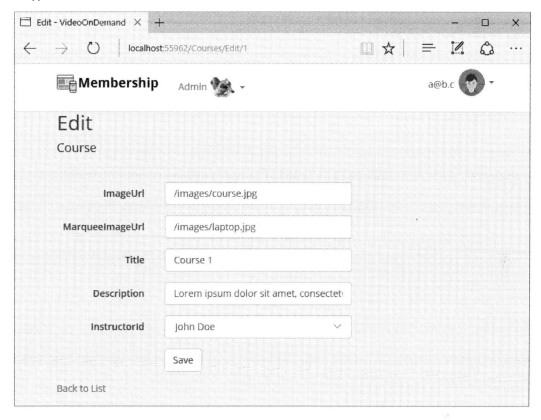

A typical **Details** view.

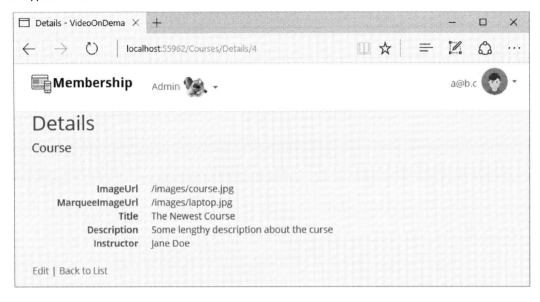

A typical **Delete** view.

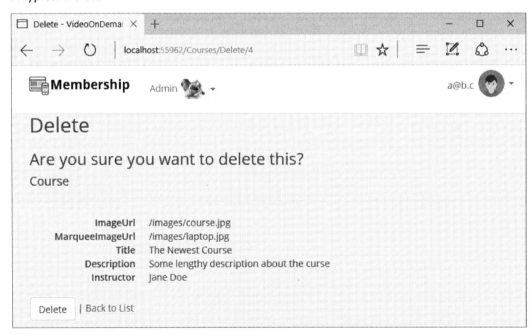

Adding Controllers and Views

The first step to interact with the database is to create the controller and its actions. This is easiest done with scaffolding through the right click-menu in the *Solution Explorer*. Let's scaffold one controller and its views together, then you can do the rest by yourself.

Sometimes when scaffolding, Visual Studio makes mistakes. For instance, the variable in LINQ statements can be added as an @-sign. If that happens, you simply replace it with an appropriate name.

```
var applicationDbContext = _context.Modules.Include(@ => @.Course);
var applicationDbContext = _context.Modules.Include(m => m.Course);
```

OR

```
var @module = await _context.Modules
if (@module == null)
```

```
var module = await _context.Modules
if (module == null)
```

1. Right click on the *Controllers* folder and select **Add-Controller**. The first time you do this a dialog will pop up, asking how to install the MVC dependencies. Select **Full Dependencies** and click the **Add** button.

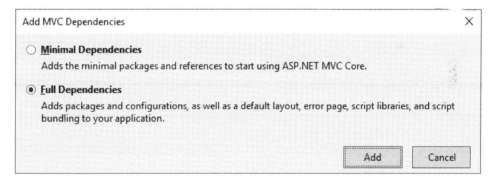

2. When the dialog has closed, right click on the same folder and select **Add-Controller**. A different dialog will be displayed, asking what template you want to use. Select **MVC Controller with views, using Entity Framework**, and click the **Add** button.

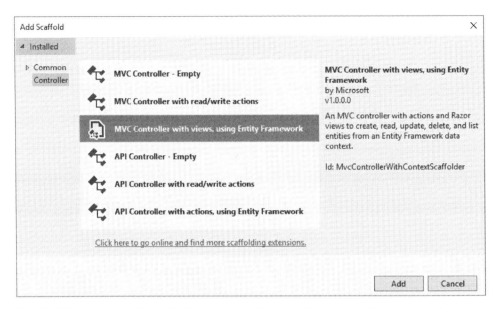

3. The **Add Controller** dialog is displayed. Select the **Course** entity class as the model in the first drop-down and **ApplicationDbContext** in the second drop-down (this is the class that is used to communicate with the database). Click the **Add** button.

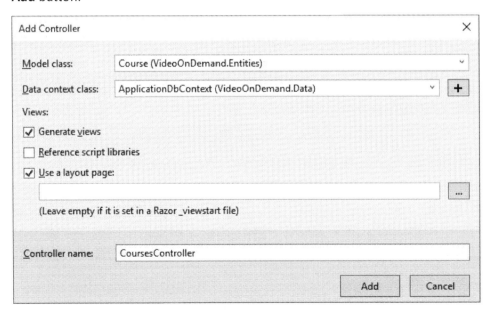

4. When the scaffolding has finished, the **CoursesController** class should have been added to the *Controllers* folder, and it should be open. There should also be a folder named *Courses* in the *Views* folder, which contains the five views associated with the controller's actions: **Create, Delete, Details, Edit,** and **Index**.

5. Open the **Delete** view and move the hidden field inside the <form> element if it has ended up outside of the form.

6. Start the application with debugging (F5).

7. Select **Course** in the **Admin** menu. This should display the **Index** view, served up by the **Index** action in the **Courses** controller.

8. Open the **CoursesController** class in Visual Studio and place a breakpoint on the **return** statement in the **Index** action. To add a breakpoint, place the cursor on the desired line of code and press F9 on the keyboard.

9. Switch to the browser and refresh the **Index** view. You should automatically be taken to Visual Studio, where the execution halts on the breakpoint.

10. Inspect the variable's content to see that the courses are loaded. This proves that the **Index** controller's action is executed before the view is displayed in the browser, and that the model passed into the view is used during the rendering process.

11. Remove the breakpoint (place the cursor on the line with the breakpoint and press F9 on the keyboard) and press F5 to continue. The view should be displayed.

12. Click the **Create New** link in the **Index** view and add a new course by filling out the form and clicking the **Create** button. Note that you are redirected to the **Index** view where the new course is displayed in the view's table.

13. Open the *SQL Server Object Explorer* and drill down to the **Courses** table. Open it and verify that the course has been added.

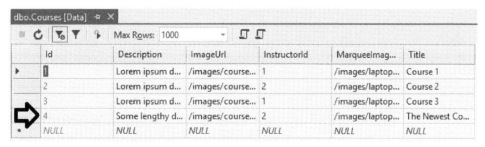

14. Switch to the browser and click the **Edit** link for the course you just added and change some data. When you click the **Save** button you will be redirected to the **Index** view where the course should be displayed with the saved changes.
15. Open the *SQL Server Object Explorer* and drill down to the **Courses** table. Open it and verify that the course data has been modified.
16. Switch to the browser and click the **Details** link and review the information. Note that there are two links below the data, one that takes the user to the **Edit** view and one that takes the user to the **Index** view. Click the **Back to List** link to get back to the **Index** view.
17. Click the **Delete** link and then the **Delete** button. This will permanently remove the course from the **Courses** table.
18. Open the *SQL Server Object Explorer* and drill down to the **Courses** table. Open it and verify that the course has been deleted.
19. Repeat steps 1-18 for all the other entity classes except the **UserCourse** class. You will find that the views for the **Video** and **Download** entities don't display the course and module values correctly, or as even the correct HTML element. The **CourseId** is displayed as an <input> element, but it should be a <select> element, to display a drop-down.

Fixing the Drop-Downs in the Views

The reason the drop-downs are displaying the wrong data, or even wrong HTML elements, is that the scaffolding couldn't determine what element to use for the **id** properties, so it defaulted to a safe element.

You didn't have that problem with the other views, because those entity classes were created with navigation properties to the relevant entities. This gives you the opportunity to learn how to send data that isn't part of the model, to the view.

You can use the dynamic **ViewData** object to send data to a view. You simply add a property to it and assign a value, and then use that property with Razor in the view.

When working with <select> lists, the data has to be converted into a **SelectList** collection. You do that by creating an instance of that class and pass in the collection or table to its constructor, along with the name of the properties that will be used for its id values and display texts.

You'll learn more about the code in the action methods after you have made these changes.

1. Open the **VideosController** class and locate the HTTP GET **Create** action.
2. Create an instance of the **SelectList** class and pass in the **Modules** table to its constructor. The second parameter tells the select list that it should send the value of the **Id** property as the selected value when a user selects an item. The third parameter tells the select list what value to display in the drop-down.
   ```
   ViewData["ModuleId"] = new SelectList(_context.Modules, "Id",
   "Title");
   ```
3. Add the same **ViewData** code on the row above the **return** statement in the HTTP POST **Create** action.
4. Refresh the browser and select **Video** in the *Admin* menu, and then click on the **Create New** link. As you can see, the **Modules** drop-down now displays titles for the values that you can select.
5. Because the course id isn't assigned by the video, it can be removed from the **Create** view altogether. Open the **Create** view and delete the <div> decorated with the **form-group** class that contains the **CourseId** elements.
   ```html
   <div class="form-group">
       <label asp-for="CourseId" class="col-md-2 control-label">
       </label>
       <div class="col-md-10">
           <input asp-for="CourseId" class="form-control" />
           <span asp-validation-for="CourseId" class="text-danger">
           </span>
       </div>
   </div>
   ```
6. Repeat steps 1-5 for the **Edit** actions.
7. Remove the **CourseId** from the **Index**, **Delete**, and **Details** views.
8. Repeat steps 1-7 for the **DownloadsController**.

The code for the altered **Create** actions in the **VideoController** class:

```csharp
public IActionResult Create()
{
    ViewData["ModuleId"] = new SelectList(_context.Modules, "Id",
        "Title");
```

```
        return View();
}

[HttpPost]
[ValidateAntiForgeryToken]
public async Task<IActionResult>
Create([Bind("Id,Title,Description,Duration,Thumbnail,Url,Position,
ModuleId,CourseId")] Video video)
{
    if (ModelState.IsValid)
    {
        _context.Add(video);
        await _context.SaveChangesAsync();
        return RedirectToAction("Index");
    }
    ViewData["ModuleId"] = new SelectList(_context.Modules, "Id",
        "Title");

    return View(video);
}
```

The code for the altered **Edit** actions in the **VideoController** class:

```
public async Task<IActionResult> Edit(int? id)
{
    if (id == null)
    {
        return NotFound();
    }

    var video = await _context.Videos.SingleOrDefaultAsync(m =>
        m.Id == id);

    if (video == null)
    {
        return NotFound();
    }

    ViewData["ModuleId"] = new SelectList(_context.Modules, "Id",
        "Title");

    return View(video);
}
```

```
[HttpPost]
[ValidateAntiForgeryToken]
public async Task<IActionResult> Edit(int id,
[Bind("Id,Title,Description,Duration,Thumbnail,Url,Position,ModuleId,
CourseId")] Video video)
{
    if (id != video.Id)
    {
        return NotFound();
    }

    if (ModelState.IsValid)
    {
        try
        {
            _context.Update(video);
            await _context.SaveChangesAsync();
        }
        catch (DbUpdateConcurrencyException)
        {
            if (!VideoExists(video.Id))
            {
                return NotFound();
            }
            else
            {
                throw;
            }
        }
        return RedirectToAction("Index");
    }

    ViewData["ModuleId"] = new SelectList(_context.Modules, "Id",
        "Title");

    return View(video);
}
```

The Index Action

A view is rendered by the ASP.NET Core framework when the corresponding action in the controller has finished building the model (if one is needed). The model is sent to the framework and is rendered with the view's HTML markup. With Razor and Tag Helpers, you can inject C# code and model data into the view at design time, which is transformed into HTML when the view is rendered.

The **Index** view in your administrator user interface is the first view the user sees when clicking a menu item in the **Admin** menu. The default **Index** view displays a table with data from the model collection, as well as links to the other views associated with the current controller.

The **Index** action might vary depending on the model data. In the following example from the **Video** controller, the **View** method that tells ASP.NET Core to render the view, is given the model as a collection of videos from the **Videos** table.

```
public async Task<IActionResult> Index()
{
    return View(await _context.Videos.ToListAsync());
}
```

In the **Courses** controller's **Index** action, a model is created with the combined data from the **Courses** table and the associated **Instructor** table by calling the **Include** method. This is possible because the **Course** entity model has an **Instructor** property.

The **Include** method loads data from a related table at the same time as the entity model is filled. A requirement is that the entity class has a property for the other entity class. It can be a one-to-one relationship or a one-to-many relationship; the difference is that the latter is a collection (see the **Course** entity class). If the **Include** method isn't called, the property will have its default value.

Property in the **Course** class:

```
public Instructor Instructor { get; set; }
```

The **Index** action:

```
public async Task<IActionResult> Index()
{
    var applicationDbContext = _context.Courses.Include(c =>
        c.Instructor);

    return View(await applicationDbContext.ToListAsync());
}
```

The Index View

As you can see from the code below, an **Index** view is just a table displaying the model data. It also has links to the other views, the <a> elements with the **asp-action** Tag Helper. Note that the **asp-controller** Tag Helper has been omitted; this is possible because ASP.NET Core keeps track of the view's controller.

The **DisplayNameFor** method will display the name of the property as a label in the view. The displayed text can be changed by using the **[Display]** attribute on the property in the entity class.

The **DisplayFor** method will display the content of the property with the HTML element type it finds most suitable for the data in the property. If the property is a collection it will use a <select> element, and if it is a string it will use an <input> element.

Add the Bootstrap class **table-condensed** to the <table> element if you want a more compact table, and the **table-striped** for alternating row colors.

```
@model IEnumerable<VideoOnDemand.Entities.Video>

@{
    ViewData["Title"] = "Index";
}

<h2>Index</h2>

<p>
    <a asp-action="Create">Create New</a>
</p>
<table class="table">
    <thead>
        <tr>
            <th>@Html.DisplayNameFor(model => model.Title)</th>
            <th>@Html.DisplayNameFor(model => model.Description)</th>
            <th>@Html.DisplayNameFor(model => model.Duration)</th>
            <th>@Html.DisplayNameFor(model => model.Thumbnail)</th>
            <th>@Html.DisplayNameFor(model => model.Url)</th>
            <th>@Html.DisplayNameFor(model => model.Position)</th>
            <th></th>
        </tr>
    </thead>
    <tbody>
```

```
@foreach (var item in Model) {
    <tr>
        <td>@Html.DisplayFor(modelItem => item.Title)</td>
        <td>@Html.DisplayFor(modelItem => item.Description)</td>
        <td>@Html.DisplayFor(modelItem => item.Duration)</td>
        <td>@Html.DisplayFor(modelItem => item.Thumbnail)</td>
        <td>@Html.DisplayFor(modelItem => item.Url)</td>
        <td>@Html.DisplayFor(modelItem => item.Position)</td>
        <td>
            <a asp-action="Edit" asp-route-id="@item.Id">Edit</a> |
            <a asp-action="Details" asp-route-id="@item.Id">
              Details</a> |
            <a asp-action="Delete" asp-route-id="@item.Id">
              Delete</a>
        </td>
    </tr>
}
</tbody>
</table>
```

The Details Action

As you can see from the code below, the **SingleOrDefaultAsync** LINQ extension method is used to fetch one video from the **Videos** table asynchronously.

When executing code asynchronously the thread is temporarily given back to the application for other work, and when the data has been fetched, the thread is returned, and the execution continues.

To execute asynchronous code, the method needs to be declared as **async** and return a **Task** or a **Task<T>**, where **T** is a type.

The **NotFound** method will return a *404 Not Found* error to the browser. There are other such methods for other eventualities, such as **Ok** for a 200 result.

```
public async Task<IActionResult> Details(int? id)
{
    if (id == null)
    {
        return NotFound();
    }

    var video = await _context.Videos
        .SingleOrDefaultAsync(m => m.Id == id);
```

```
    if (video == null)
    {
        return NotFound();
    }

    return View(video);
}
```

The Details View

As you can see from the code below, the **Details** view is basically a data list, much like the table in the **Index** view. It also has two buttons, one for returning to the **Index** view and one for opening the current video's **Edit** view.

```
@model VideoOnDemand.Entities.Video

@{
    ViewData["Title"] = "Details";
}

<h2>Details</h2>

<div>
    <h4>Video</h4>
    <hr />
    <dl class="dl-horizontal">
        <dt>@Html.DisplayNameFor(model => model.Title)</dt>
        <dd>@Html.DisplayFor(model => model.Title)</dd>
        <dt>@Html.DisplayNameFor(model => model.Description)</dt>
        <dd>@Html.DisplayFor(model => model.Description) </dd>
        <dt>@Html.DisplayNameFor(model => model.Duration)</dt>
        <dd>@Html.DisplayFor(model => model.Duration)</dd>
        <dt>@Html.DisplayNameFor(model => model.Thumbnail)</dt>
        <dd>@Html.DisplayFor(model => model.Thumbnail)</dd>
        <dt>@Html.DisplayNameFor(model => model.Url)</dt>
        <dd>@Html.DisplayFor(model => model.Url)</dd>
        <dt>@Html.DisplayNameFor(model => model.Position)</dt>
        <dd>@Html.DisplayFor(model => model.Position)</dd>
    </dl>
</div>
<div>
    <a asp-action="Edit" asp-route-id="@Model.Id">Edit</a> |
    <a asp-action="Index">Back to List</a>
</div>
```

The HTTP GET Delete Action

The HTTP GET **Delete** action is identical to the **Details** action.

The HTTP POST DeleteConfirmed Action

The HTTP POST **Delete** action is called when the **Delete** button is clicked in the **Delete** view.

First the video is fetched from the database, and then it is removed. The **SaveChanges-Async** method removes the record from the database table, then the user is redirected to the **Index** view.

```
[HttpPost, ActionName("Delete")]
[ValidateAntiForgeryToken]
public async Task<IActionResult> DeleteConfirmed(int id)
{
    var video = await _context.Videos.SingleOrDefaultAsync(m =>
        m.Id == id);
    context.Videos.Remove(video);
    await _context.SaveChangesAsync();
    return RedirectToAction("Index");
}
```

The Delete View

The **Delete** view is identical to the **Details** view, except for two things.

It has a hidden <input> element for the **Id** property. Sometimes the hidden field ends up outside of the form when scaffolding the view; if that happens, move it inside the <form> element.

```
<input type="hidden" asp-for="Id" />
```

And it has a <form> element that calls the **DeleteConfirmed** action when the user clicks the **Delete** button.

```
<form asp-action="Delete">
    <div class="form-actions no-color">
        <input type="hidden" asp-for="Id" />
        <input type="submit" value="Delete" class="btn btn-default" /> |
        <a asp-action="Index">Back to List</a>
    </div>
</form>
```

The HTTP GET Create Action

You have already altered the HTTP GET **Create** action, which is called when the **Create New** link is clicked in the **Index** view. For views where the form should be empty, like the **Create** view, the **View** method is called without a model.

In this action the dynamic **ViewData** object is used to send a list of modules to the view.

```
public IActionResult Create()
{
    ViewData["ModuleId"] = new SelectList(_context.Modules, "Id",
        "Title");
    return View();
}
```

The HTTP POST Create Action

The HTTP POST **Create** action is called when the **Create** button is clicked in the **Create** view.

If the model state is valid – that is, all mandatory controls have been filled out in the form in the **Create** view – the video is added and persisted in the database. Then the user is redirected to the **Index** view.

If the model state isn't valid, the modules are loaded into the **ViewData** object and the view is returned with the invalid model. This makes it possible to display error messages to the user while keeping the data in the form controls.

The **[ValidateAntiForgeryToken]** attribute is a security measure that checks a unique value on roundtrips to the server to make sure that the call originated on that server.

The **[Bind]** attribute determines what model properties will receive values from the client. This ensures that no illegal data enters the action.

```
[HttpPost]
[ValidateAntiForgeryToken]
public async Task<IActionResult>
Create([Bind("Id,Title,Description,Duration,Thumbnail,Url,Position,
ModuleId,CourseId")] Video video)
{
    if (ModelState.IsValid)
    {
        _context.Add(video);
        await _context.SaveChangesAsync();
```

```
            return RedirectToAction("Index");
    }

    ViewData["ModuleId"] = new SelectList(_context.Modules, "Id",
        "Title");

    return View(video);
}
```

The Create View

The **Create** view contains one form with all its controls rendered from the model data types, displaying the property data.

Form validation is added on two levels, the form level with the **asp-validation-summary** Tag Helper, and on element level with the **asp-validation-for** Tag Helper. The validation summary displays all errors reported from the model, while errors related to a specific property are displayed for each individual element. A property error could be that too many, or too few, characters have been entered, or that a value is out of range.

The form is sent to the HTTP POST **Create** action when the **Create** button is clicked.

Note that there are JavaScript libraries that can do client-side validation to avoid a round-trip to the server when validating the input controls.

```
@model VideoOnDemand.Entities.Video

@{
    ViewData["Title"] = "Create";
}

<h2>Create</h2>

<form asp-action="Create">
    <div class="form-horizontal">
        <h4>Video</h4>
        <hr />
        <div asp-validation-summary="ModelOnly"
            class="text-danger"></div>
        <div class="form-group">
            <label asp-for="Title" class="col-md-2 control-label">
            </label>
            <div class="col-md-10">
```

```
                <input asp-for="Title" class="form-control" />
                <span asp-validation-for="Title" class="text-danger">
                </span>
            </div>
        </div>
        <div class="form-group">
            <label asp-for="Description" class="col-md-2
                control-label"></label>
            <div class="col-md-10">
                <input asp-for="Description" class="form-control" />
                <span asp-validation-for="Description"
                    class="text-danger"></span>
            </div>
        </div>
        <div class="form-group">
            <label asp-for="Duration" class="col-md-2 control-label">
            </label>
            <div class="col-md-10">
                <input asp-for="Duration" class="form-control" />
                <span asp-validation-for="Duration"
                    class="text-danger"></span>
            </div>
        </div>
        <div class="form-group">
            <label asp-for="Thumbnail" class="col-md-2 control-label">
            </label>
            <div class="col-md-10">
                <input asp-for="Thumbnail" class="form-control" />
                <span asp-validation-for="Thumbnail"
                    class="text-danger"></span>
            </div>
        </div>
        <div class="form-group">
            <label asp-for="Url" class="col-md-2 control-label">
            </label>
            <div class="col-md-10">
                <input asp-for="Url" class="form-control" />
                <span asp-validation-for="Url" class="text-danger">
                </span>
            </div>
        </div>
        <div class="form-group">
            <label asp-for="Position" class="col-md-2 control-label">
            </label>
```

```
                <div class="col-md-10">
                    <input asp-for="Position" class="form-control" />
                    <span asp-validation-for="Position"
                        class="text-danger"></span>
                </div>
            </div>
            <div class="form-group">
                <label asp-for="ModuleId" class="col-md-2 control-label">
                </label>
                <div class="col-md-10">
                    <select asp-for="ModuleId" class ="form-control"
                     asp-items="ViewBag.ModuleId"></select>
                </div>
            </div>
            <div class="form-group">
                <div class="col-md-offset-2 col-md-10">
                    <input type="submit" value="Create"
                        class="btn btn-default" />
                </div>
            </div>
        </div>
    </form>

    <div>
        <a asp-action="Index">Back to List</a>
    </div>
```

The HTTP GET Edit Action

You have already altered the HTTP GET **Edit** action. It is called when the **Edit** link is clicked in the **Index** view. The **View** method is typically called with a model, because the **Edit** form should be populated by the model when it is opened.

First the **id** parameter is checked to see if it is null, and if it is, then a *404 Not Found* error is sent back to the browser.

If the id is valid, then the video matching that id is fetched asynchronously from the **Video** table in the database, using the **SingleOrDefaultAsync** method. If the result is null (no video was found for the id), then a *404 Not Found* error is sent back to the browser.

If a video was found, then the modules collection is stored in the dynamic **ViewData** object, and the video is passed to the **View** method to be rendered with the view.

```
public async Task<IActionResult> Edit(int? id)
{
    if (id == null)
    {
        return NotFound();
    }

    var video = await _context.Videos.SingleOrDefaultAsync(m =>
        m.Id == id);
    if (video == null)
    {
        return NotFound();
    }
    ViewData["ModuleId"] = new SelectList(_context.Modules, "Id",
        "Title");

    return View(video);
}
```

The HTTP POST Edit Action

The HTTP POST **Edit** action is called when the **Save** button is clicked in the **Edit** view.

If the model state and id are valid, then the video is updated and persisted in the database. Then the user is redirected to the **Index** view.

If the model state or the id are invalid, or a concurrency exception has been thrown, then the modules are loaded into the **ViewData** object, and the view is returned with the invalid model. This makes it possible to display error messages to the user while keeping the data in the form controls.

A concurrency error can occur if the record is modified by more than one user at the same time.

```
[HttpPost]
[ValidateAntiForgeryToken]
public async Task<IActionResult> Edit(int id,
[Bind("Id,Title,Description,Duration,Thumbnail,Url,Position,ModuleId,
CourseId")] Video video)
{
    if (id != video.Id)
    {
        return NotFound();
    }
```

```
if (ModelState.IsValid)
{
    try
    {
        _context.Update(video);
        await _context.SaveChangesAsync();
    }
    catch (DbUpdateConcurrencyException)
    {
        if (!VideoExists(video.Id))
        {
            return NotFound();
        }
        else
        {
            throw;
        }
    }
    return RedirectToAction("Index");
}

ViewData["ModuleId"] = new SelectList(_context.Modules, "Id", "Title");

return View(video);
}
```

The Edit View

The **Edit** view is identical to the **Create** view, apart from the text on the button, and the **asp-action** Tag Helper on the form. Here it targets the **Edit** action instead of the **Create** action.

Summary

In this chapter, you scaffolded all, but one, controller and their views. You also added and modified data in the database with the view.

Next, you will add a controller, actions, and views for the **UserCourseDTO** class.

24. The UserCourse Controller

In this chapter, you will create the **UserCourses** controller and its views, which are used to perform CRUD operations against the **UserCourses** table in the database. This controller is a bit different, in that it uses a DTO instead if an entity class. The **UserCourses** table connects users with courses.

In some cases drop-downs will display incorrect data in the views; this is something that you will have to correct. Instead of displaying the item indices, they should display the title or name.

Technologies used in this chapter
1. **C#** – To create the controller and its actions.
2. **HTML** – To create views.
3. **Entity framework** – To perform CRUD operations.

Overview

Your task is to create the **UserCourses** controller and its actions and views. This enables the user to display, add, update, and delete data in the **UserCourses** database table.

The UserCourse Controller

In this scenario where the two tables aren't linked through the entity classes, you will create the controller from scratch by adding a class called **UserCoursesController** to the *Controllers* folder. Don't use scaffolding.

The controller actions will need instances of the **ApplicationDbContext** and the **UserStore** to be able to perform CRUD operations and to look up user information in the database.

You can add these instances in different ways. One is to inject the **ApplicationDbContext** into the constructor and create an instance of the **UserStore** in the constructor. This steps away from the DI principle in that an instance of a class is created where it could be injected. However, if you scaffold the controller, you will find that that is exactly how it is implemented.

A better way is to add the **UserStore** with the necessary data types as a service to the **ConfigureServices** method in the **Startup** class. That way you will get both the **UserStore** and the **ApplicationDbContext** when injecting the **UserStore** into the constructor. There is an overload to the **UserStore** service that takes three types: **ApplicationUser**, **Identity-Role**, and **ApplicationDbContext**.

You can then store the **ApplicationDbContext** in a separate variable called **_db** for easy access.

Creating the UserCoursesController Class

1. Open the **Startup** class and locate the **ConfigureServices** method.
2. Add a singleton instance of the **UserStore** that takes the following three types, above the **AddDbContext** service: **ApplicationUser**, **IdentityRole**, and **ApplicationDbContext**.
    ```
    services.AddSingleton<UserStore<ApplicationUser, IdentityRole,
    ApplicationDbContext>>();
    ```
3. Add a class called **UserCoursesController** to the *Controllers* folder and inherit the **Controller** class. Right click on the folder and select **Add-Class**, to add the controller.
    ```
    public class UserCoursesController : Controller
    {
    }
    ```
4. Add a constructor and inject an instance of the **UserStore** service that you defined earlier. Create a class level variable called **_db** for the **ApplicationDbContext** class and assign its value from the **UserStore** instance in the constructor. Add another class level variable called **_db** of the same type as the **UserStore** instance, and assign it the injected object. This will make the database and user object available throughout the controller.
    ```
    private readonly  ApplicationDbContext _db;

    public UserCoursesController(UserStore<ApplicationUser,
    IdentityRole, ApplicationDbContext> userStore)
    {
        _db = userStore.Context;
    }
    ```

The code in the **UserCoursesController** class, so far:

```
public class UserCoursesController : Controller
{
    private readonly  ApplicationDbContext _db;
```

```
public UserCoursesController(UserStore<ApplicationUser,
IdentityRole, ApplicationDbContext> userStore)
{
    _db = userStore.Context;
}
}
```

Adding the Index Action and View

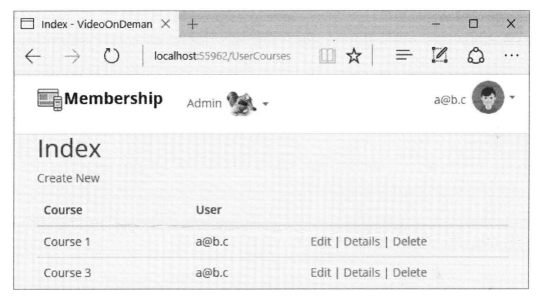

1. Open the **UserCoursesController** class.

2. Add a parameterless method called **Index** that returns **IActionResult**.
   ```
   public IActionResult Index()
   {
   }
   ```

3. Fetch all courses from the **Course** table and join in the **UserCourses** table on the **CourseId**. Use the **Select** method to create an instance of the **UserCourseDTO** class and fill it with data from the two previously mentioned tables. Use the **UserId** property from the **UserCourses** table and the **_db** instance to fetch the user's email from the **AspNetUsers** table.
   ```
   var model = _db.Courses
       .Join(_db.UserCourses, c => c.Id, uc => uc.CourseId,
   ```

```
        (c, uc) => new { Courses = c, UserCourses = uc })
    .Select(s => new UserCourseDTO
    {
        CourseId = s.Courses.Id, CourseTitle = s.Courses.Title,
        UserId = s.UserCourses.UserId,
        UserEmail = _db.Users.FirstOrDefault(u =>
            u.Id.Equals(s.UserCourses.UserId)).Email
    });
```

4. Return the **model** object with the **View** method.

```
return View(model);
```

5. Right click on the **Index** action and select **Add View**, to scaffold the **Index** view. Select the **Empty (without model)** template and make sure that it's not created as a partial view. The view will be added to a folder with the name *UserCourses* in the *View* folder.

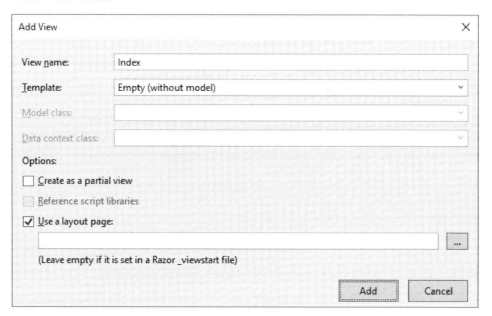

6. Run the application and select **UserCourse** from the **Admin** menu. A very spartan-looking **Index** view with the text *Index* should be displayed.

7. Delete all markup in the **Index** view you just created.

8. The **Index** view in the *Downloads* folder is very similar to the one you are creating. Open that view and copy all the content. Paste the markup into the **Index** view for the **UserCourses** controller.

9. Change the model to **IEnumerable<UserCourseDTO>**.

   ```
   @model IEnumerable<UserCourseDTO>
   ```

10. Replace the **DisplayNameFor** methods with the text **Course** and **User**
    respectively in the table header.

    ```
    <thead>
        <tr>
            <th>Course</th>
            <th>User</th>
            <th></th>
        </tr>
    </thead>
    ```

11. Relpace the erroneous **Title** and **Url** properties with the **CourseTitle** and
    UserEmail properties respectively in the **DisplayFor** methods.

    ```
    <td>@Html.DisplayFor(modelItem => item.CourseTitle)</td>
    <td>@Html.DisplayFor(modelItem => item.UserEmail)</td>
    ```

12. Change the **asp-route-id** to **asp-route-userId** for all <a> elements and assign the
    UserId property from the current item to them. Copy the **asp-route-userId** and
    add it as a second parameter called **asp-route-courseId** to all <a> elements.
    Assign the **CourseId** property from the current item to them. The rest of the
    HTTP GET actions you will add to the controller require both ids.

    ```
    <a asp-action="Edit" asp-route-courseId="@item.CourseId" asp-
    route-userId="@item.UserId">Edit</a>
    ```

The complete code in the **Index** action:

```
public IActionResult Index()
{
    var model = _db.Courses
        .Join(_db.UserCourses, c => c.Id, uc => uc.CourseId,
            (c, uc) => new { Courses = c, UserCourses = uc })
        .Select(s => new UserCourseDTO
        {
            CourseId = s.Courses.Id, CourseTitle = s.Courses.Title,
            UserId = s.UserCourses.UserId, UserEmail =
                _db.Users.FirstOrDefault(u =>
                    u.Id.Equals(s.UserCourses.UserId)).Email
        });
    return View(model);
}
```

The complete markup in the **Index** view:

```
@model IEnumerable<UserCourseDTO>

@{
    ViewData["Title"] = "Index";
}

<h2>Index</h2>

<p><a asp-action="Create">Create New</a></p>
<table class="table">
    <thead>
        <tr>
            <th>Course</th>
            <th>User</th>
            <th></th>
        </tr>
    </thead>
    <tbody>
        @foreach (var item in Model)
        {
            <tr>
                <td>@Html.DisplayFor(modelItem => item.CourseTitle)</td>
                <td>@Html.DisplayFor(modelItem => item.UserEmail)</td>
                <td>
                    <a asp-action="Edit"
                        asp-route-courseId="@item.CourseId"
                        asp-route-userId="@item.UserId">Edit</a> |
                    <a asp-action="Details"
                        asp-route-courseId="@item.CourseId"
                        asp-route-userId="@item.UserId">Details</a> |
                    <a asp-action="Delete"
                        asp-route-courseId="@item.CourseId"
                        asp-route-userId="@item.UserId">Delete</a>
                </td>
            </tr>
        }
    </tbody>
</table>
```

Adding the Details Action and View

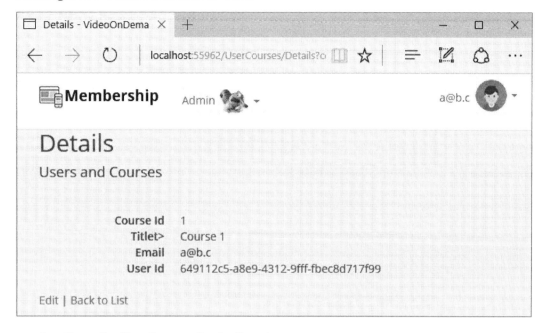

1. Open the **UserCoursesController** class.
2. Add an asynchronous method called **Details** that takes two parameters, **userId** of type **string** and **courseId** of type **int**, and return **Task<IActionResult>**.
    ```
    public async Task<IActionResult> Details(string userId,
    int courseId)
    { }
    ```
3. Return a *404 Not Found* error with the **NotFound** method if the **userId** is **null** or the **courseId** is equal to the default value for the **int** data type.
    ```
    if (userId == null || courseId.Equals(default(int)))
    {
        return NotFound();
    }
    ```
4. Copy the model variable and LINQ expression from the **Index** action and paste it below the if-block. Add a call to the **FirstOrDefaultAsync** method to select the first **UserCourseDTO** that matches the **userId** and **courseId** parameter values.
    ```
    var model = await _db.Courses
        .Join(_db.UserCourses, c => c.Id, uc => uc.CourseId,
            (c, uc) => new { Courses = c, UserCourses = uc })
    ```

```
.Select(s => new UserCourseDTO
{
    CourseId = s.Courses.Id, CourseTitle = s.Courses.Title,
    UserId = s.UserCourses.UserId,
    UserEmail = _db.Users.FirstOrDefault(u =>
        u.Id.Equals(s.UserCourses.UserId)).Email
})
.FirstOrDefaultAsync(w => w.CourseId.Equals(courseId) &&
    w.UserId.Equals(userId));
```

5. Return a *404 Not Found* error with the **NotFound** method if the **model** is **null**, which means that there was no matching **UserCourseDTO** for the ids.
```
if (model == null)
{
    return NotFound();
}
```

6. Return the **model** object with the **View** method.
```
return View(model);
```

7. Run the application and select **UserCourse** from the **Admin** menu. A very spartan-looking **Index** view with the text *Index* should be displayed.

8. Copy the **Details** view from the *Views/Downloads* folder and paste it into the *Views/UserCourses* folder. Open the view.

9. Change the model to **UserCourseDTO**.
```
@model UserCourseDTO
```

10. Change the text in the <h4> element to *Users and Courses*.

11. Replace the erroneous **Title** property with the **CourseId** property.
```
<dt>@Html.DisplayNameFor(model => model.CourseId)</dt>
<dd>@Html.DisplayFor(model => model.CourseId)</dd>
```

12. Replace the erroneous **Url** property with the **CourseTitle** property.

13. Add two more <dt> and <dd> elements for the **UserEmail** and **UserId** properties.
```
<dt>@Html.DisplayNameFor(model => model.UserEmail)</dt>
<dd>@Html.DisplayFor(model => model.UserEmail)</dd>
<dt>@Html.DisplayNameFor(model => model.UserId)</dt>
<dd>@Html.DisplayFor(model => model.UserId)</dd>
```

14. Replace the **Edit** <a> element with the one from the **Index** view. Change **@item** to **@Model**.
```
<a asp-action="Edit" asp-route-courseId="@Model.CourseId"
    asp-route-userId="@Model.UserId">Edit</a>
```

15. Save all files and refresh the browser. Select the **UserCourse** menu item in the **Admin** menu. Click on the **Details** link for one of the items in the list. The **Details** view should open and display the data for the item.

The complete code in the **Details** action:

```
public async Task<IActionResult> Details(string userId, int courseId)
{
    if (userId == null || courseId.Equals(default(int)))
    {
        return NotFound();
    }

    var model = await _db.Courses
        .Join(_db.UserCourses, c => c.Id, uc => uc.CourseId,
            (c, uc) => new { Courses = c, UserCourses = uc })
        .Select(s => new UserCourseDTO
        {
            CourseId = s.Courses.Id, CourseTitle = s.Courses.Title,
            UserId = s.UserCourses.UserId,
            UserEmail = _db.Users.FirstOrDefault(u =>
                u.Id.Equals(s.UserCourses.UserId)).Email
        })
        .FirstOrDefaultAsync(w => w.CourseId.Equals(courseId) &&
            w.UserId.Equals(userId));

    if (model == null)
    {
        return NotFound();
    }

    return View(model);
}
```

The complete code in the **Details** view:

```
@model UserCourseDTO

@{
    ViewData["Title"] = "Details";
}

<h2>Details</h2>
```

```
<div>
    <h4>Users and Courses</h4>
    <hr />
    <dl class="dl-horizontal">
        <dt>@Html.DisplayNameFor(model => model.CourseId)</dt>
        <dd>@Html.DisplayFor(model => model.CourseId)</dd>
        <dt>@Html.DisplayNameFor(model => model.CourseTitle)t>
        <dd>@Html.DisplayFor(model => model.CourseTitle)</dd>
        <dt>@Html.DisplayNameFor(model => model.UserEmail)</dt>
        <dd>@Html.DisplayFor(model => model.UserEmail)</dd>
        <dt>@Html.DisplayNameFor(model => model.UserId)</dt>
        <dd>@Html.DisplayFor(model => model.UserId)</dd>
    </dl>
</div>
<div>
    <a asp-action="Edit" asp-route-courseId="@Model.CourseId"
        asp-route-userId="@Model.UserId">Edit</a> |
    <a asp-action="Index">Back to List</a>
</div>
```

Adding the HTTP GET Create Action and View

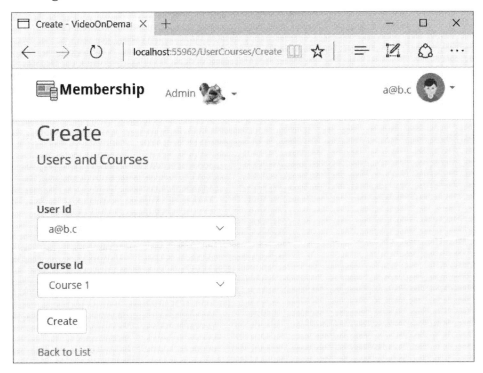

1. Open the **UserCoursesController** class.

2. Add a parameterless method called **Create** that return **IActionResult**.
```
public IActionResult Create()
{
}
```

3. Add the courses in the **Courses** table to a property called **CourseId** in the dynamic **ViewData** object.
```
ViewData["CourseId"] = new SelectList(_db.Courses, "Id",
    "Title");
```

4. Add the users in the **AspNetUser** table to a property called **UserId** in the dynamic **ViewData** object. Use the **Users** collection in the _**db** object.
```
ViewData["UserId"] = new SelectList(_db.Users, "Id",
    "Email");
```

5. Return with a call to the **View** method.
```
return View();
```

6. Copy the **Create** view from the *Views/Downloads* folder and paste it into the *Views/UserCourses* folder. Open the view.

7. Change the model to **UserCourseDTO**.
```
@model UserCourseDTO
```

8. Change the text in the <h4> element to *Users and Courses*.

9. Delete the two first **form-group** <div> elements and their content.

10. Locate the **form-group** <div> element that has the <select> element for the **ModuleId** and copy it, with its content, and paste it below the one you copied.
```
<div class="form-group">
    <label asp-for="ModuleId" class="col-md-2 control-label">
    </label>
    <div class="col-md-10">
        <select asp-for="ModuleId" class ="form-control"
            asp-items="ViewBag.ModuleId"></select>
    </div>
</div>
```

11. Replace all **ModuleId** occurrences in the first **form-group** <div> with **UserId**.
```
<div class="form-group">
    <label asp-for="UserId" class="col-md-2 control-label"></label>
    <div class="col-md-10">
        <select asp-for="UserId" class ="form-control"
```

```
                          asp-items="ViewBag.UserId"></select>
            </div>
        </div>
```

12. Save all files and refresh the browser. Select the **UserCourse** menu item in the **Admin** menu. Click on the **Create New** link. The **Create** view should open and display the data in two drop-downs. Clicking the **Create** button won't save the values because you haven't added the necessary HTTP POST **Create** action yet.

The complete code in the HTTP GET **Create** action:

```
public IActionResult Create() {
    ViewData["CourseId"] = new SelectList(_db.Courses, "Id", "Title");
    ViewData["UserId"] = new SelectList(_db.Users, "Id",
        "Email");
    return View();
}
```

The complete code in the **Create** view:

```
@model UserCourseDTO

@{
    ViewData["Title"] = "Create";
}

<h2>Create</h2>

<form asp-action="Create">
    <div class="form-horizontal">
        <h4>Users and Courses</h4>
        <hr />
        <div asp-validation-summary="ModelOnly" class="text-danger">
        </div>
        <div class="form-group">
            <label asp-for="UserId" class="col-md-2 control-label">
            </label>
            <div class="col-md-10">
                <select asp-for="UserId" class ="form-control"
                    asp-items="ViewBag.UserId"></select>
            </div>
        </div>
        <div class="form-group">
            <label asp-for="CourseId" class="col-md-2 control-label">
            </label>
```

```
            <div class="col-md-10">
                <select asp-for="CourseId" class="form-control"
                    asp-items="ViewBag.CourseId"></select>
            </div>
        </div>
        <div class="form-group">
            <div class="col-md-offset-2 col-md-10">
                <input type="submit" value="Create"
                    class="btn btn-default" />
            </div>
        </div>
    </div>
</form>

<div>
    <a asp-action="Index">Back to List</a>
</div>
```

Adding the HTTP POST Create Action

This action is called when the user clicks the **Create** button in the **Create** view, after filling out the form. The data from the client is saved to the database in the **Create** action that the form posts to.

1. Open the **UserCoursesController** class.
2. Add an asynchronous method called **Create** that returns a **Task<IActionResult>**. It should receive the data as an instance of the **UserCourse** entity and bind the **UserId** and **CourseId** from the HTML response data. Note that you can have different models for the view and the receiving HTTP POST action. ASP.NET Core will automatically map properties with the same name. Add the **[HttpPost]** and **[ValidateAntiForgeryToken]** attributes to the action.

```
[HttpPost]
[ValidateAntiForgeryToken]
public async Task<IActionResult> Create([Bind("UserId,CourseId")]
UserCourse userCourse)
{
}
```

3. Check that the model is valid with the **IsValid** property on the **ModelState** object.

```
if (ModelState.IsValid)
{
}
```

4. Add a try/catch-block inside the if-block.

```
try
{
}
catch
{
}
```

5. Add the **UserCourse** object to the **UserCourses** table, save the changes, and redirect to the **Index** action. Place the code inside the try-block.

```
_db.Add(userCourse);
await _db.SaveChangesAsync();
return RedirectToAction("Index");
```

6. Add an error to the **ModelState** object with the **AddModelError** method in the catch-block. This error will be displayed if you try to add a record that already exist in the **UserCourses** table.

```
ModelState.AddModelError("", "That combination already exist.");
```

7. Add the users and courses to the dynamic **ViewData** object below the if-block, like you did in the HTTP GET **Create** action.

```
ViewData["CourseId"] = new SelectList(_db.Courses, "Id", "Title",
    userCourse.CourseId);
ViewData["UserId"] = new SelectList(_db.Users, "Id",
    "Email");
```

8. Return with a call to the **View** method.

```
return View();
```

9. Save all files and refresh the browser. Select the **UserCourse** menu item in the **Admin** menu. Click on the **Create New** link. The **Create** view should open and display the data in two drop-downs. Select two values and click the **Create** button. The new user-course combination should be displayed in the **Index** view.

10. Try to add a combination of values that already exist in the database. The error should be displayed above the form controls.

The complete code in the HTTP POST **Create** action:

```
[HttpPost]
[ValidateAntiForgeryToken]
public async Task<IActionResult> Create([Bind("UserId,CourseId")]
UserCourse userCourse)
{
    if (ModelState.IsValid)
    {
        try
        {
            _db.Add(userCourse);
            await _db.SaveChangesAsync();
            return RedirectToAction("Index");
        }
        catch
        {
            ModelState.AddModelError("",
                "That combination already exist.");
        }
    }

    ViewData["CourseId"] = new SelectList(_db.Courses, "Id", "Title",
        userCourse.CourseId);
    ViewData["UserId"] = new SelectList(_db.Users, "Id",
        "Email");

    return View();
}
```

Adding the HTTP GET Edit Action and View

The HTTP GET **Edit** action is very similar to the **Details** action. You can copy it and modify the model to use the **SingleOrDefault** method to fetch the record that matches the passed in **UserId** and **CourseId** from the **UserCourses** table.

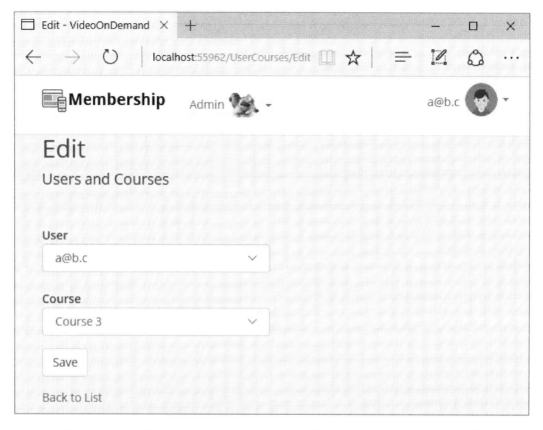

1. Copy the **Details** action and paste it below the last action in the controller class.
2. Rename the method **Edit**.
3. Replace the **model** variable's LINQ expression for one that fetches the record that matches the passed in **UserId** and **CourseId**, from the **UserCourses** table.
   ```
   var model = await _db.UserCourses.SingleOrDefaultAsync(m =>
   m.UserId.Equals(userId) && m.CourseId.Equals(courseId));
   ```
4. Add the courses and users from their respective tables to the **ViewData** object, above the **return** statement.
   ```
   ViewData["CourseId"] = new SelectList(_db.Courses, "Id", "Title");
   ViewData["UserId"] = new SelectList(_db.Users, "Id", "Email");
   ```
5. Copy the **Create** view in the *Views/UserCourses* folder and paste it into the same folder. Rename it **Edit**.
6. Change the **@model** directive to use the **UserCourse** entity class.
   ```
   @model VideoOnDemand.Entities.UserCourse
   ```

7. Change the **ViewData** title and the <h2> element to *Edit*.
8. Change the button text to *Save*.
9. Change the **asp-action** to *Edit*. This determines the action that will be called when form is submitted (the **Save** button is clicked).
10. Add the **UserId** and **CourseId** values to hidden fields. You will need them in the HTTP POST version of the action to remove the original record.
    ```
    <input type="hidden" name="originalUserId" value="@Model.UserId"
    />
    <input type="hidden" name="originalCourseId"
    value="@Model.CourseId" />
    ```
11. Run the application without debugging (Ctrl+F5).
12. Click one of the **Edit** links to display the **Edit** view. Clicking the **Save** button will not save the changes, because you haven't added the HTTP POST **Edit** action yet.

The complete code for the HTTP GET **Edit** action:

```
public async Task<IActionResult> Edit(string userId, int courseId)
{
    if (userId == null || courseId.Equals(default(int)))
    {
        return NotFound();
    }

    var model = await _db.UserCourses.SingleOrDefaultAsync(m =>
        m.UserId.Equals(userId) && m.CourseId.Equals(courseId));

    if (model == null)
    {
        return NotFound();
    }

    ViewData["CourseId"] = new SelectList(_db.Courses, "Id", "Title");
    ViewData["UserId"] = new SelectList(_db.Users, "Id",
        "Email");

    return View(model);
}
```

The complete code for the HTTP **Edit** view:

```
@model VideoOnDemand.Entities.UserCourse

@{
    ViewData["Title"] = "Edit";
}

<h2>Edit</h2>

<form asp-action="Edit">
    <div class="form-horizontal">
        <h4>Users and Courses</h4>
        <hr />
        <div asp-validation-summary="ModelOnly" class="text-danger">
        </div>
        <input type="hidden" name="originalUserId"
            value="@Model.UserId" />
        <input type="hidden" name="originalCourseId"
            value="@Model.CourseId" />
        <div class="form-group">
            <label asp-for="UserId" class="col-md-2 control-label">
            </label>
            <div class="col-md-10">
                <select asp-for="UserId" class ="form-control"
                    asp-items="ViewBag.UserId"></select>
            </div>
        </div>
        <div class="form-group">
            <label asp-for="CourseId" class="col-md-2 control-label">
            </label>
            <div class="col-md-10">
                <select asp-for="CourseId" class="form-control"
                    asp-items="ViewBag.CourseId"></select>
            </div>
        </div>
        <div class="form-group">
            <div class="col-md-offset-2 col-md-10">
                <input type="submit" value="Save"
                    class="btn btn-default" />
            </div>
        </div>
    </div>
</form>
```

```
<div>
    <a asp-action="Index">Back to List</a>
</div>
```

Adding the HTTP POST Edit Action

There are alternate ways to implement updates to the one used in this example, but because the properties being changed are part of a composite key, the **UserCourse** entity will not allow any changes. Because a composite key can't be modified, the record in the table must be replaced instead of updated. Entity Framework uses transactions, so there shouldn't be any risk of losing data.

1. Add a method called **UserCourseExist** that takes the user id and course id as parameters, and return a **bool** that specifies if the id combination exists in the **UserCourses** table.

```
private bool UserCourseExists(string userId, int courseId)
{
    return _db.UserCourses.Any(e => e.UserId.Equals(userId) &&
        e.CourseId.Equals(courseId));
}
```

2. Copy the HTTP POST **Create** action's method defiition and attributes, and paste it below the last action in the controller class. Rename the method **Edit** and add two parameters for the original user id and course id. You will need them to delete the original record.

```
[HttpPost]
[ValidateAntiForgeryToken]
public async Task<IActionResult> Edit(string originalUserId, int
originalCourseId, [Bind("UserId,CourseId")] UserCourse userCourse)
{
}
```

3. Check that the id parameters are valid, and return a *404 Not Found* if they are not.

```
if (originalUserId == null ||
originalCourseId.Equals(default(int)))
{
    return NotFound();
}
```

4. Fetch the original **UserCourse** record from the database.

```
var orignalUserCourse = await _db.UserCourses
    .SingleOrDefaultAsync(c => c.UserId.Equals(originalUserId)
    && c.CourseId.Equals(originalCourseId));
```

5. Add an if-block that checks that the modified course doesn't exist. You can't add an existing combination to the table because both ids are part of a composite table key.

```
if (!UserCourseExists(userCourse.UserId, userCourse.CourseId))
{
}
```

6. Add a try/catch-block in the if-block. Delete the original record, add the new record, and save the changes. Then redirect to the **Index** view if everything went well. Leave the catch-block empty.

```
try
{
    _db.Remove(orignalUserCourse);
    _db.Add(userCourse);
    await _db.SaveChangesAsync();
    return RedirectToAction("Index");
}
catch
{
}
```

7. Add a model state error below the if-block that tells the user that the record could not be changed.

```
ModelState.AddModelError("", "Unable to save changes.");
```

8. Add the courses and users to the **ViewData** object.

```
ViewData["CourseId"] = new SelectList(_db.Courses, "Id", "Title",
userCourse.CourseId);
ViewData["UserId"] = new SelectList(_db.Users, "Id", "Email");
```

9. Return the **userCourse** model with the **View** method call.

```
return View(userCourse);
```

10. Run the application without debugging (Ctrl+F5).
11. Open the **Edit** view and try to change the value. If successful, you should be redirected to the **Index** view, otherwise you will remain on the same view and an error message will be displayed.

The complete code for the HTTP POST **Edit** action:

```
[HttpPost]
[ValidateAntiForgeryToken]
public async Task<IActionResult> Edit(string originalUserId, int
originalCourseId, [Bind("UserId,CourseId")] UserCourse userCourse)
{
    if (originalUserId == null || originalCourseId.Equals(default(int)))
    {
        return NotFound();
    }

    var orignalUserCourse = await _db.UserCourses
        .SingleOrDefaultAsync(c => c.UserId.Equals(originalUserId) &&
            c.CourseId.Equals(originalCourseId));

    if (!UserCourseExists(userCourse.UserId, userCourse.CourseId))
    {
        try
        {
            _db.Remove(orignalUserCourse);
            _db.Add(userCourse);
            await _db.SaveChangesAsync();
            return RedirectToAction("Index");
        }
        Catch {
        }
    }

    ModelState.AddModelError("", "Unable to save changes.");
    ViewData["CourseId"] = new SelectList(_db.Courses, "Id", "Title",
        userCourse.CourseId);
    ViewData["UserId"] = new SelectList(_db.Users, "Id",
        "Email");

    return View(userCourse);
}
```

An alternate HTTP POST **Edit** action implementation:

This implementation can be used when the ids are not part of a composite table key.

```
[HttpPost, ActionName("Edit")]
[ValidateAntiForgeryToken]
public async Task<IActionResult> Edit(string originalUserId, int
originalCourseId)
{
    if (originalUserId == null && originalCourseId < 1)
    {
        return NotFound();
    }

    var studentToUpdate = await _db.UserCourses.SingleOrDefaultAsync(
        s => s.UserId == originalUserId &&
        s.CourseId == originalCourseId);

    if (await TryUpdateModelAsync<UserCourse>(studentToUpdate, "",
        s => s.UserId, s => s.CourseId))
    {
        try
        {
            await _db.SaveChangesAsync();
            return RedirectToAction("Index");
        }
        catch (DbUpdateException)
        {
            ModelState.AddModelError("", "Unable to save changes.");
        }
    }

    return View(studentToUpdate);
}
```

Adding the HTTP GET Delete Action and View

The HTTP GET **Delete** action is exactly the same as the **Details** action; copy it and change the name. The **Delete** view is very similar to the **Details** view; copy it and add a form that calls the HTTP POST **Delete** action when the **Delete** button is clicked.

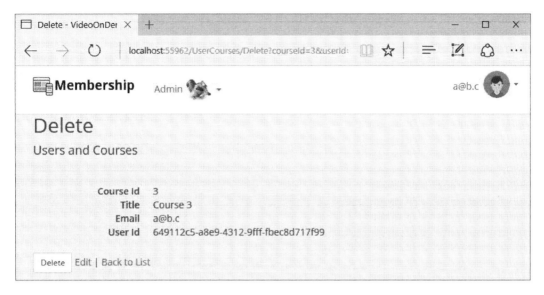

1. Copy the HTTP GET **Details** action and paste it below the last action in the controller class.

2. Rename the method **Delete**.

3. Copy the **Details** view in the *Views/UserCourses* folder and paste it into the same folder. Rename it **Delete**.

4. Change the **ViewData** title and the <h2> element to *Delete*.

5. Add a <form> element at the bottom of the view with two hidden fields for the **UserId** and **CourseId** properties. Also add a **submit** button with the text *Delete* at the bottom of the form.. Use the **asp-action** Tag Helper to target the HTTP POST **Delete** action.

```
<form asp-action="Delete">
    <input type="hidden" asp-for="UserId" />
    <input type="hidden" asp-for="CourseId" />
    <input type="submit" value="Delete"
        class="btn btn-default btn-sm" />
</form>
```

6. Move the two links to the bottom of the form and delete their <div>.

```
<a asp-action="Edit" asp-route-courseId="@Model.CourseId"
    asp-route-userId="@Model.UserId">Edit</a> |
<a asp-action="Index">Back to List</a>
```

7. Run the application without debugging (Ctrl+F5).

8. Click one of the **Delete** links to display the **Delete** view. Clicking the **Delete** button won't delete the record from the table because you haven't added the HTTP POST **DeleteConfirmed** action yet.

The complete code for the HTTP GET **Delete** action:

```
public async Task<IActionResult> Delete(string userId, int courseId)
{
    if (userId == null || courseId.Equals(default(int)))
    {
        return NotFound();
    }

    var model = await _db.Courses
        .Join(_db.UserCourses, c => c.Id, uc => uc.CourseId,
            (c, uc) => new { Courses = c, UserCourses = uc })
        .Select(s => new UserCourseDTO
        {
            CourseId = s.Courses.Id, CourseTitle = s.Courses.Title,
            UserId = s.UserCourses.UserId,
            UserEmail = _db.Users.FirstOrDefault(u =>
                u.Id.Equals(s.UserCourses.UserId)).Email
        })
        .FirstOrDefaultAsync(w => w.CourseId.Equals(courseId) &&
            w.UserId.Equals(userId));

    if (model == null)
    {
        return NotFound();
    }

    return View(model);
}
```

The complete code for the **Delete** view:

```
@model UserCourseDTO

@{
    ViewData["Title"] = "Delete";
}

<h2>Delete</h2>
```

```
<div>
    <h4>Users and Courses</h4>
    <hr />
    <dl class="dl-horizontal">
        <dt>@Html.DisplayNameFor(model => model.CourseId)</dt>
        <dd>@Html.DisplayFor(model => model.CourseId)</dd>
        <dt>@Html.DisplayNameFor(model => model.CourseTitle)</dt>
        <dd>@Html.DisplayFor(model => model.CourseTitle)</dd>
        <dt>@Html.DisplayNameFor(model => model.UserEmail)</dt>
        <dd>@Html.DisplayFor(model => model.UserEmail)</dd>
        <dt>@Html.DisplayNameFor(model => model.UserId)</dt>
        <dd>@Html.DisplayFor(model => model.UserId)</dd>
    </dl>
</div>
<form asp-action="Delete">
    <input type="hidden" asp-for="UserId" />
    <input type="hidden" asp-for="CourseId" />
    <input type="submit" value="Delete"
        class="btn btn-default btn-sm" />

    <a asp-action="Edit" asp-route-courseId="@Model.CourseId"
        asp-route-userId="@Model.UserId">Edit</a> |
    <a asp-action="Index">Back to List</a>
</form>
```

Adding the HTTP POST DeleteConfirmed Action

Because the HTTP POST action has the exact same method definition as the HTTP GET
Delete action, they can't have the same name; you can name it **DeleteConfirmed**. For the
form to be able to call the HTTP POST action using the name **Delete**, you need to add the
[ActionName] attribute with the name set to **Delete**. You also need to add the **[HttpPost]**
and **[ValidateAntiForgeryToken]** attributes.

1. Copy the method definition from the **Delete** action and paste in the code below
   the action. Add the attributes mentioned above and rename the action
   DeleteConfirmed.

```
[HttpPost, ActionName("Delete")]
[ValidateAntiForgeryToken]
public async Task<IActionResult> DeleteConfirmed(string userId,
int courseId)
{
}
```

---

2. Fetch the record that you want to delete from the database. It is the same code you used in the HTTP GET **Edit** action.
```
var userCourse = await _db.UserCourses.SingleOrDefaultAsync(m =>
m.UserId.Equals(userId) && m.CourseId.Equals(courseId));
```

3. Remove the record from the database, remembering to save the changes, and then redirect to the **Index** action.
```
_db.UserCourses.Remove(userCourse);
await _db.SaveChangesAsync();
return RedirectToAction("Index");
```

4. Run the application without debugging (Ctrl+F5).
5. Open the **Delete** view for one of the records and delete it. You should be redirected to the **Index** view after the record has been deleted.

The complete code for the HTTP POST **Delete** action:
```
[HttpPost, ActionName("Delete")]
[ValidateAntiForgeryToken]
public async Task<IActionResult> DeleteConfirmed(string userId, int
courseId)
{
    var userCourse = await _db.UserCourses.SingleOrDefaultAsync(m =>
        m.UserId.Equals(userId) && m.CourseId.Equals(courseId));
    _db.UserCourses.Remove(userCourse);
    await _db.SaveChangesAsync();
    return RedirectToAction("Index");
}
```

Authorize and Route Attributes in the Admin Controllers

To keep the admin functionality separate from the regular user interface, you can prefix the route with *admin*. To secure it from prying eyes, you add authorization to the controllers, demanding that the user must have been assigned the **Admin** role.

Using routing, you can change the URL from *[controller]/[action]* to *admin/[controller]/[action]*. This would require the user to browse to, for instance, *http://localhost:55962/admin/courses* instead of http://localhost:55962/courses. This segments your application's route in two, making the intention with each controller clear.

You change the route by adding the **Route** attribute to the controller, specifying the prefix to use at the beginning of the route. If you place the **Route** attribute on the controller class, all actions will be affected, so you might want to add the **[AllowAnonymous]** attri-bute to certain actions, to make them available to everyone.

```
[Route("admin/[controller]/[action]")]
public class CoursesController : Controller
{
}
```

The route itself doesn't prevent anyone from calling the actions and seeing the views; for that, you need to add the **[Authorize]** attribute with the **Role** parameter set to the role(s) that the user should have been assigned, to gain access to the controller's actions. In the example below, the user must belong to the **Admin** role (in the **AspNetUserRoles** table) to gain access.

```
[Authorize(Roles = "Admin")]
[Route("admin/[controller]/[action]")]
public class CoursesController : Controller
{
}
```

Changing the Route and Adding Authorization

1. Open the **UserCoursesController** class.
2. Add the **Authorize** attribute with the **Roles** parameter set to *Admin*.
   ```
   [Authorize(Roles = "Admin")]
   ```

3. Add the **Route** attribute with the *admin* prefix.
   ```
   [Route("admin/[controller]/[action]")]
   ```

4. Repeat steps 1-3 for all the administrator controllers: **CoursesController**, **DownloadsController**, **InstructorsController**, **ModulesController**, and **VideosController**.

Summary

In this chapter, you added the **UserCourses** controller without using the scaffolding feature. This is the most complex admin controller in that it uses the **AspNetUsers** table, which is not available through the **ApplicationDbContext**. You had to configure a service for the **UserStore** in the **Startup** class, and inject it in the constructor, to gain access to the **AspNetUsers** table.

You also added specific routing and authorization to the admin controllers.

Next, you will create a custom Tag Helper that displays buttons instead of the default links in the views.

25. Custom Tag Helper

Introduction

In this chapter, you will create a Tag Helper that replaces the links in the views with configurable buttons. The Tag Helper will use attributes and attribute values to configure the finished HTML elements, such as the controller, action, Bootstrap button type, what Glyphicon to display, if any, and the description on the button. The ids needed for some of the button actions will be assigned dynamically, depending on the id attributes that have been added to the Tag Helper. All ids will begin with an *id* prefix, or just **id**, if that is the name of the action parameter.

For example, if the attribute **id-courseId="1"** is added to the Tag Helper, then a URL parameter with the name **courseId** will be added to the URL, with a value of 1. If you want to add a URL parameter named **id** with a value of 2, then the Tag Helper attribute should be **id="2"**.

```
<button-container controller="Courses" actions="Edit" courseId="1">
</button-container>
http://localhost:55962/admin/Courses/Edit?courseId=1

<button-container controller="Courses" actions="Edit" id="1"></button-
container>
```

http://localhost:55962/admin/Courses/Edit?id=2

A Tag Helper is created with a C# class that creates the HTML element with C# code. It is then inserted into the views as HTML markup.

The class must inherit from the **TagHelper** class and implement a method called **Process**, which creates or modifies the HTML element. Tag Helper attributes can be added as properties in the class, or dynamically to a collection, by adding them to the HTML Tag Helper element. You will implement both scenarios in the Tag Helper you will create.

Technologies Used in This Chapter
1. **C#** – to create the Tag Helper.
2. **HTML** – To add the Tag Helper to the views.

Overview

Your task is to create a custom Tag Helper called **button-container**. You'll start with the more static approach using strings to pass in values, and then implement a more dynamic way of reading attributes and their values. The links should be displayed as Bootstrap-styled buttons with a description or a Glyphicon.

You should be able to do the following with the Tag Helper: add a controller, target multiple actions (for different buttons), add multiple descriptions, and use different Bootstrap button types and Glyphicon names. Each value should be a comma-separated list that is split up into an array, and the values from each index position in the arrays will be used to create a single button.

For example, the following Tag Helper would create two buttons. The first would have the description *Create New* and target the **Create** action in the **Courses** controller, and the second would have the description *Back to List* and target the **Index** action in the **Courses** controller.

```
<button-container controller="Courses" actions="Create,Index"
descriptions="Create New,Back to List"></button-container>
```

Implementing the Button-Container Tag Helper

The Tag Helper should be created in a class called **ButtonContainerTagHelper** located in a folder named *Tag Helpers* directly under the project node. Use the **New Item** dialog's **Razor Tag Helper** template.

You can use the **HtmlTargetElement** attribute to limit the scope of the Tag Helper to a specific HTML element type.

```
[HtmlTargetElement("my-tag-helper")]
public class MyTagHelperTagHelper : TagHelper
```

The Tag Helper will produce a <span> element with one or more <a> elements styled as buttons.

To make the Tag Helper available in views, you need to add an **@addTagHelper** directive that includes all Tag Helpers in the project assembly, to the **_ViewImports** view.

```
@addTagHelper "*, VideoOnDemand"
```

When you add the Tag Helper to the view, it's very important that you use a closing tag, otherwise the Tag Helper won't work.

```
<button-container></button-container>
```

Creating the Tag Helper

1. Add an **@addTagHelper** directive that includes all Tag Helpers in the project assembly, to the **_ViewImports** view.
   ```
   @addTagHelper "*, VideoOnDemand"
   ```

2. Add a folder named *Tag Helpers* to the project.

3. Add a **Razor Tag Helper** class called **ButtonContainerTagHelper** to the folder. Right click on the folder and select **Add-New Item**. Slelect the **Razor Tag Helper** template, name it, and click the **Add** button.
   ```
   [HtmlTargetElement("tag-name")]
   public class ButtonContainerTagHelper : TagHelper
   {
       public override void Process(TagHelperContext context,
       TagHelperOutput output)
       {
       }
   }
   ```

4. Change the **HtmlTargetElement** attribute to **button-container**. This will be the name of the Tag Helper's "element" name. It's not a real HTML element, but it looks like one, to blend in with the HTML markup. It will, however, generate a real HTML element when rendered.
   ```
   [HtmlTargetElement("button-container")]
   ```

5. Add an attribute called **Controller** to the Tag Helper, by adding a property with that name to the class. The purpose of this attribute is to add the controller name to the **href** attribute on the <a> element that the Tag Helper creates.
   ```
   public string Controller { get; set; }
   ```

6. Add an attribute called **Actions** to the Tag Helper by adding a property with that name to the class. The purpose of this attribute is to add the action name to the **href** attribute on the <a> element that the Tag Helper creates. Later, you will make it possible to add buttons for multiple actions, but for now the Tag Helper will only create one link.
   ```
   public string Actions { get; set; }
   ```

7. Add exceptions to the **Process** method, which are thrown if any of the parameters are null. Call the **Process** method in the base class below the if-statements.

```
if (context == null)
    throw new ArgumentNullException(nameof(context));
if (output == null)
    throw new ArgumentNullException(nameof(output));
base.Process(context, output);
```

8. Tell the **Process** method the element type that it should output, and add the opening element tag to the output content. Style it as an **inline-block** so that it flows with the markup it is added to. Use the **TagName** property on the **output** object to specify the Tag Helper's main element container.

```
output.TagName = "span"; // Replaces <button-container> with
<span> tag
output.Content.SetHtmlContent("<span style='min-width:100px;
display:inline-block;'>");
```

9. Add a variable named **href** to hold the finished URL that will be added to the <a> element's **href** attribute. Add another variable called **action** that you assign the **Action** property; later you will use this variable in a loop for every action name supplied to the Tag Helper.

```
var href = "";
var action = Actions;
```

10. Add an if-block that checks if the **Controller** property is not null and has content.

```
if (Controller != null && Controller.Length > 0)
{
}
```

11. Build the **href** inside the if-block using the **Controller** property and the **action** variable. If the **action** variable has content, then use its value in the **href**, otherwise use **Index** as the default action.

```
if (action != null && action.Length > 0)
    href = $@"href='/admin/{Controller}/{action}'";
else
    href = $@"href='/admin/{Controller}/Index'";
```

12. Add the **href** variable to an <a> element with the text *My link*, by calling the **AppnedHtml** method on the **output** object.

```
output.Content.AppendHtml($@"<a {href}>My link</a>");
```

13. Add the closing </span> element tag.
    ```
    output.Content.AppendHtml("</span>");
    ```

14. Open the **Index** view in the *Views/Courses* folder and add the Tag Helper below the **Create New** link. Assign *Courses* to the **controller** attribute and *Create* to the **actions** attribute.
    ```
    <a asp-action="Create">Create New</a>
    <button-container controller="Courses" actions="Create">
    </button-container>
    ```

15. Run the application without debugging (Ctrl+F5).

16. Open the **Courses Index** view. There should be a link with the text **My link** beside the **Create New** link. Click the **My link** link to open the **Create** view.

The code for the Tag Helper, so far:

```
[HtmlTargetElement("button-container")]
public class ButtonContainerTagHelper : TagHelper
{
    #region Properties
    public string Controller { get; set; }
    public string Actions { get; set; }
    #endregion

    public override void Process(TagHelperContext context,
    TagHelperOutput output)
    {
        if (context == null)
            throw new ArgumentNullException(nameof(context));
        if (output == null)
            throw new ArgumentNullException(nameof(output));

        base.Process(context, output);

        // Replaces <button-container> with <span> tag
        output.TagName = "span";
        output.Content.SetHtmlContent(
            "<span style='min-width:100px; display:inline-block;'>");

        var href = "";
        var action = Actions;
```

```
    if (Controller != null && Controller.Length > 0)
    {
        if (action != null && action.Length > 0)
            href = $@"href='/admin/{Controller}/{action}'";
        else
            href = $@"href='/admin/{Controller}/Index'";
    }

    output.Content.AppendHtml($@"<a {href}>My link</a>");

    output.Content.AppendHtml("</span>");
    }
}
```

Multiple Actions and Descriptions

1. Replace the action variable with a **foreach** loop that iterates over the comma-separated list in the **Actions** property. Use the **Split** method to create an array from the list in the property. Let the loop surround the if-block and the <a> element.
   ```
   var actions = Actions.Split(',');
   foreach (var action in actions)
   {
       ...
   }
   ```

2. Add a new property called **Descriptions** to the class.
   ```
   public string Descriptions { get; set; }
   ```

3. Split the comma-separated string in the **Description** property to a variable called **descriptions** above the **foreach** loop. Assign an empty string array if the **Description** property is null.
   ```
   var descriptions = Descriptions!= null ? Descriptions.Split(',') :
   new string[0];
   ```

4. Add a variable called **description** below the href if-block and assign it the action name. Add an if-block that checks that the **descriptions** array has the same number of records or more than the **actions** array, and assign the description for current action's array position.
   ```
   var description = action;
   if (descriptions.Length >= actions.Length)
       description = descriptions[Array.IndexOf(actions, action)];
   ```

5. Add an if-statement that checks if the description variable is empty, and assign it the **action** variable value if it is. This can happen if the user adds a comma without a description after it.
```
if(description.Length.Equals(0)) description = action;
```

6. Add the description to the <a> element.
```
output.Content.AppendHtml($@"<a {href}>{description}</a>");
```

7. Change the Tag Helper to display links for the **Create** and **Index** actions.
```
<button-container controller="Courses" actions="Create,Index"
descriptions="Create New,Back to List"></button-container>
```

8. Run the application and verify that there are two links with the provided descriptions. Play around with the descriptions and actions in the Tag Helper.

The code for the Tag Helper, so far:

```
[HtmlTargetElement("button-container")]
public class ButtonContainerTagHelper : TagHelper
{
    #region Properties
    public string Controller { get; set; }
    public string Actions { get; set; }
    public string Descriptions { get; set; }
    #endregion

    public override void Process(TagHelperContext context,
    TagHelperOutput output)
    {
        if (context == null)
            throw new ArgumentNullException(nameof(context));
        if (output == null)
            throw new ArgumentNullException(nameof(output));

        base.Process(context, output);

        // Replaces <button-container> with <span> tag
        output.TagName = "span";
        output.Content.SetHtmlContent(
            "<span style='min-width:100px; display:inline-block;'>");

        var href = "";

        var actions = Actions.Split(',');
```

```
        var descriptions = Descriptions != null ?
            Descriptions.Split(',') :
            new string[0];

        foreach (var action in actions)
        {
            if (Controller != null && Controller.Length > 0)
            {
                if (action != null && action.Length > 0)
                    href = $@"href='/admin/{Controller}/{action}'";
                else href = $@"href='/admin/{Controller}/Index'";
            }

            var description = action;
            if (descriptions.Length >= actions.Length)
                description = descriptions[Array.IndexOf(
                    actions, action)];

            if(description.Length.Equals(0)) description = action;

            output.Content.AppendHtml($@"<a {href}>{description}</a>");
        }

        output.Content.AppendHtml("</span>");
    }
}
```

URL Parameter Values

The next step will be to add ids to the URL's parameter list. You will implement this using the **TagHelperContext** object instead of adding properties to the class, because it makes more sense to do it dynamically. To implement this, you will check for attribute names beginning with *id* and fetch their values using the **AllAttributes** method on the **context** object.

1. Fetch the ids that begin with *id* from the **context** object and store them in a variable called **ids**.

   ```
   var ids = context.AllAttributes.Where(c =>
   c.Name.StartsWith("id"));
   ```

2. Add a **string** variable called **param** and a **foreach** loop that iterates over the **ids** array, below the code for the **description** attribute.

   ```
   var param = "";
   ```

```
foreach (var id in ids)
{
    ...
}
```

3. Add a variable called **splitId** inside the loop, and split the value in the **Name** property at the dash (-). It's important to know if there are any characters after the dash, or if a dash exists; if it does, then the part after the dash becomes the name of the parameter. If the name is *id* without a dash, then the parameter name is **Id**.
```
var splitId = id.Name.Split('-');
```

4. Check if the **splitId** array has one value, and assign the value in the **Value** property, prepended with the name *Id*, to the **param** variable.
```
if (splitId.Length.Equals(1)) param = $"Id={id.Value}";
```

5. Check if the **splitId** array has more than one value, and use the second value as the name. Then append the name and the value from the **Value** property to the **param** variable.
```
if (splitId.Length.Equals(2)) param +=
$"&{splitId[1]}={id.Value}";
```

6. If the string begins with an ampersand (&) then remove it. This will happen if there is no parameter named **Id**.
```
if (param.StartsWith("&")) param = param.Substring(1);
```

7. If the **param** variable contains parameter values, then insert them into the URL in the **href** vaiarble.
```
if (param.Length > 0) href = href.Insert(href.Length -
1,$"?{param}");
```

8. Open the **Index** view in the *Courses* folder and alter the Tag Helper to target the **Edit** action. Don't forget to add an id to an existing course with the **id** attribute.
```
<button-container controller="Courses" actions="Edit" id="1">
</button-container>
```

9. Run the application and select **Courses** in the **Admin** menu, to navigate to its **Index** view. Click the **Edit** link beside the **Create New** link; the **Edit** view should be displayed with the data for the course matching the id you specified in the Tag Helper.

The code in the **Process** method, so far:

```
public override void Process(TagHelperContext context,
TagHelperOutput output)
{
    if (context == null)
        throw new ArgumentNullException(nameof(context));
    if (output == null)
        throw new ArgumentNullException(nameof(output));

    base.Process(context, output);

    // Replaces <button-container> with <span> tag
    output.TagName = "span";
    output.Content.SetHtmlContent(
        "<span style='min-width:100px; display:inline-block;'>");

    var href = "";

    var actions = Actions.Split(',');
    var descriptions = Descriptions != null ? Descriptions.Split(',') :
        new string[0];
    var ids = context.AllAttributes.Where(c =>
        c.Name.StartsWith("id"));
    foreach (var action in actions)
    {
        if (Controller != null && Controller.Length > 0)
        {
            if (action != null && action.Length > 0)
                href = $@"href='/admin/{Controller}/{action}'";
            else href = $@"href='/admin/{Controller}/Index'";
        }

        var description = action;
        if (descriptions.Length >= actions.Length)
            description = descriptions[Array.IndexOf(actions, action)];
        if(description.Length.Equals(0)) description = action;

        var param = "";
        foreach (var id in ids)
        {
            var splitId = id.Name.Split('-');
            if (splitId.Length.Equals(1)) param = $"Id={id.Value}";
            if (splitId.Length.Equals(2))
                param += $"&{splitId[1]}={id.Value}";
```

```
            if (param.StartsWith("&")) param = param.Substring(1);
        }
        if (param.Length > 0)
            href = href.Insert(href.Length - 1,$"?{param}");


        output.Content.AppendHtml($@"<a {href}>{description}</a>");
    }

    output.Content.AppendHtml("</span>");
}
```

Glyphicons

The next step will be to display Glyphicons in the link. Let's try another approach where a single property determines if an icon should be displayed in the link, and fetch an appropriate icon from a collection of predefined icon names.

1. Add a **bool** property called **UseGlyps** and a dictionary collction called **ButtonGlyphs**, containing key-value pairs of action and icon names, to the class.
   ```
   public bool UseGlyphs { get; set; }
   private Dictionary<string, string> ButtonGlyphs =
       new Dictionary<string, string> {
           { "edit", "pencil" }, { "create", "th-list" },
           { "delete", "remove" }, { "details", "info-sign" },
           { "index", "list-alt" }
       };
   ```

2. Add a **string** variable called **classAttr** below the param code.
   ```
   var classAttr = "";
   ```

3. Add an if-block that checks if the **UseGlyphs** property is **true**.
   ```
   if (UseGlyphs)
   {
   }
   ```

4. Add a **string** variable called **glyph** inside the if-block. Try to fetch the glyph with a matching action name from the dictionary and store it in the **glyph** variable.
   ```
   var glyph = "";
   ButtonGlyphs.TryGetValue(action.ToLower(), out glyph);
   ```

5. Check that the **glyph** variable contain a value before adding it to the **classAttr** variable that builds a class attribute for the element. Empty the **description** variable to remove the button text.

```
if(glyph != null && glyph.Length > 0)
{
    classAttr = $"class='glyphicon glyphicon-{glyph}'";
    description = string.Empty;
}
```

6. Open the **Index** view in the *Courses* folder and add the **use-glyps** attribute to the Tag Helper.

```
<button-container controller="Courses" actions="Edit" id="1"
use-glyphs="true"></button-container>
```

7. Run the application and navigate to the **Index** view associated with the **Courses** controller and verify that the **pencil** glyphicon is visible.

The properties added to the class:

```
public bool UseGlyphs { get; set; }
private Dictionary<string, string> ButtonGlyphs =
new Dictionary<string, string>
{
    { "edit", "pencil" }, { "create", "th-list" },
    { "delete", "remove" }, { "details", "info-sign" },
    { "index", "list-alt" }
};
```

The code added to the **Process** method:

```
var classAttr = "";
if (UseGlyphs)
{
    var glyph = "";
    ButtonGlyphs.TryGetValue(action.ToLower(), out glyph);
    if(glyph != null && glyph.Length > 0)
    {
        classAttr = $"class='glyphicon glyphicon-{glyph}'";
        description = string.Empty;
    }
}
output.Content.AppendHtml($@"<a {href}><span {classAttr}></span>
{description}</a>");
```

Turning Links into Buttons

The next step will be to display the links as buttons, using Bootstrap classes.

1. Add a dictionary collection called **ButtonTypes** containing key-value pairs of action and Bootstrap button type names, to the class.

    ```
    private Dictionary<string, string> ButtonTypes =
    new Dictionary<string, string>
    {
        { "edit", "success" }, { "create", "primary" },
        { "delete", "danger" }, { "details", "primary" },
        { "index", "primary" }
    };
    ```

2. Add a **string** variable called **button** below the **UseGlyphs** if-block. Try to fetch the Bootstrap button type from the **ButtonType** collection and store the result in the **button** variable.

    ```
    var button = "";
    ButtonTypes.TryGetValue(action.ToLower(), out button);
    ```

3. Add a **string** variable called **buttonClass**.

    ```
    var buttonClass = string.Empty;
    ```

4. Add the Bootstrap classes **btn-sm** and **btn-{the fetched button type}** to the **buttonClass** variable if the button type was successfully fetched from the collection.

    ```
    if(button != null && button.Length > 0)
        buttonClass = $@"class='btn-sm btn-{button}'";
    ```

5. Add the button type to the <a> element's class attribute.

    ```
    output.Content.AppendHtml($@"<a {buttonClass} {href}><span
    {classAttr}></span>{description}</a>");
    ```

6. Run the application and navigate to the **Index** view associated with the **Courses** controller. Verify that the link is displayed as a Bootstrap button.

Styling the Views

You'll need to add a style sheet called *admin.css* where you can style the views associated with the administrator user interface. A top margin needs to be added to the <h1> element to push the conent down from the navigation bar. The right margin must be removed from the buttons, and their text decoration (underlining) should be removed. The button column in the table needs to have a fixed minimum width, with enough room for the three buttons.

While you're at it you might as well style the top margin in the regular user interface and the content in the navigation bar.

1. Add a style sheet to the *wwwroot/css* folder called *admin.css*.
2. Add links to it in the **_Layout** view and the *bundleconfig.json* file.
3. Add a selector for <a> elements decorated with the **btn-sm** Bootstrap class to the style sheet. It should remove their text decoration and border radius, to hide the link underlining and give the buttons sharp edges.

    ```
    a.btn-sm {
        text-decoration: none;
        border-radius: 0px;
    }
    ```

4. Make the button column at least 125px wide in all **Index** views associated with the administrator UI. Add a class selector called **button-col-width** to the <td> containing the buttons. Add the same selector containing the styling to the style sheet.

    ```
    .button-col-width {
        min-width: 125px;
    }
    ```

5. Add a class selector called **admin-top-margin** to the <h2> element containing the view's title in all views associated with the administrator UI. Add the same selector with a 30px top margin to the style sheet.

```
.admin-top-margin {
    margin-top: 30px;
}
```

6. Open the *menu.css* file.

7. Add a selector for **navbar-brand** and add a 21px top padding to push the logo down and align it with the **Admin** menu.

```
.navbar-brand {
    padding-top:21px;
}
```

8. Add a selector for **ul.navbar-right** and add a 8px top padding to push the right menu down to align it with the **Admin** menu.

```
ul.navbar-right {
    padding-top: 8px;
}
```

9. Add a selector for **.navbar .container** and add a 70px minimum height to make the navigation bar look uniform with regards to the menu items positions.

```
.navbar .container {
    min-height:70px;
}
```

10. Open the *membership.css* file.

11. Change the top margin to 35px for the **.membership.top-margin** selector to push the titles down in the regular user interface views.

```
.membership.top-margin {
    margin-top: 35px;
}
```

The complete code in the *admin.css* stylesheet:

```
a.btn-sm {
    text-decoration: none;
    border-radius: 0px;
}

.button-col-width {
    min-width: 125px;
}
```

```
.admin-top-margin {
    margin-top: 30px;
}
```

The selectors added to the *menu.css* stylesheet:

```
.navbar-brand {
    padding-top:21px;
}

ul.navbar-right {
    padding-top: 8px;
}

.navbar .container {
    min-height:70px;
}
```

The changes to the *membership.css* stylesheet:

```
.membership.top-margin {
    margin-top: 35px;
}
```

Replacing Links with Buttons

The next step will be to replace the links with buttons using your Tag Helper. The neat thing with using your Tag Helper is that you can make the markup look cleaner because you only need one line of markup to display many buttons.

1. Open the **Index** view in the *Views/Courses* folder.
2. Replace the **Create New** <a> element at the beginning of the view with your Tag Helper. To be able to reuse the Tag Helper in other views, you can use route data to assign the controller. Remove the <button-container> element that you have been using so far.
   ```
   <button-container
   controller="@ViewContext.RouteData.Values["controller"].ToString()
   "
   actions="Create" descriptions="Create New"></button-container>
   ```

3. Replace the three links in the table at the end of the view with your Tag Helper. These buttons should have Glyphicons. You also have to provide a value for the **id** attribute.

```
<button-container controller=
    "@ViewContext.RouteData.Values["controller"].ToString()"
    actions="Edit,Details,Delete" use-glyphs="true" id="@item.Id">
</button-container>
```

4. Repeat steps 1-3 for all **Index** views associated with the administrator user interface.

5. The **UserCourses Index** view needs some modification to work properly, because it takes two ids called **UserId** and **CourseId**, which you will have to add to the table buttons.

```
<button-container controller=
    "@ViewContext.RouteData.Values["controller"].ToString()"
    actions="Edit,Details,Delete" use-glyphs="true"
    id-userId="@item.UserId" id-courseId="@item.CourseId">
</button-container>
```

6. Open the **Details** view in the *Courses* folder.

7. Replace the **Back to Link** <a> element with your Tag Helper.

```
<button-container controller=
    "@ViewContext.RouteData.Values["controller"].ToString()"
    actions="Index" descriptions="Back to List">
</button-container>
```

8. Repeat steps 7-8 for all views associated with the administrator user interface.

9. Open the **Details** view in the *Courses* folder.

10. Remove the **Edit** <a> element.

11. Modify the Tag Helper to display both the **Back to List** button and the **Edit** button.

```
<button-container controller=
    "@ViewContext.RouteData.Values["controller"].ToString()"
    actions="Index,Edit" id="@Model.Id"
    descriptions="Back to List,Edit ">
</button-container>
```

12. Repeat steps 9-11 for all **Details** views associated with the administrator user interface.

13. Add the **UserId** and **CourseId** to the Tag Helper in the **Details** and **Delete** views in the **UserCourse** folder.

```
<button-container controller=
    "@ViewContext.RouteData.Values["controller"].ToString()"
    actions="Index,Edit" id-userId="@Model.UserId"
    id-courseId="@Model.CourseId"
    descriptions="Back to List,Edit ">
</button-container>
```

14. Run the application and verify that all the buttons in all views work properly.

An Alternate Button-Container Tag Helper

Here's the code for an alternate implementation of the **button-container** Tag Helper that is more dynamic, reading the available attributes. This is a bonus that I included to show you a different way of implementing the Tag Helper; hopefully it will give you some ideas for your own applications.

```
[HtmlTargetElement("alternate-button-container")]
public class AlternateButtonContainerTagHelper : TagHelper
{
    #region Properties
    private Dictionary<string, string> ButtonGlyphs =
        new Dictionary<string, string>
        {
            { "edit", "pencil" }, { "create", "th-list" },
            { "delete", "remove" }, { "details", "info-sign" },
            { "index", "list-alt" }
        };
        public string Controller { get; set; }
        #endregion

    public override void Process(TagHelperContext context,
    TagHelperOutput output)
    {
        if (context == null)
            throw new ArgumentNullException(nameof(context));
        if (output == null)
            throw new ArgumentNullException(nameof(output));

        base.Process(context, output);
        output.TagName = "span";
        output.Content.SetHtmlContent(
```

```
        "<span style='min-width:100px; display:inline-block;'>");

    var actions = context.AllAttributes.Where(c =>
        c.Name.StartsWith("action-"));
    var buttonTypes = context.AllAttributes.Where(c =>
        c.Name.StartsWith("btn-"));
    var buttonTexts = context.AllAttributes.Where(c =>
        c.Name.StartsWith("txt-"));
    var buttonGlyphs = context.AllAttributes.Where(c =>
        c.Name.StartsWith("gly-"));
    var glyphsForAll = context.AllAttributes.FirstOrDefault(c =>
        c.Name.Equals("glyphs")) != null;
    var buttonIds = context.AllAttributes.Where(c =>
        c.Name.StartsWith("id-"));
    var globalId = context.AllAttributes.FirstOrDefault(c =>
        c.Name.Equals("id"));

    foreach (var action in actions)
    {
        string actionName = action.Name.Substring(7);

        #region Button Type
        var buttonType = buttonTypes.FirstOrDefault(b =>
            b.Name.StartsWith($"btn-{actionName}-"));
        var btnType = buttonType == null ? "default" :
            buttonType.Name.Substring(5 + actionName.Length);
        #endregion

        #region Button Text
        var buttonText = buttonTexts.FirstOrDefault(b =>
            b.Name.StartsWith($"txt-{actionName}"));
        var btnText = buttonText == null ? string.Empty :
            buttonText.Value == null ? string.Empty :
                buttonText.Value.ToString();
        #endregion

        #region Glyphicon
        var glyph = string.Empty;
        if (glyphsForAll)
        {
            glyph = ButtonGlyphs.FirstOrDefault(g =>
                g.Key.ToUpper().Equals(actionName.ToUpper()))
                    .Value;
        }
```

```csharp
            var specificGlyph = buttonGlyphs.FirstOrDefault(b =>
                b.Name.StartsWith($"gly-{actionName}"));
            if (specificGlyph != null && specificGlyph.Value != null &&
                !specificGlyph.Value.Equals(String.Empty))
                    glyph = specificGlyph.Value.ToString();
            #endregion

            #region Ids
            var ids = globalId == null ? string.Empty :
                $"id={globalId.Value}";
            foreach (var btnId in buttonIds)
            {
                if (btnId.Value != null &&
                    !btnId.Value.Equals(string.Empty))
                {
                    ids =
                      $"{ids}&{btnId.Name.Substring(3)}={btnId.Value}";
                }
            }
            if (ids.Substring(0, 1).Equals("&")) ids = ids.Substring(1);
            var param = $"?{ids}";
            #endregion

            #region Show/hide button text and Glyphicons
            var glyphClass = "";
            if (glyph.Length > 0)
                glyphClass += $" glyphicon glyphicon-{glyph}";
            if (glyph.Length > 0 && btnText.Length > 0)
                btnText = $" {btnText}";
            #endregion

            #region Bootstrap buttona and URL
            var classAttr = $"btn-sm btn-{btnType}";
            var href = $@"/admin/{Controller}/{actionName}{param}";
            #endregion

            output.Content.AppendHtml(
                $@"<a class='{classAttr}' href='{href}'>
                    <span class='{glyphClass}'></span>{btnText}</a>");
        }

    output.Content.AppendHtml("</span>");
    }
}
```

Summary

In this chapter, you implemented a custom Tag Helper and added it to the views. You learned a more static approach using string values from Tag Helper attributes, and a more dynamic way to find out what attributes have been added, and read their values.

The purpose of the Tag Helper you created was to replace links with Bootstrap styled buttons. You can however use Tag Helpers for so much more.

Thank you for taking the time to read the book and implement the projects.

Other Titles by the Author

Books

The author has written other books and produced video courses that you might find helpful.

Books by the Author

Below is a list if the most recent books by the author. The books are available on Amazon.

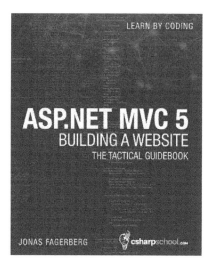

ASP.NET Core 1.1 – Building a Website: www.amazon.com/dp/1546832068

ASP.NET Core 1.1 – Building a Web API: www.amazon.com/dp/1975798929

ASP.NET MVC 5 – Building a Website: www.amazon.com/dp/B01IF63FIY

C# for Beginners: https://www.amazon.com/dp/B017OAFR8I

Video Courses

MVC 5 – How to Build a Membership Website (video course)
This is a comprehensive video course on how to build a membership site using ASP.NET MVC 5. The course has in excess of **24 hours** of video.

In this video course you will learn how to build a membership website from scratch. You will create the database using Entity Framework code-first, scaffold an Administrator UI, and build a front-end UI using HTML5, CSS3, Bootstrap, JavaScript, C#, and MVC 5. Prerequisites for this course are: a good knowledge of the C# language and basic knowledge of MVC 5, HTML5, CSS3, Bootstrap, and JavaScript.

You can watch this video course on Udemy at this URL:
www.udemy.com/building-a-mvc-5-membership-website

Store Secret Data in a .NET Core Web App with Azure Key Vault (video course)
In this Udemy course you will learn how to store sensitive data in a secure manner. First you will learn how to store data securely in a file called *secrets.json* with the User Manager. The file is stored locally on your machine, outside the project's folder structure, and is therefore not checked into your code repository. Then you will learn how to use Azure Web App Settings to store key-value pairs for a specific web application. The third and

final way to secure your sensitive data is using Azure Key Vault, secured with Azure Active Directory in the cloud.

The course is taught using a ASP.NET Core 1.1 Web API solution in Visual Studio 2015.

You really need to know this if you are a serious developer.

You can watch this video course on Udemy at this URL:
www.udemy.com/store-secret-data-in-net-core-web-app-with-azure-key-vault

97531069R00234

Made in the USA
Middletown, DE
06 November 2018